Blogging

Julie C. Meloni

in a Snap

SAMS
Teach
Yourself

Sams Publishing, 800 East 96th Street, Indianapolis, Indiana 46240 USA

Blogging in a Snap

International Standard Book Number: 0-672-32843-7

Library of Congress Catalog Card Number: 2005927568

Printed in the United States of America

First Printing: November 2005

08   07   06   4   3   2

Trademarks

Warning and Disclaimer

Bulk Sales

Sams Publishing offers excellent discounts on this book when ordered in quantity for bulk purchases or special sales. For more information, please contact

U.S. Corporate and Government Sales
1-800-382-3419
corpsales@pearsontechgroup.com

For sales outside of the U.S., please contact

International Sales
international@pearsoned.com

Acquisitions Editor
Shelley Johnston

Development Editor
Damon Jordan

Managing Editor
Charlotte Clapp

Project Editor
Seth Kerney

Copy Editor
Mike Henry

Indexer
Aaron Black

Proofreader
Jenny Matlik

Technical Editors
Parker Morse

Natalie Houston

Publishing Coordinator
Vanessa Evans

Interior Designer
Gary Adair

Page Layout
Nonie Ratcliff

Foreword

Blogging in The Stone Age

The 1952 Chuck Jones cartoon short titled "Operation: Rabbit" was the first meeting between Wile E. Coyote and Bugs Bunny. In the scene, Wile hands Bugs his business card and says, "Allow me to introduce myself. My name is Coyote. Wile E. Coyote. I am a genius, whilst you could hardly pass the entrance examination into kindergarten." The business card Wile E. presents to Bugs reads simply, "Wile E. Coyote, Genius." Later in the cartoon, after having been soundly outwitted by the cunning Bugs, Wile E. proclaims, "Allow me to introduce myself, my name is mud."

Part of the blog creation process, as you will soon learn, requires that you give your blog a name. That fated meeting between two icons of animation history popped into my head almost six years ago when I was signing up to Blogger. That's when I chose the title, "Biz Stone, Genius." In the years that followed, I became obsessed with this revolutionary new form of communication. I helped start a company that provided blogging services and I wrote articles about this new democratization of media. I couldn't stop talking about blogs to everyone I met. Not everyone shared my enthusiasm.

"Hey 'genius', I was posting articles on Usenet when you were still in diapers. Bulletin boards, email lists, and chat rooms all existed long before your precious 'blogs' started clogging up the Web. My advice to you and everyone else engaged in this endless navel gazing bacchanalia is to snap out of it and get a life. There's nothing new about blogs."

Ladies and gentlemen, welcome to my life.

The above quote is the kind of monologue I have routinely listened to with patience and humility from people who have yet to experience the significance of the powerful communication and networking medium that is blogging. Ironically, it has been my experience that those who launch into tirades like this end up being big fans of blogging. There was even some initial dissonance at Xanga, a company I helped start several years ago, when it was proposed that we focus on providing weblog services. Today, blogging providers like Blogger and Xanga have traffic rankings higher than online behemoths like

The New York Times, Apple Computer, and Craigslist. As amazing as it sounds, readership of Blogger's hosted blogs is bigger than the readership of the New York Times Online (which is even bigger than its print readership).

During my years at Google working on Blogger, attitudes relaxed and minds began to open to the idea of blogging, but there were still engineers and self-professed geeks at conferences who insisted on reminding me that they were not the least impressed. "Why are so many people making such a fuss about this so called blogging phenomenon?" they would ask me. "There is nothing so special about the technology behind blogs to warrant this much attention." My answer to them was always the same. "You're right. There's nothing new here."

Blogging is not about technology. It's about people.

Years ago I was lucky enough to get a private tour of an ancient cave in southern Spain. The group of friends I was traveling with included Donald Burgy, professor emeritus at the Massachusetts College of Art and his wife, Wellesley College professor Joy Renjilian-Burgy. It was Joy who somehow finagled us this private tour with her persuasive multilingual skills and a circuitous tale involving her asthmatic twin sons born miraculously on Christmas Day. Even now I am still impressed, as there was quite a crowd of people waiting to visit the cave. Donald Burgy has spent the better part of his career studying cave paintings all over the world and he has developed an intriguing skill—he can translate the art.

Burgy shared with me his knowledge in the dark recesses of this underground world, and something began to strike me as eerily familiar. Later, as I became immersed in the world of blogging and other forms of social software, I realized the connection. If a spear or hewn rock was hardware then those cave paintings were software and furthermore, they were social. Ancient people painted on cave walls to communicate with each other and tell stories. Deep within the caves, these paintings are protected from the elements. The stories and experiences are added to and redrawn over several millennia. In this way the paintings span the years to reach an impressively wide audience.

We tell stories and share our experiences and opinions on our blogs that reach our immediate friends and family as well as a wider group of people surfing the Web. Culture has moved online as the right kinds of tools emerge. Today communication devices are ubiquitous, and something as simple as picking up a piece of charcoal seems foreign compared to filling out a web form and clicking a button. Our tools may have changed, but we're still doing the same stuff we did 40,000 years ago. The big difference is that everything is faster now.

It doesn't matter if blogging is new or old. What matters is that we are sharing our experiences and learning from each other more now than ever before. Not until you sign up to Blogger and start posting on a regular basis will you realize what significance blogging holds for you on a personal level. On the Web you are only one search or hyperlink away from joining a network of like-minded souls. My blog has brought me to places I never would have been and introduced me to people I'm proud to call my friends. Think of your blog as a version of you online. Your web persona will teach you new things about yourself, connect you to people, and take you to places you never expected to go.

My guide through that cave in Spain was a large, mustachioed Alsatian man with a booming voice and a pair of copper divining wires up his sleeve, but you've got Julie Meloni to help you explore the world of blogging. Be thankful for that. Let Julie be your fun and helpful guide as you spelunk through all the interesting features that Blogger has to offer. Also, take a moment to appreciate that you are not shuffling through bat guano in the dark caverns of an ancient European cave. I envy you the journey you are about to make. Have fun!

—Biz Stone, Genius

About the Author

Julie C. Meloni is the technical director for i2i Interactive (http://www.i2ii.com), a multimedia company located in Los Altos, California. She has been developing web-based applications since the Web first saw the light of day and remembers the excitement surrounding the first GUI web browser. She has authored several books and articles on web-based programming languages and database topics, including the best-selling *Sams Teach Yourself PHP, MySQL and Apache All-in-One*. Julie blogs much more than she should, given her workload.

Acknowledgments

Special thanks to Mel, who got me into this blogging thing in the first place, and for everyone on my blogroll—without your posts to read, my days would be quite boring indeed. Special shout-outs for (but not limited to) Dr. B, PJM, Kathy R, Rana, Geeky Mom, Rhonda, Michelle P, Caleb, Suzan H, BrightStar, Mac, Phantom Scribbler, PZ Myers, Profgrrrrl, kmsqrd, Scribblingwoman, Scrivener, Seeker, Curtis, Stag, Juice, and GZombie.

Of course, this book would be nothing without Blogger and the good folks at Pyra Labs who built it, Google who bought it, and the current Blogger team for their continued efforts in making it a wonderful blogging platform.

Great thanks especially to all the editors and layout folks at Sams who were involved with this book for all their hard work in seeing this through! Thanks as always to everyone at i2i Interactive for their never-ending support and encouragement.

We Want to Hear from You!

As the reader of this book, *you* are our most important critic and commentator. We value your opinion and want to know what we're doing right, what we could do better, what areas you'd like to see us publish in, and any other words of wisdom you're willing to pass our way.

You can email or write me directly to let me know what you did or didn't like about this book—as well as what we can do to make our books stronger.

Please note that I cannot help you with technical problems related to the topic of this book, and that due to the high volume of mail I receive, I might not be able to reply to every message.

When you write, please be sure to include this book's title and author as well as your name and phone or email address. I will carefully review your comments and share them with the author and editors who worked on the book.

E-mail: consumer@samspublishing.com

Mail: Mark Taber
          Associate Publisher
          Sams Publishing
          800 East 96th Street
          Indianapolis, IN 46240 USA

Reader Services

For more information about this book or another Sams title, visit our website at www.samspublishing.com. Type the ISBN (excluding hyphens) or the title of a book in the Search field to find the page you're looking for.

PART I

Getting Started with Blogging

IN THIS PART:

✔Start Here

In this chapter, you'll learn some of the basics about blogging in general, beyond the specifics of using a publishing application such as Google's Blogger. This background will help you to formulate your own purpose for blogging, and will assist you in getting the most out of the process as possible.

What's a Blog?

The term *blog* is short for *weblog*, which is nothing more complicated than a World Wide Web–based journal. Don't be fooled by the use of the word *journal*—blogs are not always written by teenage girls with crushes on the latest boy bands (although that's perfectly fine if they are, of course). You'll find blogs written by parents, teachers, geeks, actors, musicians, political pundits, religious leaders, eight-year-olds, and eighty-year-olds. In other words, ordinary people write blogs and ordinary people read blogs. No special skills are required to begin your foray into blogging. You need not have a purpose or a plan. The most important thing to remember about blogging is that it is ultimately your own space, and you may do with it whatever you want.

Hopefully, what you'll want to do is participate in the greater blogging community. Unlike a simple static website, the format of a blog creates a framework upon which a community can be built. With a static website, what you see is what you get; there is no expectation of interactivity between the reader and the author or subject of the content. For instance, if you visit a website and gather corporate information or information about your favorite musician or sports team, you typically can't post a follow-up to the content or ask a question which will then be answered with authority. However, that sequence of events is exactly what the blogging community is built on: communication and conversation. People write posts, other people leave comments, more ideas are generated, and the discussion continues on another blog, and so on and so forth.

Understanding the Anatomy of a Blog

Unlike websites, which can be unpredictable with regards to content and structure, blogs tend to have very distinct elements that follow a typical order. That is, blogs contain posts, which might or might not allow for comments, and these posts are displayed with the most recent post at the beginning of the index page. Additionally, blog templates are often put together so that the display contains a sidebar column into which the blog author can put lists of links, affiliations, and other information pertinent to the author or his blog.

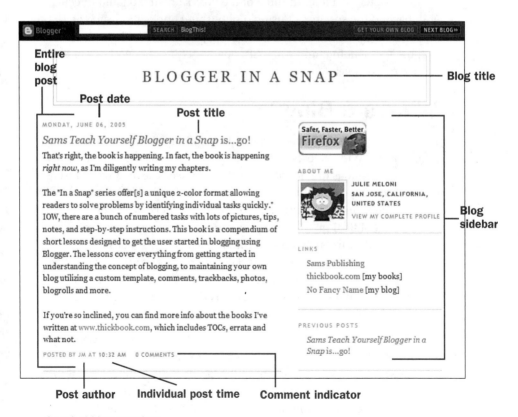

A typical blog template.

The figure shown here displays some of the typical elements you will see in a blog. Although the physical styles of blog templates—colors, fonts, and so forth—often differ between users, general structural elements remain consistent. For instance, all blogs have a title that is displayed prominently at the top of the blog main page as well as subsequent blog archive pages.

A day's worth of blog posts will begin with the posting date, followed by the title of the individual post. The content of the post comes next, and the posting time comes at the end. In the footer area of the post, where the posting time is usually displayed, you might also see the post author's name, something like posted by [yourname]. The inclusion of the post author's name is important when posting to a group blog because readers will want to know exactly which member of the group blog posted this particular bit of content. If multiple blog entries are posted on the same day, as shown in this example, each entry will fall under the single posting date heading, with the most recent post listed at the top.

As with all elements of display, the appearance of blog comments is customizable. When using Blogger's built-in commenting system, you may choose to enable or disable comments for your entire blog or just particular posts. Sometimes you might write posts that don't necessarily warrant comments, or just might not feel like opening comments for very personal posts. You'll learn more about the customization of Blogger comments, as well as third-party commenting systems, in Chapter 6, "Commenting and Trackback."

The final element shown in this example is the sidebar. Blog templates, especially the stock Blogger templates, almost always have a side column built into them, for the placement of author information, blogrolls, and other links of interest to the author. Some people use this area to personalize their blog; in addition to the basic "about me" information, you might see dynamic images that reflect the author's mood, a list of songs the author is listening to, or a list of books and movies that the author has recently enjoyed. Placing elements in the sidebar is part of editing the Blogger template itself, which you will learn about in Chapter 5, "Working with Blogger Templates."

Remaining Anonymous

You will likely encounter more pseudonymous bloggers than those who use their real names and tell you their actual geographic location. Such a blogger will often go to great lengths to protect her identity and location. You will often see pseudonyms for institutions and other locations, such as the following description from a pseudonymous academic blogger: "BrightStar is the alias of an assistant professor making her way on the tenure track. She is entering her second year on the faculty at Research University (RU) in Sleepy Town." So, throughout all the posts made by this blogger, the town in which she lives is always referenced as

"Sleepy Town" and her place of employment as "RU." Never will she say "here in Smithville" or "in the Geography Department at Northeast State Technical College" because such specifics would enable readers to discern her identity. Similarly, as this blogger leaves comments on other sites, she uses her alias instead of her real name. Additionally, as seen in this example, some pseudony- mous bloggers use a graphical image, called an *avatar*, to represent them online.

The blog of a pseudonymous blogger.

The reasons for using a pseudonym are unique for every blogger. Some people want the freedom to write whatever they want without having to worry that their friends, family, employers, and co-workers will find some scathing remarks via a Google search.

▶ DOOCE
http://www.dooce.com
Heather Armstrong is a blogger who was fired for items posted on her blog. Her blog is (and was at the time) called Dooce, which lead to creation of the slang verb *dooce*, mean- ing "to be fired from your job for items posted on your blog." Heather is not the only person ever to be fired for blogging about her job or on the job. Read your employee handbook and use good sense if you're using real names.

For others, the reasons for using a pseudonym have to do with privacy and per- sonal safety—especially when it comes to families and children. If a blogger writes about daily life and daily routines without having a masked identity, it is possible that some of the less savory individuals in this world would take advantage of these movements.

Still others might simply want to create a different persona for their life online, different than the persona that is assumed by using a real name and personal or professional description. Some of the issues described earlier might also play into the decision to remain pseudonymous, or the blogger might simply want to carve out a new niche.

Traversing the Blogosphere

Before you begin blogging on your own, you might want to spend some time investigating the communities in which you think you will possibly want to participate. You can also use this pre-blogging time to get a feel for the types of things people write about and how they go about maintaining a connection with their readers. For example, do you see bloggers allowing comments on all their posts or do they disallow comments for very personal posts? Do bloggers refer to people they know in real life by using pseudonyms or real names? Before you begin to blog, the time you spend looking around can help shape the blog you eventually build.

Finding a Community

It's simple to find a blogging community (or two, or three) in which you want to participate because everyone has an interest in something. Perhaps you are particularly passionate about technology, or you enjoy particular television shows, or you like to knit, or you work in higher education, or you're a new parent—regardless of your interests, you will find people who share them. So, where to start?

After you have identified topics or groups of people of interest to you, a starting point for discovering blogs is the old standby: the Yahoo! directory. The Yahoo! category found at http://dir.yahoo.com/Computers_and_Internet/Internet/World_Wide_Web/Weblogs/Directories/ contains a listing of numerous blog directories.

Two of the most popular entries in this Yahoo! category are the Blogwise and Technorati websites, described next:

- **Blogwise**. This website, found at http://www.blogwise.com/, is a user-submitted directory of blogs. Blogs are categorized by location and also by keyword; submissions can have unlimited keywords. You can search Blogwise by keywords or combinations of keywords, and you'll be sure to find something of interest to you.

- **Technorati**. This blog-specific search engine, found at http://www.technorati. com/, provides users with a few ways to discover new content. Use Technorati to search for keywords in blogs, specific keyword-tagged posts, find blogs that have linked to specific URLs, and more.

After using directory listings and search engines to find blogs of interest to you, you will quickly find that you can use the links within these blogs to find even more sites that you might enjoy. It is very common for bloggers to include *blogrolls* (lists of links to similar-themed blogs) blogs maintained by friends and colleagues, or simply other sites that the blogger frequently reads. You'll learn about maintaining your own blogroll in **42 Using Blogrolls.**

Making Friends and Influencing People

After you've found a blog that appeals to you, the next step is to venture out into it. You can be a silent reader—also called a *lurker*—or you can jump right into the conversation. It all depends on your own personality.

The term *lurker* is not at all pejorative. It simply means you're reading blog content and following the conversation going on in the comments section of the post, but you don't participate often (if at all). I lurk on many blogs. Sometimes it's because I don't have anything to add to the conversation—sometimes it's because I know that Jane SuperCool A-List Blogger doesn't care one whit for what I have to say. The point is this: Lurking isn't bad. In fact, it's a recommended means of entry into a new community.

Think of the Blogosphere as one big party. What happens when a stranger enters the room and loudly begins conversing with anyone who will listen? Typically, people will start slinking away, regardless of whether Loud Person has something interesting to discuss. But if a calm, quiet person sidles up to a conversation, listens for a bit, and then interjects some insightful commentary, voila! New friends are made.

Utilizing Basic Blogging Etiquette

We all want to make friends and influence people, right? Even if you write only in your own little corner of the Blogosphere, you'll be in contact with other humans, and it's important to treat your readers and fellow commenters as such. We're all human beings, and we all have something to offer to the world—just as we all have flaws. The following sections provide some guidelines to remember, which— remarkably enough—mimic etiquette in the real world.

Blogospheric Diversity

Bloggers exist on all seven continents, and virtually every demographic group on earth is represented by at least one blogger. Bloggers are very young, very old, and every age in between. Bloggers come in every shade of color between translucent white and deep ebony. Religion, sexual orientation, social class, gender—you name it, and there's a blogger out there to match any and every combination thereof.

Unless you have some sixth sense that tells you the particulars about a person based solely on a few words printed on your monitor, you will have no idea to whom you are leaving a comment or who might be reading your blog. Unless you aim to offend others or incite arguments, bear in mind this note about diversity.

That is not to say that you cannot express your opinions on your own blog or in the comment areas of other blogs. However, there is a fine line between expressing an opinion while recognizing the inherent worth of all people, and making bigoted statements with the intent to offend. Crossing or not crossing that line is a personal matter for each and every one of you.

Opinions Versus Facts

No one is "right" or "wrong" in the Blogosphere, unless there are facts in evidence that tip the scales one way or another. For instance, my car is silver. I know it is. If I say it is and a reader leaves a comment to the effect of "your car is blue," that person has obviously just lost some credibility. In this situation, I would correct the person, explaining that my car is indeed silver and I know this because I bought it, it's parked outside my house, and here, gentle reader, is a photograph of it. The example I just used is pretty lame as examples go, but it does show how to diffuse a possibly contentious conversation: offer evidence that supports the argument you are trying to make. But what if there is no evidence?

Let's say two people are arguing over whether newborn babies should ever wear polka-dotted clothes. One person might offer an opinion that her child benefited greatly from wearing polka-dotted clothes. Another person might offer an opinion that polka-dotted clothes caused tremendous mental anguish for his child and in fact is the cause of his child's developmental delay. Neither person can point to a scientific study regarding the effects of polka-dotted clothes on newborns. The two should agree to disagree, and the person who asked the question originally should consider both sides of the argument. However, if either of the opinionated parents says that he or she is right and the other person is wrong without offering factual evidence to bolster the case, that stubborn blogger is behaving badly.

Cite Your Sources

If you offer facts in evidence, use links in your posts to direct readers to the primary source of this evidence. For instance, if you are citing scientific research, link to the journal article in which the research was published. If the primary source is not available to you, link to a reputable secondary source in your post. In other words, if you are offering evidence to support your claims, provide your readers with a method to evaluate this evidence on their own.

In addition to citing sources, give credit where it is due. Perhaps you're writing a blog post about a spectacular salad you made for dinner. If you got the recipe from your mother, say so. If you got the recipe from another blogger who posted the recipe on his blog, say so with a link. The link serves several purposes: It shows you're not a salad recipe plagiarist, and it tells the original blogger that you used his recipe and enjoyed it. The act of linking also increases the page-rank of the original blogger's page in search engines that use the number of incoming links as a measure of the value of the page content.

▶ **NOTE**

In addition to citing sources within the text of your post, you can also utilize a blog-specific type of linking called *trackback*. You can learn more about trackbacks in Chapter 6.

Trollish Behavior

Trolls have been around since the first words were typed on Usenet, all those years ago. If you have spent any time on mailing lists or message boards, you've likely experienced a troll. Trolls exist for the sole purpose of "posting specious arguments, flames, or personal attacks," and they typically have no interest whatsoever in the topic at hand.

▶ **THE JARGON FILE**

http://www.catb.org/~esr/jargon/

The full definition of *troll*, and much more information on Internet jargon in general, can be found here.

It might take some time before you can immediately recognize trollish behavior. If you think a troll is baiting you into responding, you might want to post a short response to the argumentative comment by beginning with something like, "You appear to be a troll, but regardless I will briefly answer this question." You might also want to end your response with something like, "If you are not a troll, we can continue this discussion in a more civil manner." But the best way to get rid of the troll is simply to ignore it. On your own blog, if you feel a troll has posted in your comments section and want your regular readers to ignore it as well, you might post a comment that says, "Please do not feed the troll."

Additional Tips

A *successful* blog means different things to different people. Personally, my own blog is a success because it provides me with a place to chronicle people, places, and things in my life—and my handwriting is atrocious, so that was never an option. The fact that anyone at all reads my own blog is simply icing on the cake. The interaction between members of my own little blogging community is special to me because we all have things we can learn from each other. But even if no one else read my blog, I'd still be happy with it. Other people have a real need to receive comments to their posts, as a sort of validation that someone is reading their work and is moved to say something about it, and that's fine too.

However, in addition to the other elements of etiquette just discussed, there are two very blog-specific things that are considered bad form:

- **Don't ask others for a link to your blog**. If they want to link to you because they read your blog and think others would like to as well, that's their own business. Just because you link to someone doesn't mean she has to link to you. For instance, I link to Wil Wheaton's blog because I read it and enjoy it. I never expect Wil Wheaton to link to my blog, and I wouldn't ask him to do it.

▶ WIL WHEATON'S BLOG
http://www.wilwheaton.net

Wil Wheaton played Wesley Crusher on *Star Trek: The Next Generation* and Gordie in *Stand By Me*, among other things. He is still an actor, but also an author and a darn fine blogger.

- **Don't complain about a perceived lack of readership**. You might have more readers than you know because not all readers leave comments. If your regular readers feel unappreciated by such statements like, "No one reads my blog and that makes me sad," they're likely to stop coming around. If a new reader stops by and sees such a post, he might not stay because such a per-sonality trait is unappealing to some. It also calls into question the purpose of your blog. Do you write for others or for yourself? If you write for others and you believe no one is reading, doesn't that speak to a bigger issue?

To end this section on a positive note, the primary tip I can offer to you is simply to have fun. Blogging can be emotionally draining, but it can also be a raucous good time for you and newfound friends.

Using Available Blogger Resources

The good folks at Google maintain several resources for help with the Blogger application. When you visit the Blogger website (http://www.blogger.com/) you will see recent news posted on the main page. This area often calls attention to new features that have been added or scheduled downtime that might occur for maintenance. As you begin your foray into the Blogosphere, the following are some links you may want to bookmark regarding Blogger and resources for help:

- **Blogger Help**, found at http://help.blogger.com/, is the official Blogger documentation and list of Blogger How-To documents. You can also contact Blogger Support via links found here.

- **Blogger Knowledge**, found at http://www.blogger.com/knowledge/, contains articles written by Blogger developers that will help you get the most out of your blog.

- **Blogger Buzz**, found at http://buzz.blogspot.com/, is a group blog maintained by Blogger developers that posts items of interest which are generally Blogger-related.

- **Blogger Status**, found at http://status.blogger.com/, contains notifications of scheduled Blogger downtime, explanations for unscheduled outages, information about upgrades, and so on. If Blogger is acting wonky for you, this should be the first place you check to rule out any upgrades in progress.

2

Getting Started with Blogger

IN THIS CHAPTER:

The topics in this chapter are all about setting up your new blog and working with the basic configuration settings provided by the Blogger platform. Absolutely no programming, system administration, or web design skills are required—the good folks at Blogger have created a painless, World Wide Web–based interface for getting started in the world of blogging.

One of the best features of working with Blogger is the ability to change configuration settings and have these settings apply immediately after republishing your blog. These settings range from simply adding the **Email Post** icon and functionality to all your blog posts to changing the entire look and feel of your blog by selecting a new template. For instance, in only a few mouse clicks, your blog can go from pastel to primary colors and back again. If you don't like your template, try something new! Dissatisfied with your archive configuration? Change it! If you decide you want to take down a post you've already published, you can either delete it or put it in Draft mode and save the text for another day.

Before you can configure your new blog, you have to create a Blogger account— that's where this journey begins.

1 **1** ## Creating Your Blogger Account

Registering with Blogger is the first step toward creating your first blog, and it couldn't be easier, given the form-based interface for doing so. Simply point your web browser to the Blogger home page at http://www.blogger.com/ and you're good to go. There you'll see a very visible link that says **Create Your Blog Now**. Click this link to begin the process.

1 Choose a Username

The username you select will be the username with which you log in to the Blogger site. This username will not be used for identification purposes anywhere in public, so if your name is Jane Smith and you plan to blog with a pseudonym like FancyJane, you can still use janesmith as your username and the Blogosphere will be none the wiser.

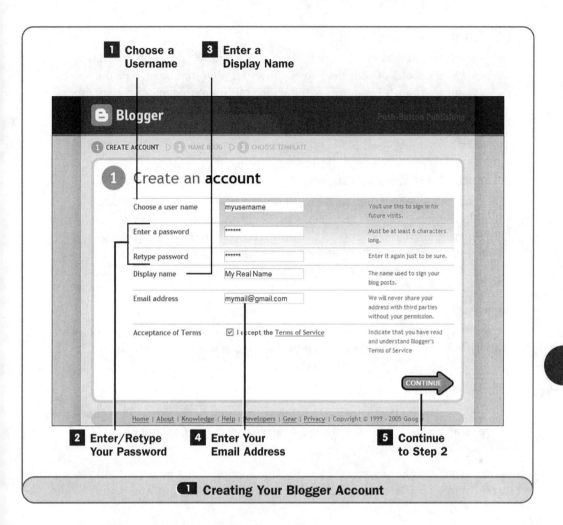

1 Choose a
    Username

3 Enter a
    Display Name

Blogger   Push-Button Publishing

1 CREATE ACCOUNT ▷ 2 NAME BLOG ▷ 3 CHOOSE TEMPLATE

1 Create an **account**

Choose a user name	myusername	You'll use this to sign in for future visits.
Enter a password	******	Must be at least 6 characters long.
Retype password	******	Enter it again just to be sure.
Display name	My Real Name	The name used to sign your blog posts.
Email address	mymail@gmail.com	We will never share your address with third parties without your permission.
Acceptance of Terms	☑ I accept the Terms of Service	Indicate that you have read and understand Blogger's Terms of Service

CONTINUE ▶

Home | About | Knowledge | Help | Developers | Gear | Privacy | Copyright © 1999 - 2005 Google

2 Enter/Retype
    Your Password

4 Enter Your
    Email Address

5 Continue
    to Step 2

1 Creating Your Blogger Account

2 Enter/Retype Your Password

Think up a password that is at least six characters long, and type it in the **Enter a Password** field. Although you're not protecting sensitive financial information, it's still a good idea to choose a good password. For instance, try to include punctuation or special characters such as an exclamation point or a pound sign, as well as numbers and a mix of uppercase and lowercase letters. You should be able to remember your password but it shouldn't be a common dictionary word, your birthday, phone number, or any other phrase that would be easy to guess. After typing the password in the **Enter a Password** field, retype it in the **Retype Password** field.

3 Enter a Display Name

The name you select and enter in the **Display Name** field will be the name used in the footer of your blog posts. This name does not have to be the same as your username. For instance, although your username might be janesmith, if you plan to blog with a pseudonym like FancyJane, enter it in this field. Your blog posts will appear as written by FancyJane, and any comments you leave on Blogger-enabled blog postings will appear as from FancyJane as well.

4 Enter Your Email Address

Enter a valid email address in the **Email Address** field. This email address will be visible to others only if you choose to enable this feature in your Blogger profile. If you are blogging with a pseudonym, you might also want to maintain a separate email address for your online identity. Many bloggers use GMail, Hotmail, or Yahoo! Mail for free and anonymous email accounts.

▶ **WEB RESOURCE**

http://mail.google.com/, http://www.hotmail.com/, http://mail.yahoo.com/
GMail, Hotmail, and Yahoo! Mail all offer free and anonymous email accounts.

5 Continue to Step 2

After reviewing the information on the first screen of the registration process and accepting the Blogger **Terms of Service**, click the **Continue** arrow to move on to the next step.

At this point, you have completed all the information about yourself. Next you must complete information specific to your blog. Click the **Continue** button to go to the next step in the process.

---

2 Naming Your Blog

✔ BEFORE YOU BEGIN	→ SEE ALSO
1 Creating Your Blogger Account	**3** Using Blogger with Third-Party Hosting
	14 Modifying Your Blogger Profile

▶ **NOTE**

The instructions in this topic assume that you are hosting your blog with Blogger. If you would like to host your blog on your own server but still use the Blogger publishing inter-face, please see **3** Using Blogger with Third-Party Hosting for information regarding the completion of the registration process.

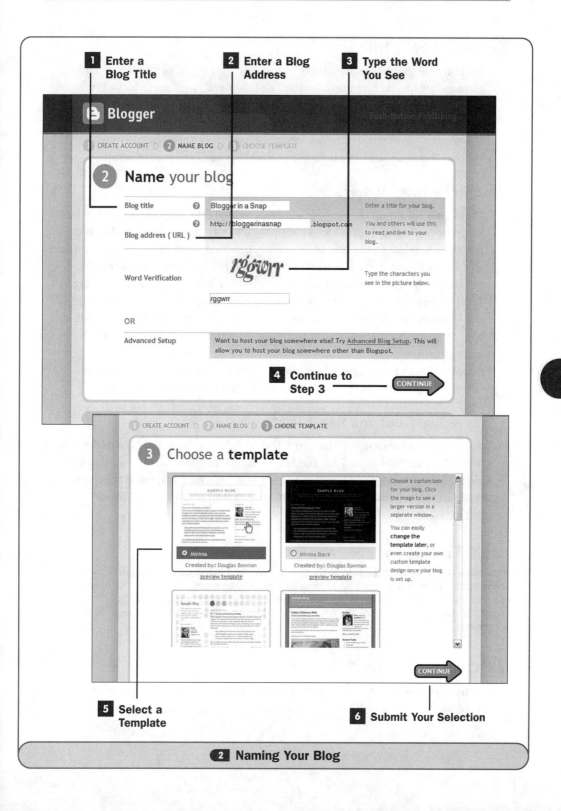

1 Enter a Blog Title

2 Enter a Blog Address

3 Type the Word You See

Blogger

Push-Button Publishing

CREATE ACCOUNT ▷ **2** NAME BLOG ▷ **3** CHOOSE TEMPLATE

2 Name your blog

Blog title	❓	Blogger in a Snap	Enter a title for your blog.
Blog address (URL)	❓	http://bloggerinasnap .blogspot.com	You and others will use this to read and link to your blog.
Word Verification		*rggwrr*	Type the characters you see in the picture below.
		rggwrr	
OR			
Advanced Setup		Want to host your blog somewhere else? Try Advanced Blog Setup. This will allow you to host your blog somewhere other than Blogspot.	

4 Continue to Step 3 — CONTINUE

CREATE ACCOUNT ▷ **2** NAME BLOG ▷ **3** CHOOSE TEMPLATE

3 Choose a template

○ Minima
Created by: Douglas Bowman
preview template

○ Minima Black
Created by: Douglas Bowman
preview template

Choose a custom look for your blog. Click the image to see a larger version in a separate window.

You can easily **change the template later**, or even create your own custom template design once your blog is set up.

CONTINUE

5 Select a Template

6 Submit Your Selection

1 Enter a Blog Title

Select a title that is meaningful to you to use as the title of your blog. You can change this title at any time, so don't feel as if you are forever locked into your blog's identity. For instance, my own blog is called No Fancy Name specifically because I couldn't think of anything spectacular to name it. However, if I ever decided to rename my blog Julie's Spectacular House o' Writing, I can do so without repercussions—it's just an account setting!

2 Enter a Blog Address

When publishing on the Blogger servers, the blog address you choose will be a hostname that is appended to a blogspot.com domain. Your blog address does not need to relate to the title of your blog, but it's a good idea if they're similar so that your blog address is easy to remember. For instance, just as the title of my blog is No Fancy Name, its address is http://nofancyname.blogspot.com/. I can simply tell someone the name of my blog, and if they're familiar with the hostname.blogspot.com convention, they'll likely find my blog without writing down the address or bookmarking it. Just like your blog title, the blog address is modifiable through your account settings. Be aware that blog addresses must be unique, which means your first choice might already be taken—so have a backup or two when you decide to set up your blog.

3 Type the Word You See

You will see a randomly displayed *captcha* followed by a text box in the **Word Verification** field. Type the letters and/or numbers exactly as you see them. This word verification step is used to ensure that you are a real person and not an automated process attempting to start a blog for nefarious reasons.

▶ KEY TERM

Captcha—An acronym that stands for *completely automated public Turing test to tell comptuers and humans apart* and refers to a type of challenge-response test used to determine whether the user is a human rather than an automated process. The word verification captcha, in which the word is displayed as a distorted image, is very common.

4 Continue to Step 3

After reviewing the information on the second screen of the registration process, click the **Continue** arrow to move on to the next step.

5 Select a Template

Blogger has several ready-made templates available for your use. You can scroll up and down in the windows to see all the choices available to you. When you see a template design that interests you, click the **Preview Template** link to launch a sample in a new browser window. Just like other blog settings, you can select a new template at any time. Do not feel as if you will be tied to your template forever; simply select a template to get started and you can change aspects of it (or the entire thing) later on.

6 Submit Your Selection

After selecting a template, click the **Continue** arrow to submit your selection and create your new blog.

After you complete the final step of the registration process, Blogger provides you with a link to continue on to post a blog entry. You can return to the main Blogger profile page by clicking the Blogger logo.

3	**Using Blogger with Third-Party Hosting**
✔ **BEFORE YOU BEGIN**	→ **SEE ALSO**
1 Creating Your Blogger Account	**14** Modifying Your Blogger Profile

3

The setup information presented in **2** **Naming Your Blog** was geared toward completing the registration process based on hosting your blog with Blogger on the blogspot.com domain. Although the majority of Blogger users stick with this all-in-one solution, if you have a custom domain name and access to web server space, you can utilize Blogger's FTP publishing feature. This feature allows you to utilize the Blogger management interface for customization and post editing—the only difference is that the act of publishing puts all files on your server rather than Blogger's servers.

The first step in publishing to your own web host is obtaining a custom domain name. Use the same guidance when selecting a domain name that you would when selecting a blog hostname: Try to make it easy to remember, and try to pick something that makes sense with regards to the content of your blog. For instance, if you plan to blog about your life as an academic, don't try to register acmeplumbing.com. Similarly—and this should be a no-brainer—if you want to maintain your anonymity, don't use your own name as your domain name.

After you decide on a short list of domain names, you must register the name with a reputable domain registration service. There are a great many of these services, with prices ranging from a few dollars per year to fifteen or twenty dollars per year. A simple Google search for "domain name registration" will yield many results, but here are three that I've worked with over the years and have no problems recommending:

- Network Solutions can be found at http://www.networksolutions.com/

- Register.com can be found at http://www.register.com/

- Domain Direct can be found at http://www.domaindirect.com/

These are only three of hundreds of possibilities for domain registration; look around and pick a company that appeals to you. If they all look the same to you, you won't go wrong with any of the three listed here.

If you plan to blog anonymously (or pseudonymously), you have to take extra steps to protect yourself if you plan to utilize a custom domain. All domain records are public information and contain three sets of addresses: one each for registrant, administrative contact, and technical contact. However, there is a domain registration service created specifically with this situation in mind: DomainsByProxy (http://www.domainsbyproxy.com/). If you purchase your domain through this service, it ensures that your privacy is kept.

After obtaining a domain name, you'll need to find a hosting provider that suits your needs. Many domain registration services also offer web hosting solution bundles, many of which provide you with everything you need to publish your blog on your own server. At the very minimum you need FTP access to your host, but other considerations include the amount of server space provided as well as the amount of bandwidth allotted to you. If you plan to host sound or video files, which are often quite large, server space will be a consideration. However, if you plan to house only your blog content, text files take up very little space; the typical 100MB of server space usually allotted for basic accounts would be plenty. Typically, hosting services simply charge you an overage fee of a few dollars per X number of megabytes over your limit.

The other consideration is your bandwidth allotment. If you are serving only the text of your blog, the bandwidth coming into and going out of your host will be minimal (unless you're wildly popular). But if you are serving sound and video files, you will use considerably more bandwidth. A basic hosting package might include anywhere from 1GB to 10GB of bandwidth on a monthly basis. But just like with server space overages, your hosting provider will simply charge you a few dollars for overages.

A good hosting solution does not have to be expensive. In fact, basic packages suitable for nonintensive blog hosting are available for $5 or $10 per month. If you become a world-famous, A-list blogger, you could find a $50 per month hosting package (or less) that would take care of your needs. Following this paragraph, I list a few hosting providers that offer stable hosting services with all the features you need (and then some). These are only a few of the hundreds and hundreds of hosting providers out there, but I've personally had some experience working with the providers listed here and could easily recommend them—unlike, say, Joe's House of Hosting, which I know nothing about.

- DreamHost, found at http://www.dreamhost.com/

- Fusion Flux, found at http://www.fusionflux.com/

- Hurricane Electric, found at http://www.he.net/

- iPowerWeb, found at http://www.ipowerweb.com/

- iValueHost, found at http://www.ivaluehost.net/

- LiveRack, found at http://www.liverack.com/

- MyHosting, found at http://www.myhosting.com/

After you set up your domain and your web hosting account, arm yourself with your FTP username, FTP password, and the directory path on the server. Those pieces are all you need to configure Blogger's FTP publishing settings.

You configure your FTP publishing settings at the time you initially create your blog, or you can change your publishing settings after your blog has been created. In this section, you'll see the steps used to set up FTP publishing during the initial blog creation sequence.

First, perform the first set of steps in **1** **Creating Your Blogger Account**, which includes visiting the Blogger home page at http://www.blogger.com/ and following the link that says **Create Your Blog Now**. When you have proceeded to the second step of the process, instead of completing the **blog title**, **blog address**, and **word verification** fields, skip over them and follow the link to **Advanced Blog Setup**.

1. Enter a title for your blog in the **Blog Title** field.

2. If you would like your blog to be linked to Blogger.com, select the **Listed** radio button. Otherwise, select the **Unlisted** radio button.

3. Enter the address of your FTP server in the **FTP Server** field. Your hosting provider might tell you to FTP to your actual domain name (for example, www.yourdomain.com), the FTP server might be ftp.yourdomain.com, or it might be something completely different. The point is that this information comes from your hosting provider.

3

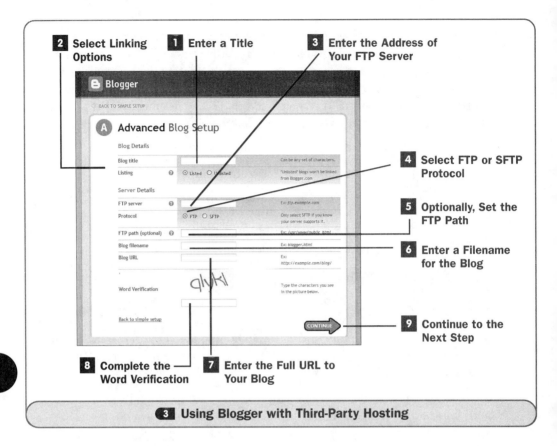

2 Select Linking Options

1 Enter a Title

3 Enter the Address of Your FTP Server

4 Select FTP or SFTP Protocol

5 Optionally, Set the FTP Path

6 Enter a Filename for the Blog

9 Continue to the Next Step

8 Complete the Word Verification

7 Enter the Full URL to Your Blog

3 Using Blogger with Third-Party Hosting

4. Select the radio button for **FTP** in the **Protocol** field, unless you are specifically told by your hosting provider to use the SFTP protocol.

5. If you have been given a specific path to use for your FTP home directory, enter it in the **FTP Path** field. If you have not been given a specific path or if the specific path is the same as your home directory, you may leave this field blank.

6. Enter a filename in the **Blog Filename** field. This filename will be used as the front page of your blog. If your blog is the only site hosted in your server space, you can enter **index.html** in the **Blog Filename** field so that when someone enters **http://www.yourdomain.com/**, they immediately see the front page of your blog. However, if your blog is part of a full website about you (or your company), you should name your front page file blog.html or something similar to avoid conflicts between the start page and the actual main page of your website.

However, if you utilize a subdirectory for your blog (which is set in the next field), you can safely use the index.html filename; no conflict will arise because the main page of your website and the main page of your blog will be in completely different directories.

7. Enter a full **Blog URL** in the field provided. This includes the protocol (http://) as well as your domain name and, optionally, blog directory name. For instance, http://www.yourdomain.com/ would be a valid blog URL, as would http://www.yourdomain.com/myBlog/. Be sure that you have created this directory on your web server.

8. Complete the **Word Verification** field by entering the words you see in the image.

9. Continue on to the next step by clicking the Continue arrow.

When you have completed this form, click the **Continue** arrow. You will select a starter template in the next step. You can scroll up and down in the browser window to view the standard Blogger templates available to you. When you see a template design that interests you, click the **Preview Template** link to launch a sample in a new browser window. You can change your template at any time during the life of your blog, as you will see in **5** **Selecting a New Template**, as well as in the topics in Chapter 5, "Working with Blogger Templates."

After selecting a template, click the **Continue** arrow to submit your selection and create your new blog. When this process is complete, Blogger provides you with a link to continue on to post a blog entry. You can return to the main Blogger profile page by clicking the Blogger logo. At this point, no files have been transferred to your server. You must create a post and publish this post before files are transferred. Additionally, you might want to modify your Blogger publishing configuration so that your FTP username and password are saved. If you do not save your FTP username and password, you will be prompted for it each time you publish a post, the blog index, or your entire blog.

If you decide to switch from hosting on the blogspot.com domain to hosting with your own service provider with your own custom domain name, all you need to do is modify your publishing settings via the Blogger management interface. After you have configured your publishing settings, the act of publishing your blog results in the publication of numerous static web pages to your new server.

To begin, log in to the Blogger management interface and select the **Change Settings** link from your Blogger dashboard. Click the **Publishing** navigational item. You will see your current settings, which will say You're publishing on blogspot.com if you haven't yet made the switch. To change your publishing option to FTP and to enter your FTP settings, click the **FTP** link. If you have already configured your blog to publish on your own server and are simply modifying your publishing settings, the FTP configuration screen will be the default screen shown to you.

▶ **NOTE**

If you need to use the SFTP protocol as instructed by your hosting provider, click the **SFTP** link instead of the **FTP** link. The subsequent form is the same for both protocols.

The FTP configuration form will look something like the following; if you have already configured your blog to publish via FTP and are here only to modify your settings, the form fields will be prepopulated with your existing information.

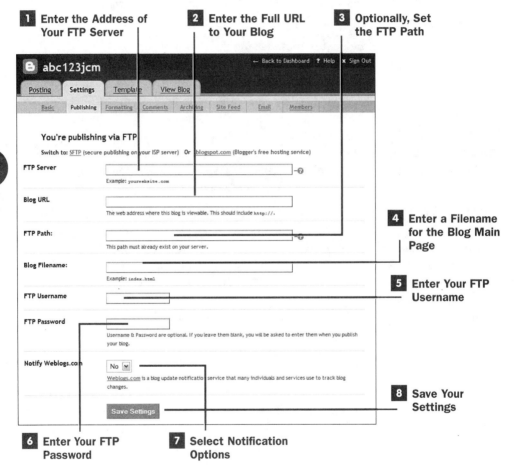

Configuring the FTP settings for an existing blog.

1. Enter the address of your FTP server in the **FTP Server** field. Your hosting provider might tell you to FTP to your actual domain name (for example, www.yourdomain.com), the FTP server might be ftp.yourdomain.com, or it might be something completely different. The point is that this information comes from your hosting provider.

2. Enter a full **Blog URL** in the field provided. This includes the protocol (http://) as well as your domain name and, optionally, blog directory name. For instance, http://www.yourdomain.com/ would be a valid blog URL, as would http://www.yourdomain.com/myBlog/. Be sure that you have created this directory on your web server.

3. If you have been given a specific path to use for your FTP home directory, enter it in the **FTP Path** field. If you have not been given a specific path or if the specific path is the same as your home directory, you can leave this field blank.

4. Enter a filename in the **Blog Filename** field. This filename will be used as the front page of your blog. If your blog is the only site hosted in your server space, you can enter **index.html** in the **Blog Filename** field so that when someone enters **http://www.yourdomain.com/**, they immediately see the front page of your blog. However, if your blog is part of a full website about you (or your company), you should name your front page blog.html or something similar name to avoid conflicts between the start page and your actual website main page.

However, if you utilize a subdirectory for your blog (refer to step 2, earlier), you can safely use the index.html filename; no conflict will arise because the main page of your website and the main page of your blog will be in completely different directories.

5. Enter your FTP username in the **FTP Username** field.

6. Enter your FTP password in the **FTP Password** field.

7. If you would like the Weblogs.com notification service to be notified when you update your blog, select **Yes** from the Notify Weblogs.com drop-down list. Otherwise, select **No**.

8. To save the changes made on this screen, click the **Save Settings** button. You will see an onscreen confirmation when the settings are saved, and at that point you must click the **Republish** button to initiate the publishing sequence.

When the publishing sequence displays its notice of completion, you can navigate away from the Blogger user interface and view your blog or work with other settings. After publishing your blog, the static files will be on your web server.

3

▶ **NOTE**

If you decide to delete your blog, going into the Blogger management interface and utilizing the **Delete This Blog** option removes your blog from the Blogger application but the static pages will remain on your server. Alternately, if you accidentally delete files from your web server, the act of republishing your entire blog through the Blogger management interface puts the content back on your server—all is not lost.

---

4   **Logging In to Blogger and Navigating the Dashboard**

✔ BEFORE YOU BEGIN	→ SEE ALSO
1 Creating Your Blogger Account	**14** Modifying Your Blogger Profile

To log into Blogger after you create an account and a blog, point your web browser to the Blogger home page at http://www.blogger.com/. There you'll see the login area in the top right of your screen.

▶ **TIP**

In addition to just being the place where you go to log in to Blogger, the Blogger main page contains links to numerous ways to increase your blogging experience. Here you'll find a scrolling list of recently updated blogs, a list of featured blogs, a link to a random "next blog," and an interface for Google's Blog Search. Additionally, you will find new Blogger features announced on the Blogger home page.

1 **Retrieve Your Username or Password**

If you have forgotten either your username or your password, click the small question mark next to the **Password** field. You will be taken to the **Forgot Your Password?** screen—which also works if you remember your password but not your username.

2 **Recover Your Password**

To recover your password, enter your username in the **Username** field and click the **Recover Password** button. Additional instructions will be sent to the email address saved in your Blogger profile.

3 **Recover Your Username**

To recover your username, enter your email address in the **Email** field and click the **Recover Username** button. Additional instructions will be sent to the email address specified. For this process to work, you must enter the same email address used to create your Blogger account.

6 Click Sign In to Continue

1 Retrieve Your Username or Password

4 Enter Your Username and Password

2 Recover Your Password

5 Check the Remember Me Box

3 Recover Your Username

7 Primary Dashboard Elements

8 Add Another Blog to Your Account

4 Enter Your Username and Password

To log in with your original username and password, enter your username in the **Username** field and your password in the **Password** field. Remember that usernames and passwords are case-sensitive, so check your Caps Lock key before typing. Your password will appear as asterisks so that anyone looking over your shoulder does not see your actual password in the text field.

5 Check the Remember Me Box

If you would like Blogger to automatically log in with your information when viewing this page on your computer, enable the **Remember Me** check box. Do not enable this check box if you are using a publicly accessible computer or a shared terminal because anyone using this machine would then have access to your Blogger account.

6 Click Sign In to Continue

After entering your username and password, and possibly checking the **Remember Me** check box, click the **Sign In** button to continue. If your login fails for some reason, such as a mistyped username or password, you are returned to the login screen and an appropriate message is shown, alerting you to your error. If your login is successful, you are sent directly to your Blogger Dashboard.

7 Primary Dashboard Elements

The Blogger Dashboard provides you with links to Blogger news and information as well as help and knowledgebase articles, links to your profile, and, most importantly, links to manage your blog posts and settings. All blogs attached to your account are shown in the primary **Blogs** area. The two icons of most importance in the Dashboard are the **New Post** and **Change Settings** icons.

You will use the **New Post** and **Change Settings** icons as starting points for much of the action that takes place through the Blogger Dashboard. However, if you want to want to edit a post, you click the **New Post** icon as well, although doing so is counter-intuitive.

8 Add Another Blog to Your Account

You can add an unlimited number of blogs to your master Blogger account. To add a new blog, click the **Create a Blog** button and you will be taken directly to step 2 of the process previously used to create a new blog. You might recall that step 2 includes providing a blog title, a blog address, and entering the word verification captcha. You then select a template and your blog will be created. This new blog immediately appears in your Blogger Dashboard, allowing you to modify its settings and begin posting to it.

---

5 **Selecting a New Template**

✔ BEFORE YOU BEGIN	→ SEE ALSO
4 Logging In to Blogger and Navigating the Dashboard	**29** Understanding the Blogger Template Structure and Editor
	33 Implementing a Third-Party Template in Blogger

The process of implementing a new Blogger template is quite simple. However, remember that any customizations you have made to your existing template must be made again to your new template. For instance, if you have edited your existing template to add links or insert advertisements, you will have to make those same edits in your new template. You can find extended information on template modifications in Chapter 5.

In this topic, you learn the mechanics of selecting a new Blogger template and carrying it through the publishing process. For example, suppose that you picked a rather plain template during the initial stages of creating your blog, and after living with it for a few posts, you decide you want to try another standard Blogger template. In a few clicks, your blog can assume an entirely new look and feel.

To begin, log in to Blogger and click the **Change Settings** icon in the **Blogs** section of the Blogger Dashboard.

5

1 Click the Template Tab

The Blogger user interface includes four top-level tabs. Click the **Template** tab to display links to the tools available for working with your template.

2 Click the Pick New Link

After clicking the **Template** tab, you will see a screen that displays your current template code, with the **Edit current** link preselected. To select a new template instead of editing your existing one, click the **Pick New** link under the **Template** tab.

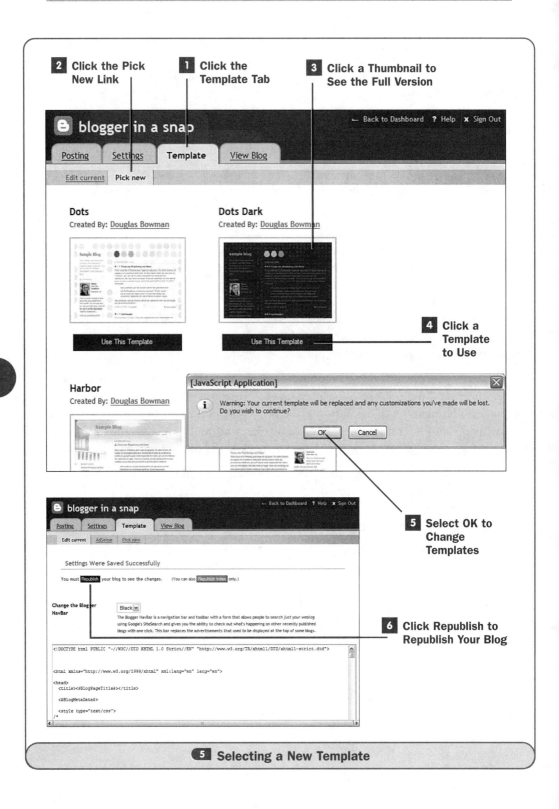

2 Click the Pick New Link

1 Click the Template Tab

3 Click a Thumbnail to See the Full Version

4 Click a Template to Use

5 Select OK to Change Templates

6 Click Republish to Republish Your Blog

5 Selecting a New Template

3 Click a Thumbnail to See the Full Version

Scroll through the list of thumbnails until you see something that catches your eye. Then click a thumbnail to see an example of a blog as if it had that particular template applied to it. The full-version example opens in a new browser window, so be sure to close that window when you finish viewing the template.

4 Select a Template to Use

After you select a template that you want to use, click the **Use This Template** button underneath the new template.

5 Click OK to Change Templates

After selecting a new template from the list of thumbnails, you are presented with a JavaScript alert asking you to verify this change. Click **OK** to accept the change, or click **Cancel** to close the alert and return to the selection screen. After you click OK, there's no going back—the template will have been applied.

6 Click Republish to Republish Your Blog

Although the new template is applied as soon as you click **OK** on the alert in the previous step, you must republish your blog to see pages with your new template applied. Click the **Republish** button to initiate the publishing sequence. When the publishing sequence displays its notice of completion, you can navigate away from the Blogger user interface and view your newly attired blog.

▶ **NOTE**

You can learn more about the designers of the standard Blogger templates by clicking their linked names in the template menu. At the personal sites of these designers, you might find ideas for implementing or extending your own template.

---

6 | **Configuring Basic Blogger Settings**

✔ BEFORE YOU BEGIN	→ SEE ALSO
4 Logging In to Blogger and Navigating the Dashboard	**20** Editing Existing Posts

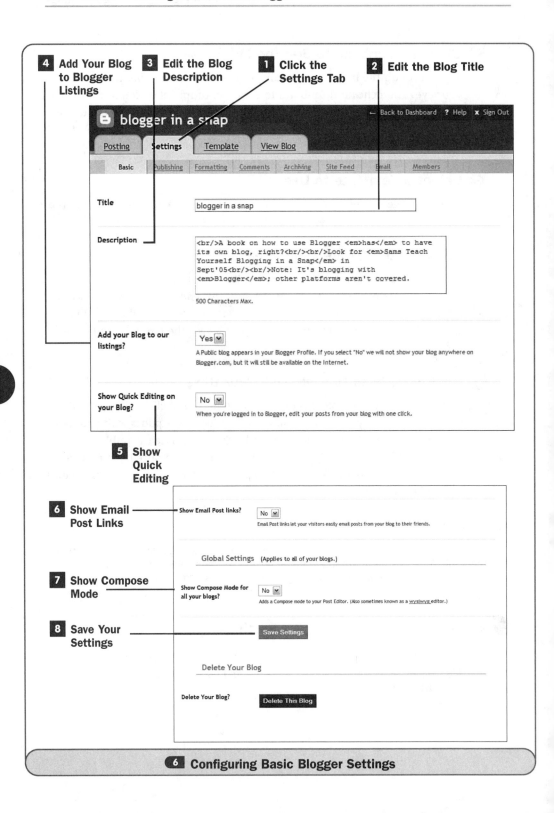

4 Add Your Blog to Blogger Listings

3 Edit the Blog Description

1 Click the Settings Tab

2 Edit the Blog Title

5 Show Quick Editing

6 Show Email Post Links

7 Show Compose Mode

8 Save Your Settings

6 Configuring Basic Blogger Settings

This topic will familiarize you with the basic configurable options under the Settings tab in the Blogger management interface. For example, suppose that you want to modify your blog title or description—just edit the existing settings and you're good to go.

To begin, log in to Blogger and click the **Change Settings** icon in the **Blogs** section of the Blogger Dashboard.

① Click the Settings Tab

The Blogger user interface includes four top-level tabs. Click the **Settings** tab to display links to the numerous configurable options. The **Basic** link will be preselected for you.

② Edit the Blog Title

You can edit the title of your blog at any time. Simply enter a new title in the **Title** field. If you have gained a wide readership, changing your blog title might cause your readership to dwindle until users realize that it is still you behind the posts. On the other hand, changing the title of your blog is sometimes a good way to jump-start a new blogging identity.

③ Edit the Blog Description

You may enter up to five hundred characters, including HTML markup, in the **Description** field. Standard Blogger templates often include a space for the blog description. You can use this space to add additional information about yourself and your blog, or you can use the space to include favorite quotes or other content that adds personalization to your blog.

④ Add Your Blog to Blogger Listings

Select Yes or No from the **Add Your Blog to Our Listings?** drop-down list. If you select Yes, your blog will be listed in your Blogger profile as well as Blogger's list of recently updated blogs (when you add a new post, that is). If you select No, your blog will appear in neither your profile nor in Blogger's list of recently updated blogs. Selecting No does not affect the publishing status of your blog or the availability of your blog to readers—this setting is applicable only to listings.

⑤ Show Quick Editing

Select Yes or No from the **Show Quick Editing on Your Blog?** drop-down list. If you select Yes, your published posts will include a link that will take you directly to the compose window so that you can edit your post. The quick edit link is visible only to you—the logged-in user and owner of the blog.

6

6   Show Email Post Links

Select Yes or No from the **Show Email Post links?** drop-down list. If you select Yes, a link will be included in your published posts that will allow you to send a note, plus the post's URL, to a specified email address. If enabled, the **Email Post** link is visible to any blog reader, and is very useful when your readers want to share good blog posts with their friends. Instead of composing an email in a separate application, readers would be able to simply click a link within your blog post, send the message, and return to your blog for further reading.

7   Show Compose Mode

Select Yes or No from the **Show Compose Mode for All Your Blogs?** drop-down list. Modifying this setting affects all blogs registered to your account. If you select Yes, the default editor for your blog posts will be the compose mode or *WYSIWYG* editor. If you select No, the Blogger editor is a more stripped-down version that allows you to enter your own HTML markup at will.

▶ **KEY TERM**

6

WYSIWYG—An acronym for *what you see is what you get*. A WYSIWYG editor helps you to produce HTML markup without requiring that you know any HTML to begin with.

8   Save Your Settings

To save the changes made on the Basic settings screen, click the **Save Settings** button. You will see a confirmation onscreen when the settings are saved, and at that point you must click the **Republish** button to initiate the publishing sequence. When the publishing sequence displays its notice of completion, you can navigate away from the Blogger user interface and view your blog or work with other settings.

One other button is visible on the Basic settings screen—the **Delete This Blog** button. Click this button only if you are absolutely sure that you want to delete the blog, its settings, and all of your posts. If you delete your blog, your posts become irretrievable.

7 **Using Blogger's Publishing Settings**	
✔ **BEFORE YOU BEGIN**	→ **SEE ALSO**
4 Logging In to Blogger and Navigating the Dashboard	**3** Using Blogger with Third-Party Hosting

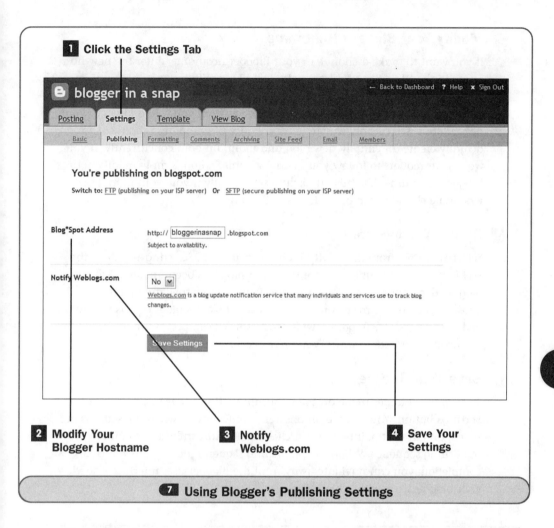

1 Click the Settings Tab

B blogger in a snap
← Back to Dashboard   **?** Help   **x** Sign Out

| Posting | Settings | Template | View Blog |

Basic   Publishing   Formatting   Comments   Archiving   Site Feed   Email   Members

You're publishing on blogspot.com

Switch to: FTP (publishing on your ISP server) Or SFTP (secure publishing on your ISP server)

Blog*Spot Address   http:// [bloggerinasnap] .blogspot.com
Subject to availability.

Notify Weblogs.com   [No ▼]
Weblogs.com is a blog update notification service that many individuals and services use to track blog changes.

[Save Settings]

2 Modify Your Blogger Hostname   **3** Notify Weblogs.com   **4** Save Your Settings

7 Using Blogger's Publishing Settings

The standard Blogger publishing settings are relevant for publishing on the blogspot.com domain. In **3** **Using Blogger with Third-Party Hosting**, you can learn about publishing via FTP to a different host. In this topic, only two additional publishing settings are discussed; both are accessible via the Settings tab in the Blogger management interface.

To begin, log in to Blogger and click the **Change Settings** icon in the **Blogs** section of the Blogger Dashboard.

1 **Click the Settings Tab**

The Blogger user interface includes four top-level tabs. Click the **Settings** tab to display links to the numerous configurable options. The **Basic** link will be preselected for you, so click the **Publishing** link to access the publishing settings.

2 Modify Your Blogger Hostname

If you want to make a change in your Blogger hostname, enter the new hostname in the **Blog*Spot Address** field. Just like modifying your blog name, you might experience a drop in readership when you change your blog address. Blogger does not include any redirects from your old address to your new address, so the only way to leave a notice of an address change is to actually create an entirely new blog and maintain both concurrently. If you want your readers to follow you to a new home, do not simply modify your Blogger hostname. Use this publishing setting only if you want to make a wholesale change from one address to the other.

3 Notify Weblogs.com

Select Yes or No from the **Notify Weblogs.com** field. Selecting Yes alerts the Weblogs.com notification service that your blog has been updated. Many blog readers monitor Weblogs.com and visit blogs as they are updated because readers like fresh content. If you select No, Weblogs.com is not notified of your update. To gain a wide readership, it's important to utilize all the notification services to which you have access.

4 Save Your Settings

To save the changes made on the Publishing settings screen, click the **Save Settings** button. You will see an onscreen confirmation when the settings are saved, and at that point you must click the **Republish** button to initiate the publishing sequence. When the publishing sequence displays its notice of completion, you can navigate away from the Blogger user interface and view your blog or work with other settings.

8 Working with Blogger's Formatting Settings

✔ BEFORE YOU BEGIN	→ SEE ALSO
4 Logging In to Blogger and Navigating the Dashboard	10 Setting Up Blogger Archives 30 Identifying Elements in the Blogger Template Source

The Blogger formatting settings represent the largest grouping of settings for blog display. In this group of settings, you can modify date and time formats for timestamps, change language encoding for your text, implement a template for individual posts, and much more.

To begin, log in to Blogger and click the **Change Settings** icon in the **Blogs** section of the Blogger Dashboard.

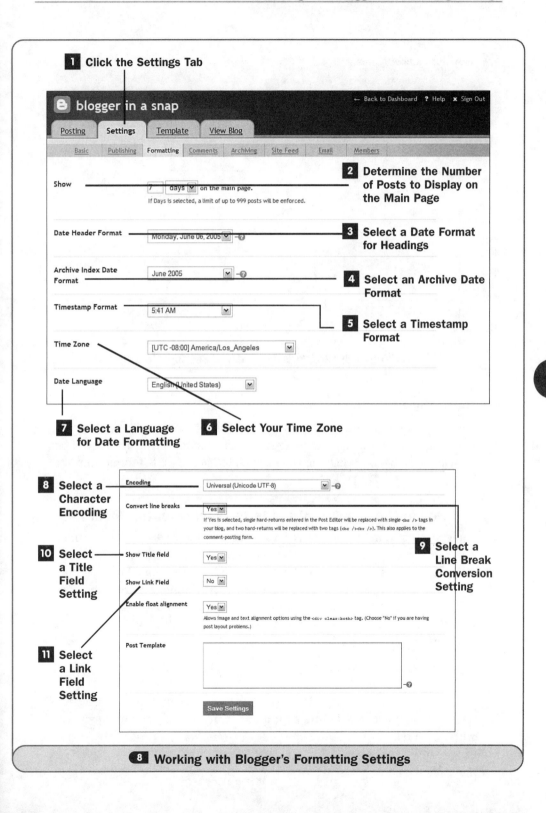

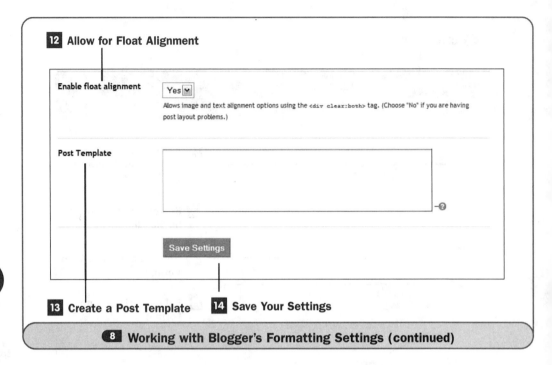

12 **Allow for Float Alignment**

Enable float alignment   Yes ▾

Allows image and text alignment options using the `<div clear:both>` tag. (Choose "No" if you are having post layout problems.)

Post Template

Save Settings

13 Create a Post Template   **14** Save Your Settings

8 Working with Blogger's Formatting Settings (continued)

1 ## Click the Settings Tab

The Blogger user interface includes four top-level tabs. Click the **Settings** tab to display links to the numerous configurable options. The **Basic** link will be preselected for you, so click the **Formatting** link to access the formatting settings.

2 ## Determine the Number of Posts to Display on the Main Page

You can enter a number of days or a number of posts to display on the main page of your blog. In the **Show** field, enter the number in the text field and select either Days or Posts from the drop-down list. The number of posts on the main page of your blog should not be overwhelming: You want the page to load quickly, but it should not be limited to just a few days' worth of posts because new readers will want to get a feel for your writing before venturing into your blog's archives.

If you utilize a day-based setting such as 7 Days rather than a setting equivalent to a number of posts, Blogger will impose a limit of 999 total posts on the main page of your blog. However, if you write 999 posts in just seven days, I recommend going outside for a brisk walk and reacquainting yourself with the world!

3 Select a Date Format for Headings

All blog posts are displayed within a date-based grouping, and the **Date Header Format** field is used to determine the style of this date. You can select from numerous examples of date-based headings, from a full day-and-date heading such as Monday, June 06, 2005, to simply Monday, or 6.06.2005, and so on.

4 Select an Archive Date Format

In addition to the posts on your main page, all posts are part of an archive that Blogger automatically keeps for you. The size of the archive itself—daily, weekly, monthly—is controlled through an archive setting; the **Archive Date Format** field determines how that archive will be displayed to the reader. For instance, if you have set up monthly archives, the options in the **Archive Date Format** drop-down list are relevant for that type of display.

As shown in this example, June 2005 is selected from the drop-down list. This means that the user can access a month-based archive by following a link in the blog to **June 2005** (as well as **July 2005** and so on). Other options in the drop-down list include the full range of dates (06/01/2005 – 06/30/2005), different methods for displaying the month (such as 06/2005, 06.2005), and so on.

5 Select a Timestamp Format

Every blog post is timestamped with its publishing date and time, and this timestamp is shown in the footer of your blog post unless you specifically remove that code from your blog template. In the **Timestamp Format** field, you can customize the appearance of this timestamp. Your timestamp can include only the time, as shown here, or it can include the full date as well, such as 6/05/2005 07:25:45 AM. If you have selected a full date in the **Date Header Format** setting, it is unnecessary to repeat the full date in the post's timestamp, but to each his own. You will often see a full date in the date heading, and then simply a timestamp such as 5:41 AM in the post footer.

6 Select Your Time Zone

Although not directly displayed on your blog, having the correct **Time Zone** setting is relevant for timestamping your posts. If you are blogging at 5 a.m. in Los Angeles, it's 8 a.m. in New York City. Your timestamp should reflect your local time, so in the **Time Zone** field you should select [UTC –08:00 America/Los_Angeles] and not [UTC –05:00 America/New_York] unless you want all of your timestamps to be in New York time. If you have a large, worldwide readership you might want to set the **Time Zone** field to [UTC +05:00 GMT], which would stamp all your posts in Greenwich Mean Time.

8

7 Select a Language for Date Formatting

The names of months and days are easily localized in software applications, given there are a standard number of days and months ready for translation. As such, Blogger offers you the ability to display your date header in any of a number of different languages: If your blog is in English, you can display the date in German, or if your blog is in French, you may display the date in Russian if you want. For instance, if I have selected a full date header via the **Date Header Format** field and English from the **Date Language** drop-down list, my date header would show up like Friday, June 24, 2005. But if I selected German from the **Date Language** drop-down list, that particular date would be displayed as Freitag, Juni 24, 2005.

8 Select a Character Encoding

You may compose your blog posts in any language, but after you've decided to use a particular language, it's important not to change the **Character Encoding** setting because it affects how your posts are stored in the Blogger databases. Therefore, if you plan to compose your posts in languages other than English—which is the default setting—be sure to change this setting immediately after creating your blog.

8

▶ WEB RESOURCE
http://www.i18nguy.com/markup/right-to-left.html
The folks in Blogger Support have identified a good tutorial for composing and implementing bi-directional text in XHTML. If you plan to compose your blog in Arabic or Hebrew, this tutorial will be of great use to you.

9 Select a Line Break Conversion Setting

When Yes is selected from the **Convert Line Break** drop-down list, the Blogger Post Editor will automatically insert a <br/> tag in place of a hard return. So, if you use two hard returns to separate paragraphs while typing, Blogger will insert two <br/> tags. If No is selected from the drop-down list, you will be responsible for inserting your own hard returns or other paragraph markup.

10 Select a Title Field Setting

If Yes is selected from the **Show Title Field** drop-down list, a text field will appear in the Post Editor as you create your post, allowing you to provide a title. If No is selected from the **Show Title Field** drop-down list, no text field will appear in the Post Editor.

Changing the value of **Show Title Field** does not affect any posts that have already been published; it affects only the options available in the Post Editor from the time the change is made.

11 Select a Link Field Setting

The **Show Link field** setting works in tandem with a specific Blogger template tag, which you can learn more about in **30** **Identifying Elements in the Blogger Template Source**. If Yes is selected from the **Show Link Field** drop-down list, a text field will appear in the Post Editor, allowing you to provide an additional link which will then be displayed in your post. The placement of the post field is determined by a specific template modification. If No is selected from the **Show Link Field** drop-down list, no additional text field will appear in the Post Editor.

12 Allow for Float Alignment

The **Enable Float Alignment** field is relevant for users who experience display issues with their Blogger templates, especially when posting images. If Yes is selected from the **Enable Float Alignment** drop-down list, Blogger will continue to insert a specific DIV tag into the post template. This tag comes into play when inserting photos using Blogger Images, but might cause problems with certain templates when images are not inserted. If No is selected from the **Enable Float Alignment** drop-down list, the DIV tag will be suppressed.

This is a setting that you won't know you need to modify until you post a few entries, with and without images, and notice if your template looks wonky. If you are experiencing a large amount of whitespace in your posts, set **Enable Float Alignment** to Yes and see whether that fixes the problem.

13 Create a Post Template

If you find yourself repeating certain elements of code or if you keep a Post-It note filled with certain oft-used bits of HTML, simply enter those items in the **Post Template** textarea. This template has nothing to do with your overall Blogger template. Instead, it's simply a chunk of code that will appear in the Blogger Post Editor each time you create a new post. You might or might not use that code, and if you do not use it you can simply delete it as you type something else.

A good example of a post template would be if you post something every day in a table format. Instead of having to type the code for the table over and over each day, or save it in a separate file and then copy and paste it when

8

you're ready to use it, you can enter the basic code as a post template. Then when you open the Post Editor to type a new entry, the table code would be ready and waiting for you to complete it.

14 Save Your Settings

To save the changes made on the Formatting settings screen, click the **Save Settings** button. You will see an onscreen confirmation when the settings are saved, and at that point you must click the **Republish** button to initiate the publishing sequence. When the publishing sequence displays its notice of completion, you can navigate away from the Blogger user interface and view your blog or work with other settings.

---

9   **Configuring Blogger's Comments Settings**

✔ BEFORE YOU BEGIN	→ SEE ALSO
4 Logging In to Blogger and Navigating the Dashboard	**13** Setting Up Groups and Members in Blogger
	34 Using Blogger's Commenting System
	38 Implementing the Haloscan Commenting and Trackback System

8

Comments play an important role in the Blogosphere: They are the primary way in which your readers will interact with you. Depending on the type of post that you write, readers might engage you in discussion or debate, offer support during trying situations, or just engage in friendly, conversational chatter with you as well as other readers.

To begin, log in to Blogger and click the **Change Settings** icon in the **Blogs** section of the Blogger Dashboard.

1 Click the Settings Tab

The Blogger user interface includes four top-level tabs. Click the **Settings** tab to display links to the numerous configurable options. The **Basic** link will be preselected for you, so click the **Comments** link to access the commenting settings.

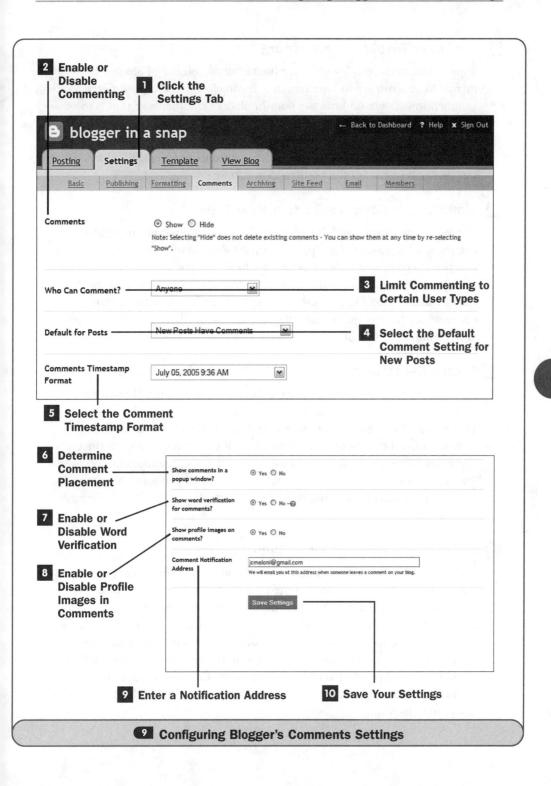

2 Enable or Disable Commenting

1 Click the Settings Tab

3 Limit Commenting to Certain User Types

4 Select the Default Comment Setting for New Posts

5 Select the Comment Timestamp Format

6 Determine Comment Placement

7 Enable or Disable Word Verification

8 Enable or Disable Profile Images in Comments

9 Enter a Notification Address

10 Save Your Settings

9

9 Configuring Blogger's Comments Settings

2 Enable or Disable Commenting

The **Comments** field allows you configure the overall use of Blogger comments. As you can see in later topics, you can elect to use a third-party commenting system and not the built-in Blogger comments. If that is the case, select the **Hide** radio button in the **Comments** field. If you want to use Blogger's built-in comments, select the **Show** radio button. If you select the **Show** radio button, you will still be able to disable comments on a post-by-post basis as part of the post creation process.

3 Limit Commenting to Certain User Types

The **Who Can Comment?** drop-down list allows you to limit the ability to comment to specific reader types. You might want to allow anyone and everyone to comment on your posts, in which case you would select Anyone from the drop-down list. If you want to restrict commenting to registered Blogger users, select Only Registered Users. Finally, if you want to restrict commenting to only those users who are also members of your blog, select Only Members of this Blog.

4 Select the Default Comment Setting for New Posts

As mentioned in step 2, when comments are enabled, you still have the opportunity to enable or disable comments on a post-by-post basis. The **Default for Posts** drop-down list determines the default setting of the radio button that will be visible in the Post Editor. If you select New Posts Have Comments from the **Default for Posts** drop-down list, the radio button in the Post Editor will be preselected to enable comments. If you select New Posts Do Not Have Comments from the **Default for Posts** drop-down list, the opposite will be true.

5 Select the Comment Timestamp Format

Much like selecting the timestamp format under the formatting options, you can customize the appearance of the comment timestamps. Unlike a post, which typically has a date heading displayed and is only ever attached to a single date, users may leave comments over a period of days and weeks. As such, a timestamp format such as 09:36AM is useless because you have no idea what day the comment was left for you. In this example, I've selected a format such as July 05, 2005 09:36AM from the **Comments Timestamp Format** drop-down list so that I will know the actual date of the comment in addition to its time.

6 Determine Comment Placement

The **Show Comments in a Popup Window?** field allows you determine the placement of the interface for viewing and leaving comments. If you select the **Yes** radio button, all comment-related activity will go on in a small pop-up window. If you select the **No** radio button, clicking the link to view or leave a comment will take you to a new web page.

7 Enable or Disable Word Verification

The implementation of a word verification feature in Blogger comments is an attempt to combat spammers who might otherwise take the opportunity to leave a "comment" to your post that is nothing more than a link to their spamblogs or other spam-like websites. If you require word verification before leaving a comment, spammers will not be able to use automated spam tools to leave a comment on your post because they must type the characters shown in an image—something a computer cannot read. Therefore, spammers must actually do the spamming manually, going through the word verification process each time—something they are unlikely to do.

If you decide to enable word verification for Blogger comments—and I recommend that you do so—select the **Yes** radio button in the **Show Word Verification for Comments?** field. The default setting is **No**, meaning that no users—spammers or otherwise—will be required to complete a word verification test before leaving a comment on your blog.

8 Enable or Disable Profile Images in Comments

Blogger users have the option of uploading an image as part of their user profiles. This image could be a photograph, a cartoon, or virtually anything the user chooses. When a registered Blogger user with an image in his or her profile leaves a comment through the Blogger commenting system, this profile image might also be displayed. Whether or not profile images are shown for comments on your blog is entirely up to the blog owner (you!) through the **Show Profile Images on Comments?** field. If you select the **Yes** radio button, profile images will be displayed. If you select the **No** radio button, profile images will not be displayed.

9 Enter a Notification Address

To receive notification when someone leaves a comment to one of your blog posts, enter a valid email address in the **Comment Notification Address** field. The notification email will include the blog title and date in the subject field, and the content of the comment in the email body. Additionally, the email will include a direct link to the post to which the comment is attached. You can then choose to respond privately via email, or publicly via a comment of your own.

🔟 Save Your Settings

To save the changes made on the Comments settings screen, click the **Save Settings** button. You will see an onscreen confirmation when the settings are saved, and at that point you must click the **Republish** button to initiate the publishing sequence. When the publishing sequence displays its notice of completion, you can navigate away from the Blogger user interface and view your blog or work with other settings.

---

10 | **Setting Up Blogger Archives**

✔ BEFORE YOU BEGIN	→ SEE ALSO
4 Logging In to Blogger and Navigating the Dashboard	**30** Identifying Elements in the Blogger Template Source

9

Your blog consists of not only the posts on your main page, but also the pages and pages of posts that make up your archives. In this small group of settings, you can modify the time frame for your archives, as well as enable a setting that creates attractive *permalinks* for your individual blog posts.

▶ KEY TERM

Permalinks—"Permanent links" created for individual blog posts. Permalinks allow you to provide direct access to individual blog posts rather than saying something like "go to the entry for June 27th, 2005 and look for the third post."

To begin, log in to Blogger and click the **Change Settings** icon in the **Blogs** section of the Blogger Dashboard.

1 Click the Settings Tab

The Blogger user interface includes four top-level tabs. Click the **Settings** tab to display links to the numerous configurable options. The **Basic** link will be preselected for you, so click the **Archiving** link to access the archiving settings.

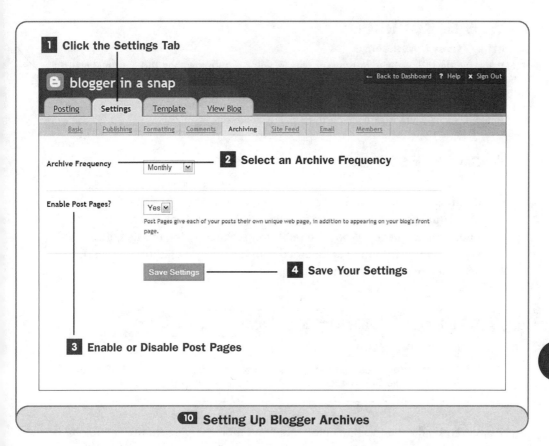

10 Setting Up Blogger Archives

2 Select an Archive Frequency

You can create daily, weekly, or monthly archives by selecting the correspon-ding entry from the **Archive Frequency** drop-down list. In this example, I have selected Monthly archives so that all my posts from a particular month are grouped together as one large page of archived posts.

3 Enable or Disable Post Pages

Post pages are enabled by selecting Yes from the **Enable Post Pages?** drop-down list. By doing so, you ensure that each individual blog entry will be given a permalink that contains either the post title or the first few words of the post (if no title exists). For instance, I have a post called "Busy Busy Busy" on my primary blog and, with post pages enabled, the permalink to the post is http://nofancyname.blogspot.com/2005/07/busy-busy-busy.html. If post pages were disabled, the permalink URL would be the domain name, plus the archive page name (2005_07_01_nofancyname_archive.html) with an ID value appended to it (something like #8792878374387). As you can imagine, post pages provide much tidier URLs.

WEB RESOURCE

http://www.tinyurl.com/

Using the tinyURL website or browser plug-in, you can turn any long URL into a short URL that never expires. Although Blogger post pages are easier to deal with than permalinks created without post pages enabled, they're still pretty long. I turned the URL to my "Busy Busy Busy" post referenced earlier into this tiny URL: http://tinyurl.com/cwlfs. It doesn't make any sense, but it sure is shorter!

4 Save Your Settings

To save the changes made on the Archiving settings screen, click the **Save Settings** button. You will see an onscreen confirmation when the settings are saved, and at that point you must click the **Republish** button to initiate the publishing sequence. When the publishing sequence displays its notice of completion, you can navigate away from the Blogger user interface and view your blog or work with other settings.

10

11 Enabling and Publishing Site Feeds

✔ BEFORE YOU BEGIN	→ SEE ALSO
4 Logging In to Blogger and Navigating the Dashboard	**49** Providing an External RSS Feed
	50 Using an RSS Aggregator

Using web syndication technologies, more and more people actually read blogs through a feed reader rather than a web browser. These XML-formatted data-streams are primarily used for news aggregation and content indexing. Blogger enables all users with the ability to provide an Atom feed for their blogs.

To begin, log in to Blogger and click the **Change Settings** icon in the **Blogs** section of the Blogger Dashboard.

1 Click the Settings Tab

The Blogger user interface includes four top-level tabs. Click the **Settings** tab to display links to the numerous configurable options. The **Basic** link will be preselected for you, so click the **Site Feed** link to access the feed-related settings.

2 Enable or Disable Site Feed

Select Yes or No from the **Publish Site Feed** drop-down list. If Yes is selected, Blogger will publish an Atom feed for your blog. If No is selected, no feed will be provided. Site feeds are highly recommended for all blogs.

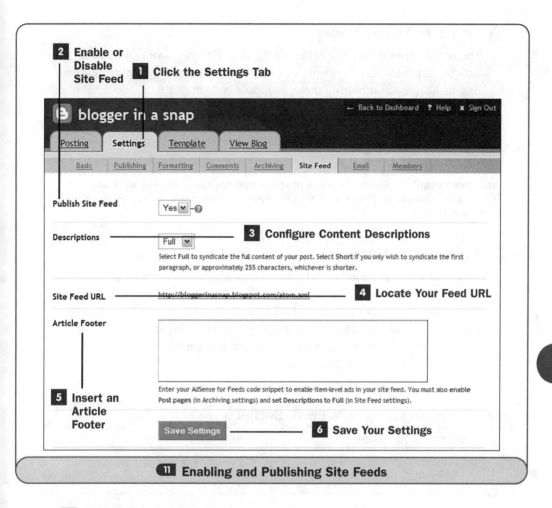

blogger in a snap   ← Back to Dashboard   ? Help   ✗ Sign Out

| Posting | Settings | Template | View Blog |

Basic   Publishing   Formatting   Comments   Archiving   **Site Feed**   Email   Members

Publish Site Feed   Yes ▾ ❼

Descriptions ————   Full ▾   **3** Configure Content Descriptions

Select Full to syndicate the full content of your post. Select Short if you only wish to syndicate the first paragraph, or approximately 255 characters, whichever is shorter.

Site Feed URL ————   http://bloggerinasnap.blogspot.com/atom.xml   **4** Locate Your Feed URL

Article Footer

Enter your AdSense for Feeds code snippet to enable item-level ads in your site feed. You must also enable Post pages (in Archiving settings) and set Descriptions to Full (in Site Feed settings).

5 Insert an Article Footer

Save Settings ————   **6** Save Your Settings

3 Configure Content Descriptions

Atom feeds may contain the entire text of your blog post or simply the first paragraph. Full-text descriptions are recommended unless you are specifically trying to drive traffic to your website as opposed to simply having blog readers. Readers who want to comment on the content they read via your feed will still click through to your site to do so. To enable full-text descriptions, select Full from the **Descriptions** drop-down list. Otherwise, select Short from the **Descriptions** drop-down list.

4 Locate Your Feed URL

If an Atom feed has been enabled, the URL will be displayed in the **Site Feed URL** field. Use this URL for reference whenever you need to make a link to your site feed.

5   Insert an Article Footer

The **Article Footer** field is specifically for bloggers who have registered for the AdSense for Feeds service offered by Google. In addition to being a registered user of AdSense and placing the appropriate code in this field, you must also enable full-text descriptions and post pages.

▶ WEB RESOURCE
http://www.google.com/adsense/

Learn more about the Google AdSense program, and register if you like what you see. After you register, you will have access to the code to paste in the **Article Footer** field referenced here.

6   Save Your Settings

To save the changes made on the Site Feed settings screen, click the **Save Settings** button. You will see an onscreen confirmation when the settings are saved, and at that point you must click the **Republish** button to initiate the publishing sequence. When the publishing sequence displays its notice of completion, you can navigate away from the Blogger user interface and view your blog or work with other settings.

11

---

12   **Configuring Blogger's Email Settings**

✔ BEFORE YOU BEGIN	→ SEE ALSO
4 Logging In to Blogger and Navigating the Dashboard	**44** Creating a Moblog

The Email options under the Settings tab number only two and are completely unrelated. Additionally, neither of these email-related settings affects the email address associated with your Blogger account or the email address associated with comments you receive through your blog posts. However, these two email-related functional elements provide you with a method for extending your blogging capabilities.

To begin, log in to Blogger and click the **Change Settings** icon in the **Blogs** section of the Blogger Dashboard.

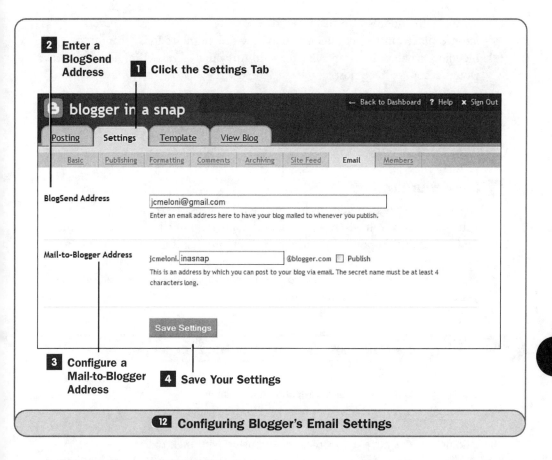

12 Configuring Blogger's Email Settings

1 Click the Settings Tab

The Blogger user interface includes four top-level tabs. Click the **Settings** tab to display links to the numerous configurable options. The **Basic** link will be preselected for you, so click the **Email** link to access the feed-related settings.

2 Enter a BlogSend Address

The email address entered in the **BlogSend Address** field will be used when you successfully publish a new blog post. When a new post is published, the content of the post will be sent to the address specified in this field. The notification will include the blog title and post title in the subject field, and the content of the post and a direct link to the new post in the body of the email.

3 Configure a Mail-to-Blog Address

You can post to your blog simply by sending an email to a specified address. In the **Mail-to-Blogger Address** field, a text field awaits a secret word used to complete the address. For instance, the example shows the secret word *inasnap* placed in the text field, making the full email address for mail-to-blogging jcmeloni.inasnap@blogger.com. Any email sent to that address would become a blog post.

When checked, the **Publish** field enables automatic posting to your blog. By leaving this check box unchecked, your emailed blog posts will remain in Draft mode until you manually publish them via the Blogger World Wide Web–based interface.

4 Save Your Settings

To save the changes made on the Site Feed settings screen, click the **Save Settings** button. You will see an onscreen confirmation when the settings are saved, and at that point you must click the **Republish** button to initiate the publishing sequence. When the publishing sequence displays its notice of completion, you can navigate away from the Blogger user interface and view your blog or work with other settings.

12

13 **Setting Up Groups and Members in Blogger**

✔ **BEFORE YOU BEGIN**

4 Logging In to Blogger and Navigating the Dashboard

Blogs do not always have a one-to-one relationship with their authors—sometimes more than one person has access to post on a particular blog. While traversing the Blogosphere, you might see blogs that are maintained by two or three people at all times, or you could see instances when the primary owner of a blog has granted temporary posting rights to someone else while the primary owner is out of town or away from his or her computer for an extended period of time.

You might also come across a blog that is truly a group blog, in which numerous people have posting rights and the blog is set up as a type of discussion group. This type of blog is most often seen when blogs are used in classroom settings. In those instances, professors will provide an assignment to the class that requires everyone to post on a particular topic, and everyone else must comment on the posts of others. When a blog is used in a classroom setting, it's typical to see 20 or 30 different members attached to a single blog, with the professor as the overall blog administrator.

To create a group blog or simply grant posting rights to another user, log in to Blogger and click the **Change Settings** icon in the **Blogs** section of the Blogger Dashboard.

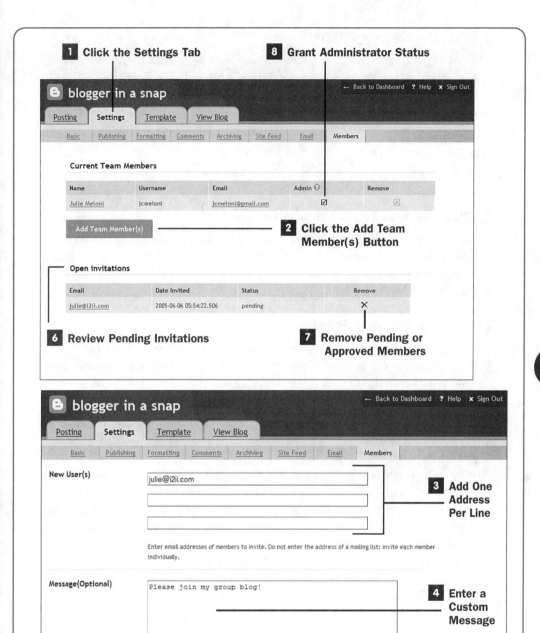

1 Click the Settings Tab

The Blogger user interface includes four top-level tabs. Click the **Settings** tab to display links to the numerous configurable options. The **Basic** link will be preselected for you, so click the **Members** link to access the member-related settings.

▶ **NOTE**

As blog owner, you will be listed automatically as the Admin for the group blog.

2 Click the Add Team Member(s) Button

The process of adding new members includes sending a Blogger-generated invitation to the prospective member and having them follow the instructions in that email. To send invitations to one or more potential members, click the **Add Team Member(s)** button.

3 Add One Address Per Line

The interface for sending invitations includes three text fields in the **New User(s)** section. You can send invitations for up to three potential users at one time by entering their email addresses in these text fields. If you want to send invitations to more than three users, simply return to this form and complete the **New User(s)** section for as many potential users as you have.

4 Enter a Custom Message

Although an optional field, it's a good idea to provide additional information in the **Message** field. The content you provide in this field will be sent along with the invitation to join your blog. It would be worthwhile to add your own contact information if the potential new user has questions or concerns, and also you might think about adding a few ground rules or expectations to which the new users would be expected to adhere.

5 Save Your Settings

To initiate the invitation process, click the **Save Settings** button. At that point, invitations are sent to the email addresses specified in the **New User(s)** field. When a user accepts or declines your invitation to join your group blog, an email will be sent to the address listed in your account profile.

6 Review Pending Invitations

In addition to receiving a notification of a change of status for your potential users, you can also review the pending invitations in the **Open Invitations** section of the **Members** page. If a user has already declined your invitation, their invitation will not appear in this area. However, anyone who has yet to accept or reject your invitation will appear in this area along with the date he or she was invited.

7 Remove Pending or Approved Members

If an invitation has been sitting in the Open Invitations queue for quite some time or if you need to rescind access for an existing user, you can click the X icon in the **Remove** column. Any user can be removed, except for the overall owner and administrator of the blog (that would be you). As you can see in this example, the X icon in the **Remove** column is inaccessible for the primary administrative user.

8 Grant Administrator Status

You can grant administrative access to any user by checking the box in the **Admin** column. When granted administrative access, a user may modify the template and setting for the group blog and also edit or delete any post made by any other group member. As you can imagine, you must only grant administrative access to trusted users.

14

---

14   Modifying Your Blogger Profile

✔ **BEFORE YOU BEGIN**

4 Logging In to Blogger and Navigating the Dashboard

Although your Blogger profile does not have anything directly to do with your blog or the blogging process, keeping your profile up-to-date enables your readers to learn more about you. Additionally, potential new readers might find your blog simply by browsing lists of related interests, favorite movies and music, or even geographic location. Your profile can be as cryptic or chock full of information as you want it to be because not all the profile fields are required.

To edit your profile, log in to Blogger and click the **Edit Profile** link in the upper-right corner of the Blogger Dashboard. This area will include your profile image (if available) and your Blogger display name.

1 Edit the Privacy Settings

2 Edit the Identity Settings

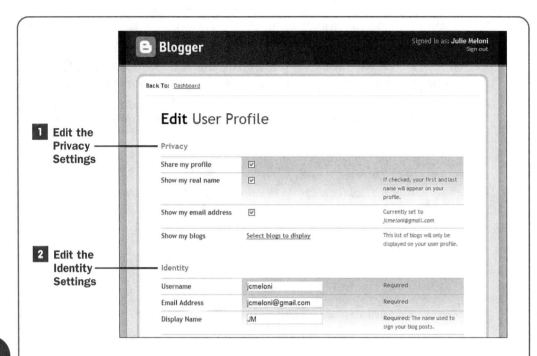

3 Add a Photograph to Your Profile

4 Attach an Audio Clip to Your Profile

5 Edit the General Settings

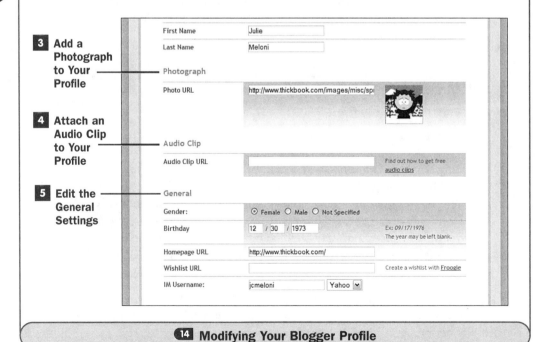

14 Modifying Your Blogger Profile

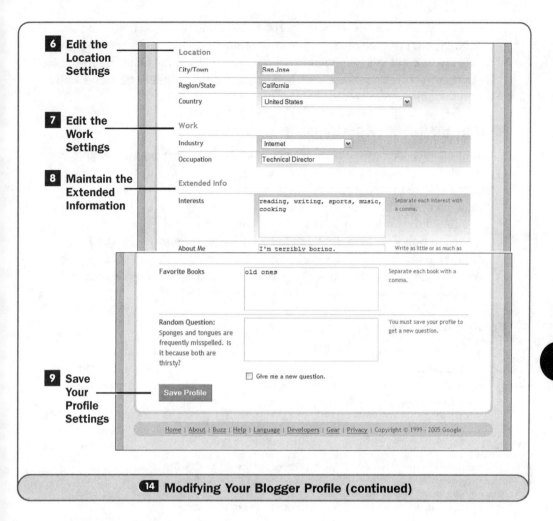

6 Edit the Location Settings

7 Edit the Work Settings

8 Maintain the Extended Information

9 Save Your Profile Settings

14 **Modifying Your Blogger Profile (continued)**

1 Edit the Privacy Settings

The four privacy-related settings have to do with the manner in which elements are displayed in your Blogger profile. These begin with the **Share My Profile** check box: If it is not checked, your profile will not be shared with the public. Next is the **Show My Real Name** check box, and check this box if you want Blogger to show your real first and last name on your user profile. If the **Show My Real Name** check box is unchecked, your display name will be used instead. The **Show My Email Address** check box determines whether your registered email address will be made public on your profile. Providing an email address is important to foster communication between you and your readers, but this address might easily land in the hands of a spammer. It is recommended that you display a contact email address but use a good spam filter on your incoming mail. The final setting in this section is the list of blogs that are to be displayed on your profile. Clicking the **Select Blogs to Display** link will take you to a page containing a list of the blogs you own or of which you are a member. You can choose to display links to all, none, or a combination thereof on your Blogger profile.

2 Edit the Identity Settings

Your identity settings should look very familiar; they were required during your initial Blogger registration process. A required field, your **Username**, is used to log in to Blogger but can be changed here. Next up are two more required fields: your **Email Address** and your **Display Name**. The **Display Name** is different from your **First Name/Last Name** "real name" because it is used to sign your blog posts and in Blogger-based commenting. The **First Name/Last Name** text fields are not required, but when they're completed and the **Show My Real Name** check box is checked in the previous section, this "real name" will be displayed in your user profile.

3 Add a Photograph to Your Profile

If you provide a URL to a small image file, that image will be shown in your profile page. If you leave the **Photo URL** field blank, no image will be displayed. In this example, an image is part of my profile and is also shown here in the Edit Profile form.

▶ **NOTE**

You can learn more about obtaining a URL for an image in **28** Other Methods for Inserting Images into Posts. Although your Blogger account profile is quite different than a blog post, Topic 28 discusses the act of externally hosting an image and retrieving a URL for it, which you need for this particular profile setting.

4 Attach an Audio Clip to Your Profile

If you would like to provide your users with an audio clip of some sort—your own voice, a song, someone else's voice, and so on—enter the URL in the **Audio Clip URL** field.

5 Edit the General Settings

The settings in the **General** section are not required, but if present they are displayed at the beginning of your Blogger profile. Select the appropriate radio button for the **Gender** field, and enter the month and day (the year is optional) in the **Birthday** field. You can also specific an additional **Homepage URL** if you have a website besides your blog. If you have a

Froogle wishlist, you can enter the URL in the **Wishlist URL** field, providing your users with a quick reference for potential birthday gifts. Finally, if you want users to have instant message access to you, enter your **IM Username** and select the type of messenger platform used.

▶ WEB RESOURCE
http://www.google.com/frghp

Froogle is a Google-provided service that is essentially a search engine for items available for sale online. Froogle searches the Internet and returns a list of the best prices and most highly ranked sellers for items on your shopping list.

6 Edit the Location Settings

If you enter a **City/Town** and **Region/State** and then select a country from the **Country** drop-down list, this location information will be presented in your Blogger profile. The text for each entry will be transformed into a link, and when that link is clicked you (and other users) will be able to see other Blogger members who reside in the same city, region, and country. For instance, if I enter **San Jose** in the **City/Town** field and then view my profile, I can click the words San Jose and see a list of all other registered Blogger users who live there.

7 Edit the Work Settings

If you select an entry from the **Industry** drop-down list and provide text in the **Occupation** text field, this work-related information will be presented in your Blogger profile. The text for each entry will be transformed into a link, and when that link is clicked you (and other users) will be able to see other Blogger members who share your profession. For instance, if I select Internet from the **Industry** drop-down list and then view my profile, I can click the word Internet and see a list of all other registered Blogger users, worldwide, who work in this industry.

8 Maintain the Extended Information

The **About Me** field can contain anything you want to say about yourself, up to 1,200 characters. This paragraph of text will be displayed on your Blogger profile. The other fields in the **Extended Information** section require that you separate your entries with commas, as shown here. For instance, in the **Interests** field I have listed five items separated by a comma. The same requirement holds true for the **Favorite Movies**, **Favorite Music**, and **Favorite Books** fields. Just like the **Location** and **Work** settings, the entries listed in these areas will become links—hence the need to separate the entries

14

with commas. For instance, I have entered *The Incredibles* as one of my favorite movies. When I view my Blogger profile, *The Incredibles* will be a link I can follow to find other Blogger users who also like that movie.

The **Random Question** is a truly random (and usually strange) question generated by Blogger, which you may or may not choose to answer. If you do not like the random question you were given, simply select the **Give Me a New Question** check box and you will be given a new one the next time you visit the **Edit Profile** screen after saving your profile.

9 Save Your Profile Settings

To save the changes you have made to your Blogger profile, click the Save Profile button. Your new profile will be immediately viewable to you and all others.

14

3

All About Posting

IN THIS CHAPTER:

The art of blogging requires you to actually write something, which you might or might not post to your blog. Because it's your blog, you might write something and decide not to post it, or you might write something, post it, and a few hours later decide that maybe it's best to remove the post. Or you might write and post something that people comment on, and yet you go back and edit it later—because the argument you made was unclear, or the facts changed, or you decide you want to add pictures or links to your post. All of these actions lead you to one place: the Blogger management interface for posts.

Because your blog is *your blog*, you can write on any topic you please and as often as you like. Or you can go days and days without blogging a word. You should feel no pressure regarding the volume and frequency of blog posts you produce unless you're attempting to make a living from blogging. In this case there are a few more books you should probably read a few more books regarding journalism, law, privacy, and so forth. Assuming that you're not going that route (at least not yet!), remember blogging should be an enjoyable experience, not something that fills you with a sense of dread. If you feel you have some sort of writer's block, write about it! Your faithful readers will likely jump in and offer advice—some good, some not so good—and before you know it you'll be back to your old self.

After you've decided on a writing topic, you might decide to write an essay or you might decide that a quick post with just a link and some general commentary would do the trick just as well. Regardless, always remember to make your arguments as clear as possible and offer evidence and citations where appropriate. Many blog posts are brief remarks along the lines of "Jane uncovered this really interesting bit of information about XYZ. Here's where you can go read more about it," with hyperlinks embedded where appropriate. Other blog posts are long remarks about topics of great interest to the reader, and even more blog posts are simply accounts of events in the blogger's life. Blogs that are entirely personal are likely to have a low but loyal readership, whereas a blog that utilizes a combination of topics and types of posts—essays, personal accounts, quick hits, and so forth—is more likely to attract a larger and more varied readership. Neither type of blog is necessarily better or worse than the other, and the Blogosphere is large enough for all types.

▶ NOTE

All the topics in this chapter assume that you have registered your blog and can log in to the Blogger Dashboard and begin posting.

15 Creating a Post Using the Blogger Editor in Compose Mode

✔ BEFORE YOU BEGIN	→ SEE ALSO
6 Configuring Basic Blogger Settings	**18** Using the Recover Post Feature **19** Understanding the Blogger Publishing Process **25** Inserting Images into Your Posts Using Blogger

When creating a post by using the Blogger editor in Compose mode, you have access to numerous buttons that can be used to modify the text elements of your message. Additionally, the Blogger editor can assist you with inserting hyperlinks and images into your post. Using Compose mode is helpful if you want to apply formatting to posts but do not have the HTML skills necessary to do so.

To begin, log in to Blogger and click the **New Post** icon in the **Blogs** section of the Blogger Dashboard.

1 Select the Compose Tab

If the **Compose** tab is not already selected, you must click this tab to switch to Compose mode. You can switch between Compose mode and Manual mode at any point during the composition of your post.

▶ **NOTE**

If you do not see the Compose tab in the Blogger editor, you have not selected Yes from the **Show Compose Mode for All Your Blogs?** drop-down list in the Basic settings.

2 Enter a Title

The title of your post should be relevant to your post content. You can use special characters as well as HTML in the **Title** text field, which is useful if you're discussing a book or movie and want to italicize the title. However, the formatting buttons that are available in the Compose mode editor are applicable to only the body of your post, not the title. Therefore, if you want to insert hyperlinks or HTML formatting into your post title, you have to do it manually.

▶ **NOTE**

The title of your post is also used to formulate the permalink URL if you selected Yes from the **Enable Post Pages?** drop-down list in the Archiving settings.

15

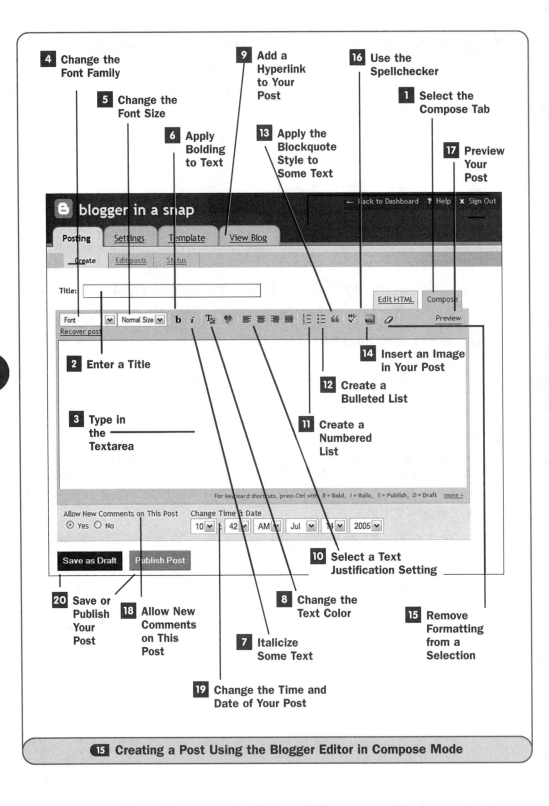

4 Change the Font Family

5 Change the Font Size

6 Apply Bolding to Text

9 Add a Hyperlink to Your Post

13 Apply the Blockquote Style to Some Text

16 Use the Spellchecker

1 Select the Compose Tab

17 Preview Your Post

2 Enter a Title

3 Type in the Textarea

14 Insert an Image in Your Post

12 Create a Bulleted List

11 Create a Numbered List

10 Select a Text Justification Setting

20 Save or Publish Your Post

18 Allow New Comments on This Post

7 Italicize Some Text

8 Change the Text Color

15 Remove Formatting from a Selection

19 Change the Time and Date of Your Post

15 Creating a Post Using the Blogger Editor in Compose Mode

3 Type in the Textarea

The textarea contains the text that you type, which will become the body of your post. When HTML formatting is applied to this text using the tools provided by the editor, the text will be displayed as formatted. For instance, if you type some text and then apply bold formatting to it, the textarea will display the text as bold.

If you switch from Compose mode to Manual mode, the text will be plain but with the appropriate HTML surrounding it. If you modify text in Manual mode by applying HTML formatting to it and then switch to Compose mode, the text will retain its formatting.

4 Change the Font Family

If you would like to change the font family used for the text of your post, select a new family from the **Font** drop-down list. From that point, all typed text will be in that font family unless you decide to change it midstream. If you want to change the font family for only a specific portion of your typed text, highlight that text with your mouse and then select the new family from the **Font** drop-down list.

Avoid changing the font family too often within the body of your post. To avoid eyestrain for your readers, use a different font for section headings or to set off a special area of your text, such as a long quote.

15

5 Change the Font Size

If you would like to change the font size used in the text of your post, select a size from the **Size** drop-down list. From that point, all typed text will be in that size unless you decide to change it halfway through. If you want to change the font size for only a specific portion of your typed text, highlight that text with your mouse and then select the new size from the **Size** drop-down list.

Avoid changing the font size too often within the body of your post. Some examples of acceptable, modified font size include using a larger font size to indicate a subheading within your post, or using a smaller font size to indicate footnotes.

6 Apply Bolding to Text

If you would like some of your text to appear bolded, highlight the selected text with your mouse and then click the **Bold** icon. You can combine bolded text with additional formatting, such as italics and differently colored text.

7 Italicize Some Text

If you would like some of your text to appear italicized, highlight the selected text with your mouse and then click the **Italics** icon. You can combine italicized text with additional formatting, such as bold and differently colored text.

8 Change the Text Color

To change the color of some of your text, highlight the portion to be colored and click the **Text Color** icon. A secondary menu will appear, containing several basic colors from which you can choose. When you use your mouse to click a color, color formatting will be applied to the text you had previously highlighted.

9 Add a Hyperlink to Your Post

You can use the **Hyperlink** button to assist in the creation of a hyperlink. If you select some text before clicking the **Hyperlink** button, the selected text will be surrounded by the HTML for the link. However, if you do not select any text, the HTML for the link will be placed in the textarea and you will have to manually place the cursor between the opening and closing <a></a> tags before typing the linked text.

When you click the **Hyperlink** button, you will see a prompt to enter a URL. The http:// will already be present in the text field of the prompt, so if you are pasting a full URL, be sure to paste over the prepopulated comment. If you paste a full URL in addition to the prepopulated content, your actual URL will be something like http://http://someurl.com/, which is invalid. When you have entered the URL, click the **OK** button and the editor will apply your link code.

10 Select a Text Justification Setting

If you would like to change the text justification of your text, select one of the justification options: right-justified, center-justified, left-justified, or fully justified. From that point, all typed text will be justified accordingly, unless you decide to change it midstream. If you want to change the text justification for only a specific portion of your typed text, highlight that text with your mouse and then select a new justification option.

11 Create a Numbered List

There are two methods for creating a numbered list as part of your post. Before you begin typing your list, click the **Numbered List** button. The first numbered list item will automatically appear with the cursor positioned after

15

the number. Type the text for that item and then press the Enter key. A new list item will appear each time you press Enter, until you click the **Numbered List** button again to turn off the formatting.

The second option for creating a numbered list is simply to type your list items, press Enter after each item, highlight the list with your mouse, and click the **Numbered List** button. The numbered list style will be applied to the selected text.

12 Create a Bulleted List

There are two methods for creating a bulleted list as part of your post. Before you begin typing your list, click the **Bulleted List** button. The first list item will automatically appear with the cursor positioned after the number. Type the text for that item, and then press the Enter key. A new list item will appear each time you press Enter, until you click the **Bulleted List** button again to turn off the formatting.

The second option for creating a bulleted list is simply to type your list items, pressing Enter after each item, highlight the list with your mouse, and click the **Bulleted List** button. The bulleted list style will be applied to the selected text.

13 Apply the Blockquote Style to Some Text

The blockquote style is typically used to set off a long quote that you want to include as part of your post. To apply the blockquote style, click the **Blockquote** button before pasting the quoted text; or paste the quoted text, select it with your mouse, and then click the **Blockquote** button. When your post is published, blockquoted text will usually be indented on both sides to distinguish it from the main post, but the actual style definition for the <blockquote></blockquote> tag is in your style sheet.

14 Insert an Image in Your Post

Click the **Image Insertion** button to launch Blogger's image insertion interface. For more information on this functionality, please see **25** Inserting Images into Your Posts Using Blogger.

15 Remove Formatting from a Selection

If you have applied formatting to some text and you want to remove the formatting entirely, highlight the text and click the **Remove Formatting** button. The selection will revert to its base state in which all formatting has been removed.

15

However, you do not have to remove all layers of formatting before applying new formatting to your text; any new formatting of the same type simply replaces the previous formatting. For instance, perhaps you have formatted some text as bold and red. If you want the text to be italicized and blue, simply highlight the text, click the **Bold** button to deselect bold formatting, click the **Italics** button to utilize italicized formatting, and select a blue color chip from the **Text Color** menu. The underlying HTML code will be changed appropriately.

16 Use the Spellchecker

After your post has been written, you can use Blogger's built-in spellchecker to catch any spelling errors you might have made. Click the **Spellchecker** button to launch the spellchecker application, which acts similarly to typical spellchecker, built into standard word processing programs. The Blogger spellchecker will highlight a problematic word and offer suggestions for changing it. You can select a word from the list of selections, propose your own change, ignore the suggestion, and tell the spellchecker to learn the problematic word.

If you change a word via the spellchecker, it will be modified in the textarea of your post. When you have finished with the spellchecker, click the **Finish** button to return to your post.

17 Preview Your Post

To see an approximation of how your post will look when published, click the **Preview** link. Previewing your post is part of the overall publishing process, and for more information please see **19 Understanding the Blogger Publishing Process**.

18 Enable or Disable Comments for This Post

If Blogger commenting is enabled for your blog, you will see this option for allowing reader comments on a post-by-post basis. Select the radio button next to **Yes** if you would like readers to be able to comment on your post, and the radio button next to **No** if you would like comments to be closed.

19 Change the Time and Date of Your Post

You can select a new time and date for your post, which is useful if you began a post and didn't finish it until hours or days later. Unless they're changed, the time and date of the post are the time and date it was started, not finished. You can set the time and date to something in the future or something in the past. If the post is future-dated, it will remain at the top of your index page until that date and time passes. If the post is dated in the past, it will be published in the appropriate order in your archives.

20 Save or Publish Your Post

When you have finished typing and formatting your post—either in its entirety or in a draft version—the next step is to save or publish the post. If you want to save your post in draft format so that you can put the finishing touches on it at a later date, click the **Save as Draft** button. If you are ready to publish your post to the masses, click the **Publish Post** button.

You will learn more about the publishing process itself in **19 Understanding the Blogger Publishing Process**.

---

16 Creating a Post Using the Blogger Editor in Manual Mode

✔ BEFORE YOU BEGIN	→ SEE ALSO
6 Configuring Basic Blogger Settings	**18** Using the Recover Post Feature
	19 Understanding the Blogger Publishing Process
	25 Inserting Images into Your Posts Using Blogger

16

If you prefer a hands-on approach to text formatting, in which you type your own HTML and utilize custom styles, using the Blogger editor in Manual mode will appeal to you. Although this version of the editor contains a few buttons for use as shortcuts for some basic formatting, by and large the look and feel of your post is left up to you.

To begin, log in to Blogger and click the **New Post** icon in the **Blogs** section of the Blogger Dashboard.

1 Select the Edit HTML Tab

Select the **Edit HTML** tab to switch the Blogger editor to Manual mode. You can switch between Compose mode and Manual mode at any point during the composition of your post.

▶ NOTE

If you do not see the **Edit HTML** tab in the Blogger editor, you have not selected Yes from the **Show Compose Mode for All Your Blogs?** drop-down list in the Basic settings. If the selected value of the **Show Compose Mode for All Your Blogs?** drop-down list is No, your editor will default to Manual mode.

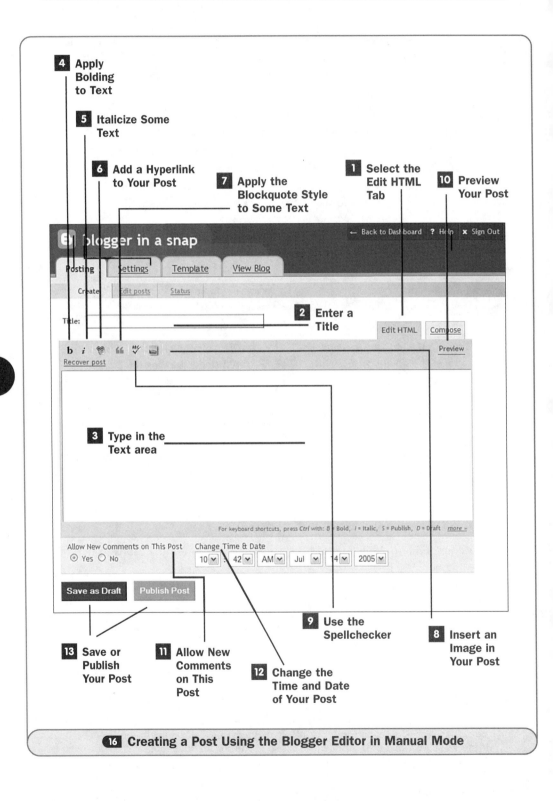

4 Apply Bolding to Text

5 Italicize Some Text

6 Add a Hyperlink to Your Post

7 Apply the Blockquote Style to Some Text

1 Select the Edit HTML Tab

10 Preview Your Post

2 Enter a Title

3 Type in the Text area

9 Use the Spellchecker

8 Insert an Image in Your Post

13 Save or Publish Your Post

11 Allow New Comments on This Post

12 Change the Time and Date of Your Post

16 Creating a Post Using the Blogger Editor in Manual Mode

2 Enter a Title

The title of your post should be relevant to your post content. You can use special characters as well as HTML in the **Title** text field, which is useful if you're discussing a book or movie and want to italicize the title. Although the **Bold** and **Italics** buttons are available when working with the editor in Manual mode, these formatting buttons are applicable only to the body of your post, not the title. Therefore, if you want to insert hyperlinks or HTML formatting into your post title, you'll have to do it manually.

▶ **NOTE**

The title of your post is also used to formulate the permalink URL if you select Yes in the **Enable Post Pages?** drop-down list in the Archiving settings.

3 Type in the Textarea

The textarea contains the text that you type, which will become the body of your post. When using the Blogger editor in Manual mode, you must manually insert all HTML code you want to use in your post, with the possible exception of line breaks. If you select Yes for **Convert Line Breaks** in the Formatting settings, Blogger will insert <br /> tags every time you press the Enter key.

You can also utilize the formatting-related options described in the next five steps but, in general, if you're using Manual mode to prepare your posts, it's likely you'll be coding with your own brand of HTML all along the way.

▶ **NOTE**

You can learn more about utilizing your own styles in **31** Defining and Implementing Custom Styles.

4 Apply Bolding to Text

If you would like some of your text to appear bolded, highlight the selected text with your mouse and then click the **Bold** icon. You can combine bolded text with additional formatting, such as italics and differently colored text.

5 Italicize Some Text

If you would like some of your text to appear italicized, highlight the selected text with your mouse and then click the **Italics** icon. You can combine italicized text with additional formatting, such as bold and differently colored text.

16

6 Add a Hyperlink to Your Post

You can use the **Hyperlink** button to assist in the creation of a hyperlink. If you select some text before clicking the **Hyperlink** button, the selected text will be surrounded by the HTML for the link. However, if you do not select any text, the HTML for the link will be placed in the textarea and you will have to manually place the cursor between the opening and closing <a></a> tags before typing the linked text.

When you click the **Hyperlink** button, you will see a prompt to enter a URL. The http:// will already be present in the text field of the prompt, so if you are pasting a full URL, be sure to paste over the prepopulated comment. If you paste a full URL in addition to the prepopulated content, your actual URL will be something like http://http://someurl.com/, which is not a valid URL. When you have entered the URL, click the **OK** button and the editor will apply your link code.

7 Apply the Blockquote Style to Some Text

The blockquote style is typically used to set off a long quote that you want to include as part of your post. To apply the blockquote style, click the **Blockquote** button before pasting the quoted text; or paste the quoted text, select it with your mouse, and then click the **Blockquote** button. When your post is published, blockquoted text will usually be indented on both sides to distinguish it from the main post, but the actual style definition for the <blockquote></blockquote> tag is in your style sheet.

8 Insert an Image in Your Post

Click this button to begin Blogger's image insertion interface. For more information on this functionality, please see **25 Inserting Images into Your Posts Using Blogger**.

9 Use the Spellchecker

After your post has been written, you can use Blogger's built-in spellchecker to catch any spelling errors you might have made. Click the **Spellchecker** button to launch the spellchecker application, which acts similarly to typical spellchecker functionality built into standard word processing programs. The Blogger spellchecker will highlight a problematic word and offer suggestions for changing it. You can select a word from the list of selections, propose your own change, ignore the suggestion, and tell the spellchecker to learn the problematic word.

16

If you change a word via the spellchecker, it will be modified in the textarea of your post. When you have finished with the spellchecker, click the **Finish** button to return to your post.

10 Preview Your Post

To see an approximation of how your post will look when published, click the **Preview** link. Previewing your post is part of the overall publishing process, and for more information please see **19** **Understanding the Blogger Publishing Process**.

11 Enable or Disable Comments for this Post

If Blogger commenting is enabled for your blog, you will see this option for allowing reader comments on a post-by-post basis. Select the radio button next to **Yes** if you would like readers to be able to comment on your post, and the radio button next to **No** if you would like comments to be closed.

12 Change the Time and Date of Your Post

You can select a new time and date for your post, which is useful if you begin a post and don't finish it until hours or days later. Unless they're changed, the time and date of the post are the time and date it was started, not finished. You can set the time and date to something in the future or something in the past. If the post is future-dated, it will remain at the top of your index page until that date and time passes. If the post is dated in the past, it will be published in the appropriate order in your archives.

13 Save or Publish Your Post

When you have finished typing and formatting your post—either in its entirety or in a draft version—the next step is to save or publish the post. If you want to save your post in draft format so that you can put the finishing touches on it at a later date, click the **Save as Draft** button. If you are ready to publish your post to the masses, click the **Publish Post** button.

You will learn more about the publishing process itself in **19** **Understanding the Blogger Publishing Process**.

17

17 Using Keyboard Shortcuts in the Blogger Editor

✔ **BEFORE YOU BEGIN**

15 Creating a Post Using the Blogger Editor in Compose Mode
16 Creating a Post Using the Blogger Editor in Manual Mode

If you are using the Blogger editor in either Compose or Manual mode, there are several keyboard shortcuts you can use in lieu of using your mouse. A few of these shortcuts are standard shortcuts found in Windows-based programs, so you might be familiar with their use.

Even if you choose not to use keyboard shortcuts while composing your blog posts, it's important to be aware of them—especially the **Publish Post** shortcut. The last thing you want to do is inadvertently publish your post before it is complete! Sure, you can just navigate to your list of posts, select the one that was prematurely published, and save it in draft mode, but that's an awful lot of extra clicks.

▶ **NOTE**

It's also important to be aware of your web browser's shortcut key combinations, which are unique to your browser type and thus out of the scope of this book. The Blogger interface has a few built-in elements to ensure that you don't lose posts—namely, the Recover Post feature you'll learn about in **18** **Using the Recover Post Feature**.

- **Bold.** To apply bold formatting to selected text, use the Ctrl+B key combination.
- **Italics.** To apply italicized formatting to selected text, use the Ctrl+I key combination.
- **Blockquote.** To apply blockquote formatting to selected text, use the Ctrl+L key combination.
- **Undo.** The Ctrl+Z key combination will undo your last action.
- **Redo.** The Ctrl+Y key combination will redo your last action. In web browsers, the Ctrl+R key combination reloads the page, so do not mistakenly use Ctrl+R for a redo action.
- **Insert hyperlink.** Use the Ctrl+Shift+A key combination to launch the hyperlink creation prompt.
- **Preview mode.** Use the Ctrl+Shift+P key combination to switch your post editor to Preview mode. When in Preview mode, use the same key combination to return to Edit mode.
- **Save as draft.** Use the Ctrl+D key combination to save your post as a draft.
- **Publish post.** Use the Ctrl+S key combination to start the publishing process that will result in your post appearing on your blog. In Windows programs, Ctrl+S is reserved for the Save function, so although you might naturally associate Ctrl+S with saving a document, remember that this shortcut not only saves, it also publishes. If you want to save your post without publishing, use Ctrl+D to save it as a draft.

18 | **Using the Recover Post Feature**

✔ **BEFORE YOU BEGIN**

15 Creating a Post Using the Blogger Editor in Compose Mode
16 Creating a Post Using the Blogger Editor in Manual Mode

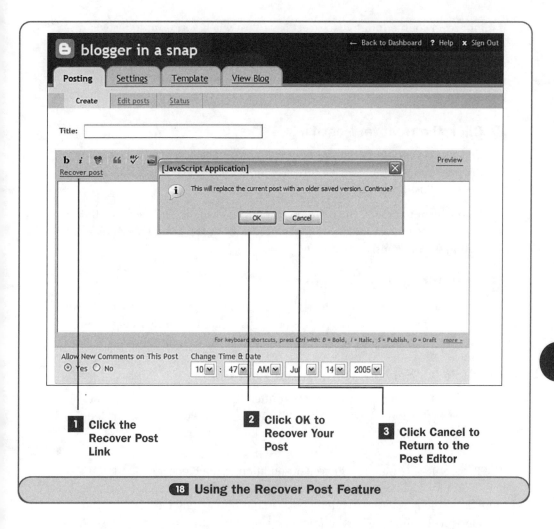

B blogger in a snap ← Back to Dashboard ? Help ✗ Sign Out

| Posting | Settings | Template | View Blog |

Create Edit posts Status

Title:

b *i* 🌐 ❝ ✌ ▢   Preview
Recover post

[JavaScript Application]   ✗

ⓘ This will replace the current post with an older saved version. Continue?

OK   Cancel

For keyboard shortcuts, press Ctrl with: B = Bold, I = Italic, S = Publish, D = Draft *more »*

Allow New Comments on This Post   Change Time & Date
⊙ Yes ○ No   10 ⌄ : 47 ⌄ AM ⌄ Ju ⌄ 14 ⌄ 2005 ⌄

1 Click the
Recover Post
Link

2 Click OK to
Recover Your
Post

3 Click Cancel to
Return to the
Post Editor

18

18 Using the Recover Post Feature

If you've spent any time on the Internet—and for the sake of argument I'm assuming you have—you know that sometimes your connection drops, websites become unreachable, your web browser decides to quit on you, you accidentally navigate off the page, and so on and so forth. If you compose your posts directly in the Blogger post editor, your worst nightmare might be an Internet connection that breaks while you're attempting to save a post, or a web browser that shuts down before you have a chance to click the **Publish Post** button.

Blogger has a feature that might eliminate some of the lost posts in those situations. As you type in the textarea of the Blogger post editor, the characters are saved in a cookie associated with your web browser and the blog you were working on at the time. If something happens and you need to recover your post, log back in to Blogger and click the **New Post** icon in the **Blogs** section of the Blogger Dashboard.

It might seem counterintuitive to select **New Post** when you want to recover a post that might exist somewhere in the ether, but the fact is that the information stored in your cookie has not become an actual, saved post. The following steps will lead you to your recovered post, if you perform them within 30 minutes of losing your connection to Blogger.

1 Click the Recover Post Link

Under no circumstances should you type anything in the textarea before clicking this link! If you want to recover the text stored in your cookie, click the **Recover Post** link. You will see a prompt as in step 2.

If you begin to type in the textarea before you click the **Recover Post** link, the contents of the cookie will be replaced with the text you type, thus eliminating the previously saved text.

2 Click OK to Recover Your Post

If you click the **OK** button, the stored text will be extracted from your cookie and placed in the textarea. At this point, you might want to immediately save the post as a draft to eliminate the possibility of losing the post again.

3 Click Cancel to Return to the Post Editor

If you decide not to recover your text after all, click the **Cancel** button to return to the post editor. You can still choose to recover your text, as long as you do not begin to type in the textarea before doing so.

The Recover Post feature is an excellent addition to the Blogger editor, but it should not be relied on to save your text in all instances. The cookie can only store three kilobytes of text, so long posts might not be fully recovered. If you plan to write a long blog post, it might be worthwhile to compose the post offline in a text editor and simply paste the contents into the Blogger interface when you complete your composition.

19   Understanding the Blogger Publishing Process

✔ BEFORE YOU BEGIN

15 Creating a Post Using the Blogger Editor in Compose Mode
16 Creating a Post Using the Blogger Editor in Manual Mode

1 Preview Before Posting

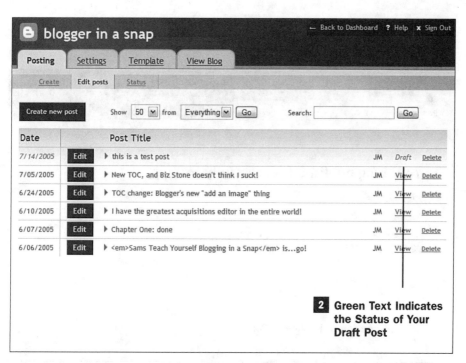

2 Green Text Indicates the Status of Your Draft Post

19 Understanding the Blogger Publishing Process

3 The Publishing Process Indicator

4 Confirmation of Published Post

19 Understanding the Blogger Publishing Process (continued)

The Blogger publishing process is quick and painless, but it's important to understand the steps involved. Let's assume that you have created a post using the Blogger editor—either in Compose mode or Manual mode—and you are ready for this post to show up on your blog.

But wait—*are* you ready? We pick up the process in step 1, assuming that you have clicked on the **Preview** link in the Blogger editor.

1 Preview Before Posting

After clicking the Preview link in the Blogger editor, your view will change to an approximation of how your post will look when published. The preview is an approximation and not an accurate depiction because the preview interface does not take into consideration the specific styles used in your blog template.

For instance, if you use Compose mode to create your post, your preview is more likely to look like the final version that will appear on your blog because the WYSIWYG editor marks up the text as you go and this markup is independent of your stylesheet. If you create your post using Manual mode, you are likely applying styles that are available only in your stylesheet and therefore not available to the preview function.

This is not to say the preview function is useless; you will still be able to view your post outside of the editing interface, which makes it much easier to proofread. When you have completed the proofreading process, you can switch back to the editor by clicking the **Hide Preview** link; you can click the **Save as Draft** button to save the post without publishing it; or you can click the **Publish Post** button to release your post into the wild.

▶ **NOTE**

Previewing your post is not a required step in the publishing process, but if you are at all concerned about the readability of your text, give it a once-over via the preview function.

2 Green Text Indicates the Status of Your Draft Post

When you save a post as a draft, it will appear in your list of posts (the **Edit Posts** navigation item under the **Posting** tab) but it will not appear on your blog. It will remain in this state until you explicitly click the **Publish Post** button in the Blogger editor. All draft posts are indicated by green text—the date of the post is in green, as is the word *Draft*, which appears in place of the **View** link in your post management interface.

3 The Publishing Process Indicator

The process indicator appears any time your blog is published—after publishing a post, publishing your index, or republishing your entire blog. Publishing a single post is a very quick process, so you might see the indicator go from 0% to 100% in just a few seconds. But when you need to republish the index page or even the entire blog, the process will take a bit longer. Do not navigate away from the process indicator as it refreshes, just allow it to run its course.

▶ **NOTE**

Manually republishing the index republishes the index page and your site feed—the two most important areas as far as your general readers are concerned. Manually republishing your entire blog refreshes all the post pages and archive pages in addition to the index page and your site feed—you can understand why this would take a bit longer than republishing only the index page. If you make changes to your template, and those changes affect all pages, you should republish your entire blog so that the changes are applied appropriately. If your template changes are confined to only the main page, republishing only the index would be an appropriate choice.

4 Confirmation of Published Post

You will see a success message when the publishing process has been successfully completed. If you would like to see a list of all the affected pages, click the **Details** link. From this page you also can click the **View Blog** link to see your newly published blog, or you can click one the **Republish Index Only** or the **Republish Entire Blog** button to start the publishing process over again.

The latter actions are often used when a failure occurs in the publishing process. On rare occasions, the Blogger application will be unable to make a connection to the databases that holds the content, and in that case the publishing process will fail. Instead of seeing a success message, you will see a failure message; text following the **Details** link will describe the reason for the failure, which you can use when communicating with Blogger Support.

---

20 | Editing Existing Posts

✔ BEFORE YOU BEGIN

15 Creating a Post Using the Blogger Editor in Compose Mode
16 Creating a Post Using the Blogger Editor in Manual Mode

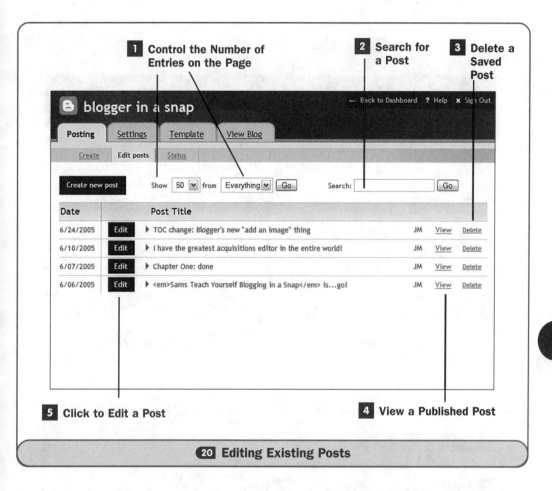

1 Control the Number of Entries on the Page

2 Search for a Post

3 Delete a Saved Post

5 Click to Edit a Post

4 View a Published Post

If you write a post and save it in draft mode, or even if you have already published a post and want to add or modify its text, you can navigate the Edit Posts menu to select a specific post to edit. Somewhat counterintuitively, the quickest way to get to the Edit Posts menu is to click the **New Post** icon in the **Blogs** section of the Blogger Dashboard. From there, click the **Edit Posts** subnavigation item. Steps 1–5 detail some of the actions you can take in this interface.

1 Control the Number of Entries on the Page

You can use the two visible drop-down menus to determine how many posts you want to show in the **Edit Posts** menu. You can select 5, 10, 25, 50, 100, or 300 posts from the first drop-down list, and Everything, Drafts, or Current in the second drop-down list. So, if you want to show only the first five posts saved as drafts, in descending order by date, you would select 5 and Drafts from the drop-downs and click the **Go** button. *Current* posts are those that are published, and *Everything* includes both draft and published posts.

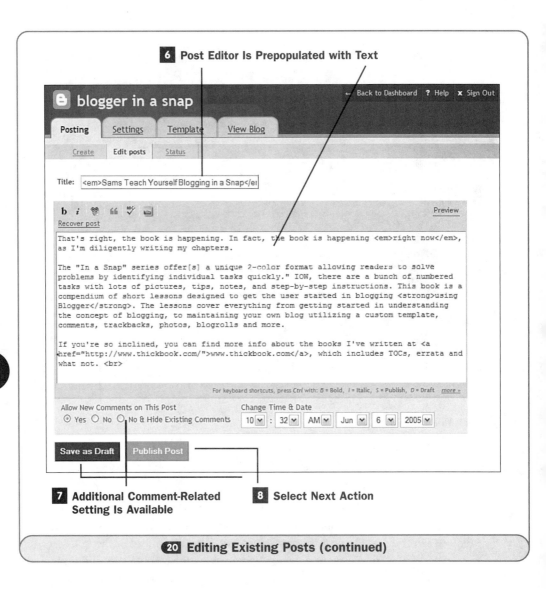

6 Post Editor Is Prepopulated with Text

7 Additional Comment-Related Setting Is Available

8 Select Next Action

20 Editing Existing Posts (continued)

2 Search for a Post

If you want to search for a particular post by keyword, enter the keyword in the Search text field and click the **Go** button. Only those posts matching your keyword will be displayed in the **Edit Posts** list. This is a particularly handy search tool because it also matches bits of code that you have typed along with your post text. For instance, suppose that you have linked to a specific URL in several of your posts, but you know for a fact that the URL has changed. You can use the search interface to look for the string `<a href="http://www.oldaddress.com">`, which you can then replace manually in each post.

3 Delete a Saved Post

The **Edit Posts** list also provides you with an option to delete a particular post. To delete a post, click the **Delete** link. This action will take you to a confirmation page to ensure that you really want to delete the post and didn't accidentally click the **Delete** link.

4 View a Published Post

To view a post that has been published, click the **View** link for that post in the **Edit Posts** list. The **View** link will open a new browser window, showing the post as it appears on your blog.

▶ **NOTE**

You can also view a draft or published post in Preview mode by clicking the right-pointing arrow next to the post title in the Edit Posts interface. The content of the post, lacking any style sheet–based design, will dynamically appear in the Edit Posts interface so that you can get a quick idea of the content you've written to determine whether you need to click through to the post editor.

5 Click to Edit a Post

To launch the Blogger editor to edit a particular post, click the **Edit** button next to the name of the post you want to edit.

6 Post Editor Is Prepopulated with Text

After the Blogger editor is launched, the original post title and text will populate their respective areas of the editor. From this point you can use the Blogger editor in Compose or Manual mode to edit your post as if you were writing it for the first time—all editor features are available to you.

7 Additional Comment-Related Setting Is Available

If Blogger commenting is enabled for your blog, the Blogger editor will include an option for allowing reader comments on a post-by-post basis. You can select the radio button next to **Yes** if you would like readers to be able to comment on your post, and the radio button next to **No** if you would like comments to be closed. When editing a post that has been published, one additional feature will be available to you: No & Hide Existing Comments. Select this radio button to close comments for this post and hide any comments that have been left through the Blogger commenting interface.

20

8   Select Next Action

When you finish editing your post, you can either save it or publish the post as if you were creating it for the first time. If you want to save your post in draft format so that you can put the finishing touches on it at a later date, click the **Save as Draft** button. If you are ready to publish your post to the masses, click the **Publish Post** button.

---

21   Creating Expandable Blog Posts

✔ BEFORE YOU BEGIN	→ SEE ALSO
15 Creating a Post Using the Blogger Editor in Compose Mode **16** Creating a Post Using the Blogger Editor in Manual Mode	**30** Identifying Elements in the Blogger Template Source

Some of us are rather verbose bloggers, and some readers are turned off when a very long post is fully visible on your blog index page. The solution to this is to modify your Blogger template so that you can create expandable blog posts. *Expandable* blog posts are that those that contain a link to the full version. When expandable blog posts are used, the reader will see only a small portion of the text—a *teaser*—followed by a link that will take them to the individual post page.

Please follow these steps closely because even the smallest typo in your code will cause it not to work. Before you begin, ensure that your selection for **Enable Post Pages?** is Yes in your Archiving settings. If it is not, make it so and republish your blog before continuing.

▶ **WEB RESOURCE**

http://nofancyname.blogspot.com/2005/02/making-expandable-blog-posts-in.html

If you want to cut and paste the code rather than type it, you can visit my original blog entry on the subject.

The first modification you must make is to your Blogger template. You will learn more about working with the Blogger template in Chapter 5, "Working with Blogger Templates," so for now just follow closely. To get to the template editing interface, select **Change Settings** from your Blogger Dashboard, and then click the **Template** tab. You will see a textarea that contains your template code.

20

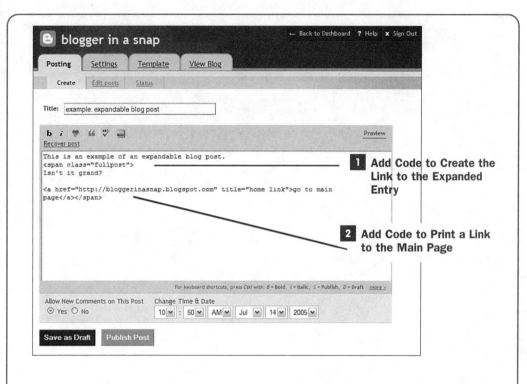

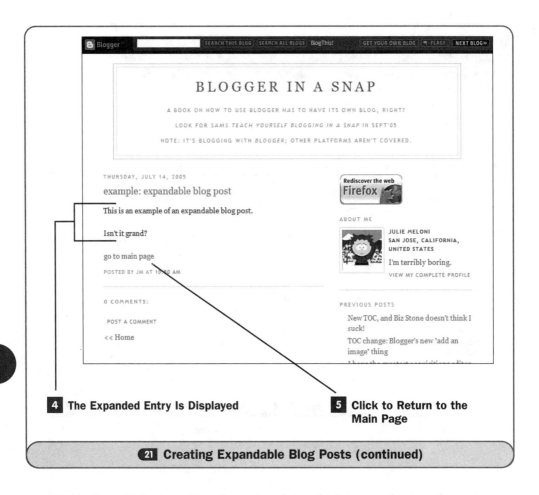

4 The Expanded Entry Is Displayed

5 Click to Return to the Main Page

21 Creating Expandable Blog Posts (continued)

Within the stylesheet portion of your template, which is near the top of your template and is enclosed between the `<style></style>` tag pair, add the following lines:

```
<MainOrArchivePage>
span.fullpost {display:none;}
</MainOrArchivePage>

<ItemPage>
span.fullpost {display:inline;}
</ItemPage>
```

This code is a mixture of Blogger code and standard stylesheet entries. The two conditional Blogger template tag pairs are `<MainOrArchivePage>` `</MainOrArchivePage>` and `<ItemPage></ItemPage>`. Based on these conditions—whether the user is viewing the main page or archive page or whether the user is viewing an individual post page—Blogger will print a different style sheet definition for the span.fullpost class. With these stylesheet entries, you conditionally define the span.fullpost entity as either displayed or not displayed, depending on which page is viewed—you want the full entry to be displayed on only the individual post page.

The next modification to your Blogger template occurs directly after the closing style tag (</style>) and before the closing head tag (</head>). Add the following lines of code:

```
<script type="text/javascript">
var memory = 0;
var number = 0;
</script>
```

These lines of code initialize two JavaScript variables, memory and number, and sets their initial values to 0. These variables will be used in a JavaScript code snippet that determines when to show the link to the full post.

Next, scroll through your template code and look for this Blogger template tag:

```
<$BlogItemBody$>
```

21

Directly after it, place this Blogger template tag/JavaScript snippet:

```
<MainOrArchivePage>
<script type="text/javascript">
spans = document.getElementsByTagName('span');
number = 0;
for(i=0; i < spans.length; i++){
     var c = " " + spans[i].className + " ";
     if (c.indexOf("fullpost") != -1) {
          number++;
     }
}

if(number != memory){
     document.write('<a href="<$BlogItemPermalinkUrl$>">[link text]
                    ➥</a><br>');
}

memory = number;
</script>
</MainOrArchivePage>
```

By surrounding this bit of JavaScript with the `<MainOrArchivePage>` `</MainOrArchivePage>` tag pair, you ensure that it will be printed on only main or archive pages and not individual post pages. This bit of JavaScript scans through the HTML used in a particular post, and collects all the `<span></span>` tags used by the author. The code then examines those `<span></span>` tags to see whether any are defined with the class of `"fullpost"`—this was defined previously in the style sheet and will be used within the blog post itself. If the JavaScript encounters text surrounded by the `<span class="fullpost"></span>` tags, it increments one of those placeholder variables you saw earlier (number, to be exact). When the JavaScript has finished looking for `<span></span>` tags, it compares the value of number with the other placeholder value (memory). If these numbers are *different*, meaning that number has been incremented because a `<span class="fullpost"></span>` element has been found, the JavaScript produces a link. That link is your Read More link.

Let's look at the line of JavaScript that writes the link to the page:

```
document.write('<a href="<$BlogItemPermalinkUrl$>">[your text]
          ➥</a><br>');
```

You should replace [your text] with whatever you would like the link text to be. Additionally, you can add any style to the `<a></a>` tag by using a class attribute. After these changes are made, click the **Save Template Changes** button, and then click the **Republish** button. You can now move on to creating a post that utilizes this new functionality.

The following steps assume that you have logged in to Blogger and selected **New Post** from your Blogger dashboard.

1 Add Code to Create the Link to the Expanded Entry

After you have typed the opening of your blog entry—the teaser text, if you will—place the `<span class="fullpost">` opening tag in the spot where you would like to see the link to the full post. When the post is published and viewed, the link to Read More (or whatever text you use in your template) will be located wherever the `<span class="fullpost">` opening tag is placed.

2 Add Code to Print a Link back to the Main Page

After the `<span class="fullpost">` opening tag, type the remainder of your blog post. Before typing the closing `</span>` tag, create a link that will take the user back to the main page of your blog when they are finished reading your extended entry. For example:

```
<p><a href="http://yourblog.blogspot.com">go home now</a></p>
```

After this last bit of code is added, click the **Publish Post** button to publish the post to your blog.

3 Click to Expand the Post and Read Additional Text

When your blog post is published, you will see the link to the full post appears where you placed the `<span class="fullpost">` opening tag while typing your text. You will also notice that all the text you typed after the `<span class="fullpost">` opening tag is hidden from view. The user will see this only if they click through to the expanded entry.

4 The Expanded Entry Is Displayed

When users click on the link to the extended entry—in this case, a link that says `continue reading...`—they will be taken to the individual post page. The link to the extended entry will be replaced by the text of the extended entry itself.

5 Click to Return to the Main Page

In the extended entry portion of the post, you can see the link created by performing step 2—adding a link back to the index page. Clicking this link will take users back to your index page, where they can continue reading your other blog posts without the clutter of a long blog post that takes up most of the visible space.

21

PART II

Fun with Blog Layouts

IN THIS PART:

4

Using Basic HTML and Working with Images

IN THIS CHAPTER:

The set of features provided in the Blogger post editor is suitable for quite a lot of people. Many bloggers are content with using the Compose mode of the Blogger post editor to create the minimal HTML markup for their post, but other bloggers want to add a little pizzazz or personalization to their content. The topics in this chapter provide some instruction with regard to the use of additional markup in your posts, and also to the addition of images to your posts using any of a number of image-hosting services.

Think of these topics as a step up from using the buttons in the Blogger post editor, but they do not require a full-fledged understanding of HTML and custom style sheets. You'll learn more about custom style sheets in Chapter 5, "Working with Blogger Templates," and you can also find additional reference information in Appendix A, "HTML Fundamentals," and Appendix B, "CSS Fundamentals."

Several topics in this chapter have to do with including images in your blog posts. There is no requirement that your blog posts contain images, but sometimes these things liven up your blog and allow you to connect further with your readers. For anonymous/pseudonymous bloggers, the utilization of images in blog posts requires a additional consideration: Are there any identifying features in your shared images, either of yourself or your location? You can take additional steps to preserve your anonymity while using various image-hosting services, and those steps will be discussed during their relevant topics. But being an anonymous blogger does not preclude you from personalizing your blog posts using markup or other basic design features, which is what the topics in this chapter will cover.

22

▶ **NOTE**

All topics in this chapter assume that you are familiar with the Blogger post editor (either **Compose** or **Manual** mode) and have successfully posted to your blog.

---

22 | **Using Paragraphs, Blockquotes, and List Markup in Your Posts**

✔ **BEFORE YOU BEGIN**

15 Creating a Post Using the Blogger Editor in Compose Mode

16 Creating a Post Using the Blogger Editor in Manual Mode

→ **SEE ALSO**

31 Defining and Implementing Custom Styles

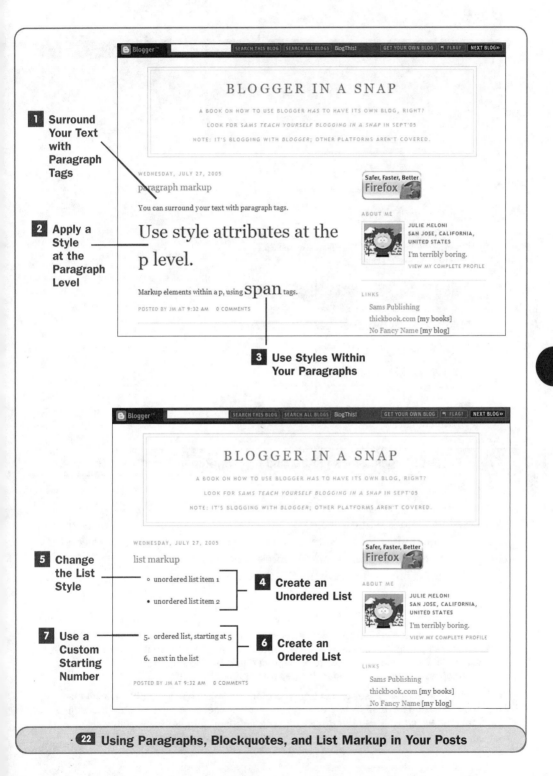

1 Surround Your Text with Paragraph Tags

2 Apply a Style at the Paragraph Level

3 Use Styles Within Your Paragraphs

5 Change the List Style

4 Create an Unordered List

7 Use a Custom Starting Number

6 Create an Ordered List

22

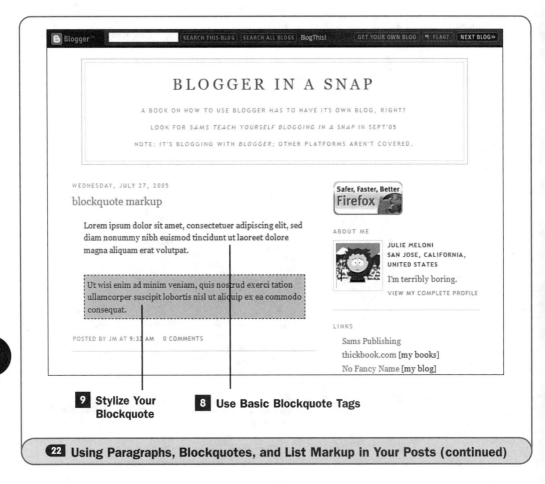

22

22 Using Paragraphs, Blockquotes, and List Markup in Your Posts (continued)

When creating a post using the Blogger editor in Compose mode, you have access to numerous buttons that can be used to modify the text elements of your blog post. In addition, the Blogger editor can assist you with inserting hyperlinks and images into your post. Using Compose mode is helpful if you want to apply formatting to posts but do not have the HTML skills necessary to do so.

▶ NOTE

When using Manual mode of the Blogger post editor in conjunction with block-level elements such as paragraphs, lists, and blockquotes, you might also want to ensure the **Convert Line Breaks** setting is set to No. You can find this setting on the **Settings** tab, **Formatting** navigation item, in your Blogger management interface.

If **Convert Line Breaks** is set to Yes and you mark up your posts using block-level elements like those described in this topic, your post will contain extra line breaks around your content, which will result in a post with a great deal of extraneous whitespace.

The following steps show sample HTML code used to create the content within the posts you see in the figures. You can follow along by logging in to Blogger and clicking the **New Post** icon in the **Blogs** section of the Blogger Dashboard, and then selecting the **Edit HTML** tab to switch to Manual mode if that mode is not your default.

▶ **TIP**

This topic refers to CSS styles and classes, which you can learn more about in Appendix B, "CSS Fundamentals." If you want to learn more about the HTML elements described in this topic, take a look at Appendix A, "HTML Fundamentals." If CSS styles and classes are unfamiliar to you, please glance at Appendix B before continuing in this topic.

1 Surround Your Text with Paragraph Tags

In HTML, a paragraph is created using the `<p></p>` tag pair; these tags should surround the text that is your paragraph. For example:

```
<p>You can surround your text with paragraph tags.</p>
```

When using the `<p></p>` tag pair, a line break is automatically assumed by the browser both before the start tag and after the end tag. This means you do not have to insert a line break (`<br/>`) before or after the paragraph tags. If you create several paragraphs in your post, the act of using the `<p></p>` tag pair ensures the proper spacing.

2 Apply a Style at the Paragraph Level

You can utilize the `style` attribute of an HTML tag to apply specific style elements to just one tag. For example, the following `style` attribute creates a paragraph with 36px text:

```
<p style="font-size: 36px;">Use style attributes at the
➥ p level.</p>
```

Because this particular style is attributed to only the text contained within its `<p></p>` tag pair, the paragraphs before it or after it will be in their normal style (or another specifically defined style). You can also replace the `style` attribute with a `class` attribute defined in your style sheet. For instance, if you defined a class called `bigtext` as `font-size: 36px` and applied the code like so

```
<p class="bigtext">Use style attributes at the p level.</p>
```

the resulting text would look exactly the same.

22

3 Use Styles Within Your Paragraphs

The text contained within a paragraph does not have to be plain vanilla text. You can use <b></b> and <i></i> tags around various pieces of text within a paragraph or other block element to add bolding and italics, respectively. You can also create your own styles by surrounding text with <span></span> tags that use a specific style or class attribute. For instance, the following code displays as a paragraph in normal text, but with a very large font size for the word span.

```
<p>Markup elements within a p, using
➥<span style="font-size: 36px;">span</span> tags.</p>
```

4 Create an Unordered List

Although *unordered* is the technical term for this type of list, these are commonly known as *bullet* lists because the default item indicator is a small bullet. The HTML for the unordered list shown here is

```
<ul>
<li>unordered list item 1</li>
<li>unordered list item 2</li>
</ul>
```

Unordered lists consist of individual list items surrounded by the <ul></ul> tag pair. Each list item is surrounded by the <li></li> tag pair.

5 Change the List Style

You can change the item indicator on a per-item basis by adding a style attribute to the opening <li> tag. In the following example, you can see the style attribute used to display the circle instead of the default bullet:

```
<li style="list-style-type: circle;">unordered list item 1</li>
```

Other options for the list-style-type style, as it relates to unordered lists, are none, disc, and square. The none style does what you imagine it would— it does not place an indicator before the item. The disc style is rendered as what we typically refer to as a *bullet* or *filled circle*. The square style uses a small filled square as the item indicator.

6 Create an Ordered List

An ordered list follows the same structure as an unordered list, but the tag pair for an ordered list is <ol></ol> instead of <ul></ul>. The HTML for the ordered list shown here is

```
<ol>
<li>ordered list</li>
<li>next in the list</li>
</ol>
```

No special list-style-type is used for these list items, so the default style (decimal) is used. Other options for ordered lists are decimal-leading-zero, lower-roman, upper-roman, lower-alpha, and upper-alpha. Using decimal-leading-zero would result in items numbered 01, 02, 03, and so on. The lower-roman and upper-roman styles would use Roman numerals as your item numbers, such as i, ii, iii if lowercase, and I, II, III if uppercase. The lower-alpha and upper-alpha styles would result in items numbered such as a, b, c if lowercase and A, B, C if uppercase. Using a combination of all of these styles, as well as nested lists, allows you to create a hierarchical outline such as those produced by word processing programs.

7 Use a Custom Starting Number

To start your ordered list at a specific point, use the start attribute in the opening <ol> tag:

```
<ol start="5">
```

If no list style is specified, your list items will begin with the number five. If you specify a different type of list style, the fifth item of that type will be used. For instance, if you use the upper-alpha style, the fifth alphabetical letter is E; therefore the first item in this particular ordered list would be indicated with an E.

8 Use Basic Blockquote Tags

The <blockquote></blockquote> tag pair is often used to surround long quotes included in your posts. Without any additional style definition, the standard blockquoted text will appear indented on both sides, relative to your other paragraphs.

9 Stylize Your Blockquote

To really set your blockquoted text apart from your other paragraphs, you can add elements of style to it. The following code was used to produce the second example shown in the figure:

```
<blockquote style="border: 1px dashed black; padding: 5px;
➥background-color: grey;">Utwisi enim ad minim veniam, quis
➥nostrud exerci tation ullamcorper suscipit lobortis nislut
➥aliquip ex ea commodo consequat.</blockquote>
```

22

Think of the `<blockquote></blockquote>` tag pair as creating an invisible box around your content. You can make the box visible by attributing styles to the borders and background as well as padding to the text it contains. You can learn more about borders, colors, and padding of elements in Appendix B.

---

23   Creating Hyperlinks in Your Posts

✔ BEFORE YOU BEGIN	→ SEE ALSO
15 Creating a Post Using the Blogger Editor in Compose Mode	**31** Defining and Implementing Custom Styles
16 Creating a Post Using the Blogger Editor in Manual Mode	

If you only learn one bit of HTML during your blogging lifetime, learn how to create a hyperlink. Without hyperlinks, there would be no World Wide Web because it is through these links that connections are made. The Blogger post editor—in both Compose and Manual modes—contains a button to assist you in the creation of a hyperlink, but you can also hand-code your own links while typing your post. After you learn the structure of the link code, you can use it without the assistance of the Blogger editor to leave comments on other blogs.

The following steps show how to create hyperlinks using the Blogger post editor. You can follow along by logging in to Blogger and clicking the **New Post** icon in the **Blogs** section of the Blogger Dashboard.

▶ TIP

To learn more about the various states of hyperlinks, take a look at Appendix A, "HTML Fundamentals."

1 Highlight the Text You Want to Link

Using the **Hyperlink** button in the Blogger post editor, you can turn text into a hyperlink at any point during the creation of your post. If you type the content of your post and then go back to fill in the links, start by highlighting the text you want to turn into a link.

2 Click the Hyperlink Button

To create a hyperlink, click the **Hyperlink** button. A prompt will appear, with the `http://` portion of the hyperlink already in place.

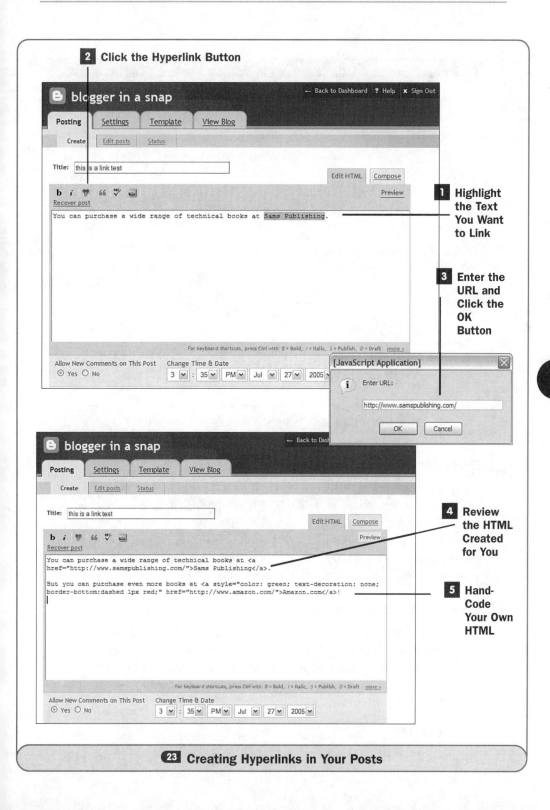

2 **Click the Hyperlink Button**

1 Highlight the Text You Want to Link

3 Enter the URL and Click the OK Button

4 Review the HTML Created for You

5 Hand-Code Your Own HTML

23

23 Creating Hyperlinks in Your Posts

6 Review the Links in Your Published Posts

23 Creating Hyperlinks in Your Posts (continued)

3 Enter the URL and Click the OK Button

If you are pasting a full URL into this text field, be sure to paste over the pre-populated content. If you paste a full URL in addition to the prepopulated content, your actual URL will be something like http://http://someurl
.com/, which is not a valid URL. When you have entered the URL, either through pasting it or typing it on your own, click the **OK** button. The editor will apply your link code and the prompt will disappear.

4 Review the HTML Created for You

If you have selected text to turn into a link, as in step 1, the selected text will now be surrounded by the HTML for the link. However, if you did not select any text before clicking the **Hyperlink** button and entering a URL, you have to manually place the cursor between the opening and closing <a></a> tags before typing the linked text.

5 **Hand-Code Your Own HTML**

The hyperlink function in the Blogger post editor creates the most basic link code. After the link code has been placed in your editor or you have typed it yourself, you can modify it by adding style or class attributes. In this example, a style attribute has been added, which will result in this link appearing in green text, without a standard underline, and with a red dashed bottom border.

▶ **NOTE**

You can learn more about styles and classes in Appendix B, "CSS Fundamentals."

6 **Review the Links in Your Published Posts**

After publishing a post containing hyperlinks, review the post to ensure that the hyperlinks are correct. This review can include tests ranging from visually inspecting the linked text to clicking the individual links and verifying they go to the correct places.

24

24 **Creating Tables in Your Posts**

→ **SEE ALSO**

31 Defining and Implementing Custom Styles

While blogging, you might encounter a time when you want to present text that is best displayed in a table format. The Blogger post editor does not contain a table creation wizard, but a basic table contains only a few elements and its syntax is easy to understand. The following steps show how to create a basic table in HTML. You can follow along by logging in to Blogger and clicking the **New Post** icon in the **Blogs** section of the Blogger Dashboard.

24 Creating Tables in Your Posts

1 Stylize Your Table Elements

For this example, I added the following elements to my Blogger template's style sheet so that I could quickly reference the styles by name instead of repeating the style attributes within in the HTML.

```
table              {border: 1px solid black; width: 350px;}
td                 {border: 1px solid black; padding: 5px}
td.LeftAlignHdr    {font-weight: bold; text-align:left;
                   ➥background-color: #CCCCCC;}
td.CenterAlignHdr  {font-weight: bold; text-align:center;
                   ➥background-color: #CCCCCC;}
td.LeftAlign       {font-weight: normal; text-align:left;}
td.CenterAlign     {font-weight: normal; text-align:center;}
```

The first item defines the table as being 350 pixels wide and having an outer border which is 1 pixel wide and solid black in color. The remaining styles are for the table data cells themselves. The second entry states that all table data cells should have a 1 pixel solid black border, and padding should be placed on all four sides; that is, the text inside the cell should have five pixels of whitespace on its top, right, bottom, and left sides.

The remaining four items define specific types of table data cells. The LeftAlignHdr and CenterAlignHdr classes will be used for the column head-ings—the text will appear in a bold font, either left or center aligned, and on a grey background. The LeftAlign and CenterAlign classes will be used for the remaining table data cells, and the text with them will be of normal weight and aligned either to the left or to the center.

▶ **TIP**

You can learn more about styles and classes in Appendix B, "CSS Fundamentals."

A table is encompassed by the `<table></table>` tag pair:

```
<table cellspacing="0">
[table rows and cells go here]
</table>
```

The `cellspacing` attribute used in the preceding code ensures that the table rows and columns have no extra spacing between them. In the figure, you can see the results of the application of these table styles.

2 Create Table Rows

A table row is enclosed by the `<tr></tr>` tag pair. Table rows contain table data cells:

```
<table cellspacing="0">
<tr>
[table cells go here]
</tr>
</table>
```

The HTML for table rows should be repeated for as many rows as you have in your table. Remember to close the table row tag pair before you start a new one.

24

3 Create Column Headings

In this example, the column headings are created by applying the LeftAlignHdr and CenterAlignHdr styles to the <td></td> tag pair:

```
<table cellspacing="0">
<tr>
<td class="LeftAlignHdr">TEAM</td>
<td class="CenterAlignHdr">WINS</td>
<td class="CenterAlignHdr">LOSSES</td>
<td class="CenterAlignHdr">PCT</td>
</tr>
</table>
```

The column headers are table data cells, much like the table data cells that will follow—the difference is in the style applied to them. Just as I reminded you to close your <tr></tr> tags, be sure to close your <td></td> tags as well.

4 Populate Your Table with Data

The following code is all that was used to create the table you see in the figure. Each row contains four table data cells, and the table itself contains six rows.

24

▶ **TIP**

For more information regarding table data cells, including row and column spanning, please see Appendix A, "HTML Fundamentals."

```
<table cellspacing="0">
<tr>
<td class="LeftAlignHdr">TEAM</td>
<td class="CenterAlignHdr">WINS</td>
<td class="CenterAlignHdr">LOSSES</td>
<td class="CenterAlignHdr">PCT</td>
</tr>
<tr>
<td class="LeftAlign">San Diego</td>
<td class="CenterAlign">50</td>
<td class="CenterAlign">50</td>
<td class="CenterAlign">.500</td>
</tr>
<tr>
<td class="LeftAlign">Arizona</td>
<td class="CenterAlign">49</td>
<td class="CenterAlign">54</td>
```

```
<td class="CenterAlign">.476</td>
</tr>
<tr>
<td class="LeftAlign">Los Angeles</td>
<td class="CenterAlign">46</td>
<td class="CenterAlign">54</td>
<td class="CenterAlign">.460</td>
</tr>
<tr>
<td class="LeftAlign">San Francisco</td>
<td class="CenterAlign">43</td>
<td class="CenterAlign">57</td>
<td class="CenterAlign">.430</td>
</tr>
<tr>
<td class="LeftAlign">Colorado</td>
<td class="CenterAlign">36</td>
<td class="CenterAlign">63</td>
<td class="CenterAlign">.364</td>
</tr>
</table>
```

▶ **NOTE**

When hand-coding your own HTML you might also want to ensure the **Convert Line Breaks** setting is set to No. You can find this setting under the **Settings** tab, **Formatting** navigation item, in your Blogger management interface.

If **Convert Line Breaks** is set to Yes and you create a table with your elements clearly delimited such as those just shown, your post will contain extra line breaks and thus extra whitespace between your table rows. If you keep **Convert Line Breaks** set to Yes, you can eliminate this extra whitespace by typing your HTML without line breaks, such as the following:

```
<table><tr><td>text</td></tr></table>
```

25 Inserting Images into Your Posts Using Blogger

You can use images to spice up your blog posts or to share a slice of life with your readers. Blogger provides users with a simple tool to assist in the storage of placement of these images. The following steps show how to place an image in your post, using the Blogger post editor. You can follow along by logging in to Blogger and clicking the **New Post** icon in the **Blogs** section of the Blogger Dashboard.

25

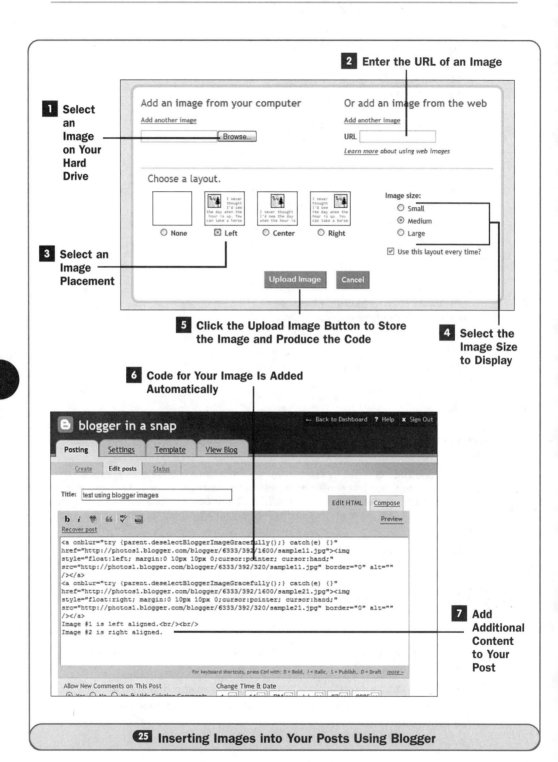

2 Enter the URL of an Image

1 Select an Image on Your Hard Drive

3 Select an Image Placement

5 Click the Upload Image Button to Store the Image and Produce the Code

4 Select the Image Size to Display

6 Code for Your Image Is Added Automatically

7 Add Additional Content to Your Post

25 Inserting Images into Your Posts Using Blogger

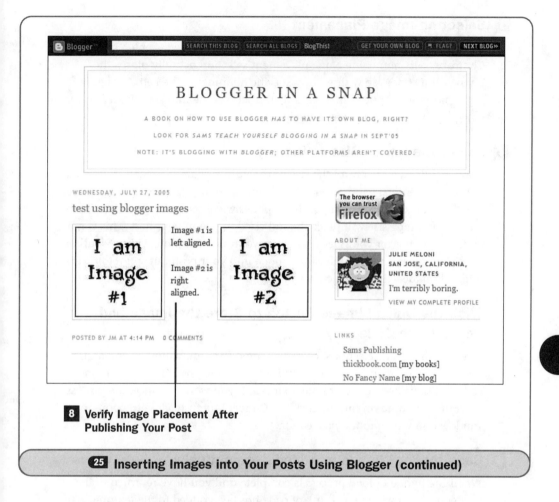

8 Verify Image Placement After Publishing Your Post

25 Inserting Images into Your Posts Using Blogger (continued)

1 Select an Image on Your Hard Drive

Click the **Browse** button and navigate the directory structure of your hard drive to find the image you would like to upload. If you want to add more than one image from your hard drive, click the **Add Another Image** link to display additional form fields.

2 Enter the URL of an Image

You can use the Blogger image insertion tool to add an image to your post even if it is hosted elsewhere. If you want to add more than one image from an external URL, click the **Add Another Image** link to display additional form fields.

3 Select an Image Placement

You have several options for image placement: None, Left, Center, and Right. Contrary to its name, the None placement selection actually places the image—it just does so without any specific alignment. The Left, Center, and Right placement options include code that aligns the image to the left, center, or right of the post area, respectively.

4 Select the Image Size to Display

Allowing Blogger to control the size of the displayed image means you need not have an image-editing program of your own. If you have uploaded a raw image that is 640 pixels long and 480 pixels wide, selecting the **Large** radio button for image size will place the full-sized image in your post. This is not optimal, neither for your viewers nor for your blog template. Using **Small** or **Medium** places a reasonably sized image into your post, but still retains the original image—the image code will include a link to it.

5 Click the Upload Image Button to Store the Image and Produce the Code

After making your selections, click the **Upload Image** button to upload the image, close the pop-up window, and return to the post editor. The image code will have been added to the textarea. If you want to cancel the process without uploading an image, click the **Cancel** button to close the pop-up window and return to the post editor.

6 Code for Your Image Is Added Automatically

When the image upload process is complete and you have returned to the post editor, you will see a chunk of code has been added to the textarea. The core elements of this text are the HTML code for including an image and the HTML code for a hyperlink wrapped around this image code, which (when published) will create an image linked to a larger version of itself. Within this code are various attributes that control placement of the image.

7 Add Additional Content to Your Post

Although experimenting with the image placement code is not recommended unless you thoroughly understand it, you can add your own content to the rest of the post and style it as you will.

8 Verify Image Placement After Publishing Your Post

When you have completed the publishing process, take a look at your blog post. Are the images aligned properly? Do they fit? If you are unhappy with

25

your image placement, remember you can simply edit your post and republish it—the images will have been uploaded once, and there will be no need to go through the image upload process again.

---

26 | **Inserting Images into Your Posts Using Flickr**

→ SEE ALSO

28 Other Methods for Inserting Images into Posts

Flickr is a popular online photo management application with both free and paid accounts. Account holders have numerous tools at their disposal, as well as the abilities to browse and comment on other users' photos and to set privacy levels and copyrights. Learn more online at http://www.flickr.com/.

Flickr users can register their blog details and create a seamless process for posting photos from Flickr to Blogger using Flickr's Blog This tool. To associate your Blogger-based blog with your Flickr account, first log in to Flickr, go to the **Account** page, and follow the link to **Your Blog**. Click the **Set Up a New Blog** link. The first question asks your blogging platform (Blogger), and the second question asks you to enter your Blogger username and password. Using your username and password, Flickr retrieves a list of the blogs associated with your account. If you have more than one blog, you are asked to select the specific blog you want to set up at this time. You can associate as many blogs as you have with your Flickr account, but you must go through the setup process for each blog. After selecting a blog, you are asked to confirm the blog details before saving the information in your Flickr account.

After you have at least one blog associated with your Flickr account, you can seamlessly post photos from Flickr to Blogger by using the Blog This tool, as shown in the following steps:

1 Click Blog This

When browsing photos on Flickr—either yours or someone else's—one of the tools available to you is Blog This. As you find an image you want to blog about, click the **Blog This** link on the photo's page.

2 Select a Blog

Clicking the **Blog This** link invokes a drop-down list containing the names of blogs associated with your account. Select the name of a blog to continue, or click **Cancel** to end the **Blog This** process.

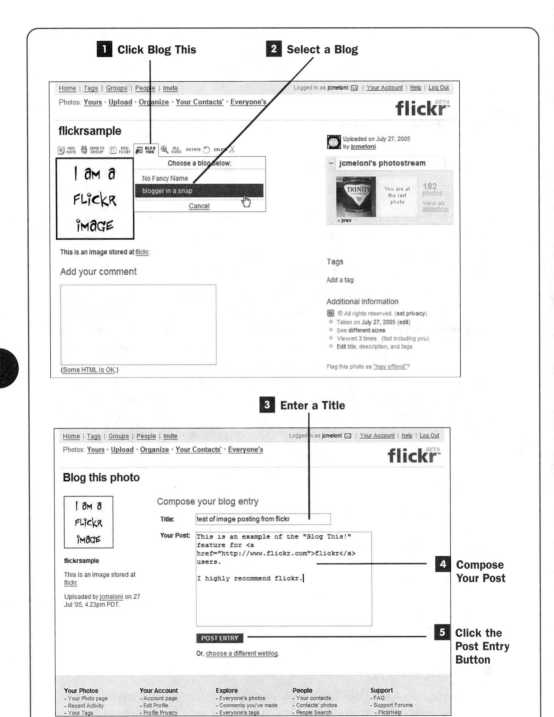

26 Inserting Images into Your Posts Using Flickr

6 **Receive Confirmation of a Successful Post**

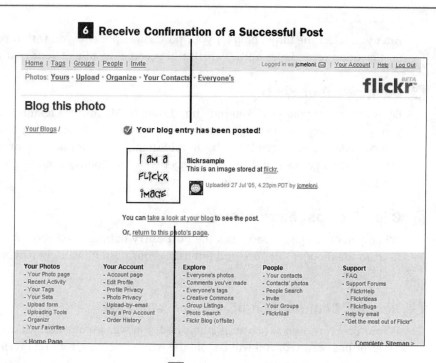

8 **Verify the Post Contents and Image Alignment**

7 **Go to Your Blog**

3 Enter a Title

After you select the target blog for your post, Flickr presents you with a basic post creation form. Enter a title, which will become the title of your post.

4 Compose Your Post

Enter the text of your post. You may hand-code HTML into the textarea. If you typically rely on the Blogger editor in Compose mode, remember that you can edit the post after it has been published. Enter minimal text at this time and then go back and use the Blogger editor in Compose mode if you need help with the HTML coding.

5 Click the Post Entry Button

When you are ready to post, click the **Post Entry** button. The Flickr form connects to the Blogger interface and publishes your post, all without leaving the Flickr site.

6 Receive Confirmation of a Successful Post

If your post has been successfully published, you will see a confirmation. If an error has occurred, you will be told the reason for the error and given the opportunity to try again.

7 Go to Your Blog

After publishing your post, follow the **Take a Look at Your Blog** link to view the newly published post. You can also return to the photo page and continue navigating within Flickr.

8 Verify the Post Contents and Image Alignment

Go to your blog and verify that the Flickr image and post text are just as they should be. If you need to make changes, simply edit your post via the Blogger interface and republish it.

Whether you upload your own photo or someone else's, part of the standard Flickr-posted content will be the name of the image and the linked name of the image owner. This is akin to giving credit where credit is due and should be kept in your blog post, especially when you are not the original owner of the image.

▶ TIP

Flickr also provides HTML for inserting an image in your blog post if you decide not to use the direct-to-blog interface. To get this HTML, click the **All Sizes** icon when viewing an image. Under the image you will see a simple URL, which you can then place in an `<img/>` tag, and a chunk of HTML that you can paste in its entirety in your blog post.

26

▶ **NOTE**

Additional blog-related settings in Flickr can be found by going to your account page and selecting **Your Blogs**. There you can set default image placement for all your uploaded photos, among other things.

---

27 | **Inserting Images into Your Posts Using PhotoBucket**

→ **SEE ALSO**

28 Other Methods for Inserting Images into Posts

PhotoBucket is a popular online photo management application with both free and paid accounts. Learn more online at http://www.photobucket.com/.

PhotoBucket users can register their blog details and subsequently post photos from PhotoBucket to Blogger. To associate your Blogger-based blog with your PhotoBucket account, first log in to PhotoBucket and click the **Blog Options** button. From there, select your blogging platform (Blogger) from the drop-down menu and click the **Add** button. Next, enter your Blogger username and password. Using your username and password, PhotoBucket will retrieve a list of the blogs associated with your account. If you have more than one blog, you will be asked to select the specific blog you want to set up at this time. You can associate as many blogs as you have with your PhotoBucket account, but you must go through the setup process for each blog. After selecting a blog, you are asked to confirm the blog details before saving the information in your PhotoBucket account.

After you have at least one blog associated with your PhotoBucket account, you can post photos from PhotoBucket to Blogger by using the **Blog** button as shown in the following steps:

1 **Click the Blog Button to Create a Post from PhotoBucket**

When browsing within your own PhotoBucket album, click the **Blog** button to initialize the interface for posting to your blog.

2 **Select a Blog**

Clicking the **Blog** button will take you to the Post to Blog form. Select the target blog from the drop-down list containing the names of blogs associated with your account.

27

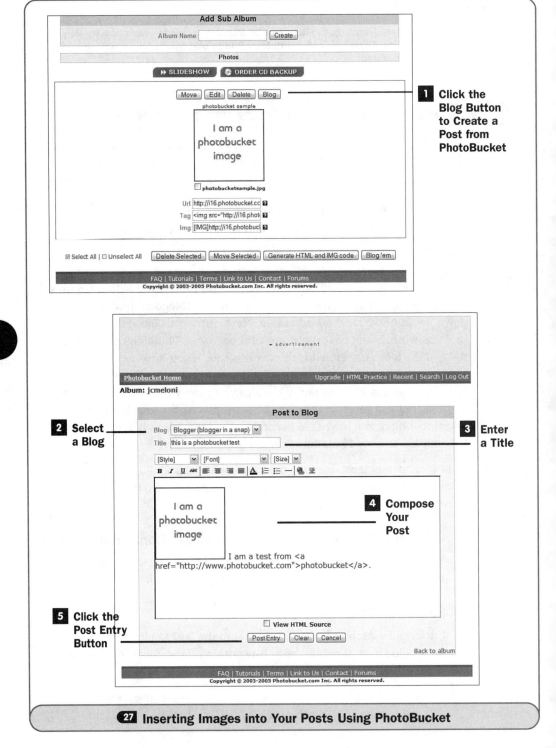

27   **Inserting Images into Your Posts Using PhotoBucket**

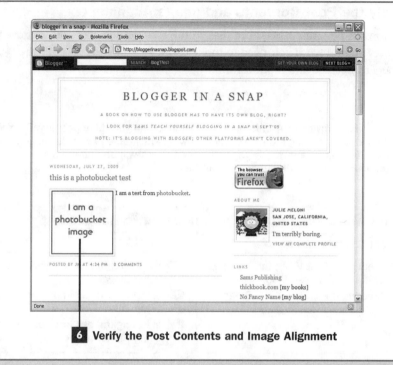

6 Verify the Post Contents and Image Alignment

27 Inserting Images into Your Posts Using PhotoBucket (continued)

27

3 Enter a Title

In the Post to Blog form, enter a title in the text field. That title will become the title of your post.

4 Compose Your Post

Enter the text of your post in the textarea provided. The default form contains a minimal WYSIWYG editor, which you can use in lieu of the Blogger editor in Compose mode. If you prefer to hand-code the HTML, check the **View HTML Source** check box to switch modes.

5 Click the Post Entry Button

When you are ready to post, click the **Post Entry** button. The PhotoBucket form will connect to the Blogger interface and publish your post, all without leaving the PhotoBucket site. If your post successfully publishes, you will see a confirmation. If an error occurs, you will be told the reason for the error and given the opportunity to try again.

6 Verify the Post Contents and Image Alignment

Go to your blog and verify that the PhotoBucket image and post text are just as they should be. If you need to make changes, edit your post via the Blogger interface and republish it.

▶ **TIP**

PhotoBucket also provides HTML for inserting an image in your blog post if you decide not to use the direct-to-blog interface. When viewing any image in your gallery, the URL to the image as well as an `<img/>` tag with the URL in it will be underneath the gallery image. You can use this code directly in your blog post.

27

28 Other Methods for Inserting Images Into Posts

✔ BEFORE YOU BEGIN	→ SEE ALSO
15 Creating a Post Using the Blogger Editor in Compose Mode	**25** Inserting Images into Your Posts Using Blogger
16 Creating a Post Using the Blogger Editor in Manual Mode	**26** Inserting Images into Your Posts Using Flickr
	27 Inserting Images into Your Posts Using PhotoBucket

In addition to hosting images, you have options on Blogger, or other image-hosting services such as Flickr and PhotoBucket, which offer an interface to posting to your blog. If you have access to a web server, you can host images there and simply refer to them via the `<img>` HTML tag, using the full URL to the image. For instance, you might use an image-hosting service without a direct-to-blog interface. In that instance, you can obtain the URL to your image and manually create the appropriate HTML to include this image in your post.

In addition to Flickr and PhotoBucket, the following image hosting services are just a few of the numerous services that offer free accounts and external linking:

- ImageShack, at http://imageshack.us/
- TinyPic, at http://tinypic.com/
- Village Photos, at http://www.villagephotos.com/

The key phrase is external linking, which means that you will have a URL to an image, such as http://the.server.name/imagename.jpg. Armed with this URL, you can insert inline images into your blog posts or your blog template.

Although the image tag has several attributes, the only required attribute is src or the source location of the image—the external URL, for example.

Other attributes that you should use, but are not required, include `height`, `width`, and `alt-text` attributes. For instance, the following defines an image that is 200 pixels wide, 200 pixels high, with alternative text of `myImage`:

```
<img src="http://the.server.name/imagename.jpg" width="200" height="200"
alt="myImage"/>
```

Specifying the height and width of the image allows the browser to render the page while leaving the correct space for the photo that might not be ready to load at the time the browser encounters the `<img>` tag.

▶ NOTE

In Appendix B, "CSS Fundamentals," you'll learn how to set additional properties for `<img>` tag attributes by using styles such as padding, margins, and borders.

28

5

Working with Blogger Templates

IN THIS CHAPTER:

Although Blogger provides more than 30 different templates that you can apply to your blog, there will come a time when you want to customize something within your standard Blogger template. This customization could be as simple as removing the placeholder links that appear in new Blogger templates. Or you might want to change something in your style sheet, such as the font size of the text within your posts. Or you might want to add images within a sidebar area. All of these actions—and more—can be performed by editing your template via the Blogger template editor, which is found under the **Template** tag in the Blogger management interface.

The topics in this chapter will familiarize you with the general structure of a Blogger template and how this single template controls the appearance of your blog main page, archive page, and post pages. You'll also learn some tips for implementing a completely customized Blogger template; that is, one not provided by Blogger but created by either you or a third-party template designer.

If your blog is meant to be your personal online presence, it stands to reason that you should be able to customize it however you see fit—the topics in this chapter are meant to give you the basic knowledge to do just that.

▶ **NOTE**

All topics in this chapter assume that you are familiar with navigating around the Blogger management interface.

29	**Understanding the Blogger Template Structure and Editor**
✔ **BEFORE YOU BEGIN**	→ **SEE ALSO**
4 Logging In to Blogger and Navigating the Dashboard	**30** Identifying Elements in the Blogger Template Source

All changes to your Blogger template occur through the Blogger template editor. Such changes range from simple style sheet modifications to full template replacements. To begin, log in to Blogger and click the **Change Settings** icon in the **Blogs** section of the Blogger Dashboard. Click the **Template** tab to display navigational items; **Edit Current** is the default landing page and, in this instance, is where you should be.

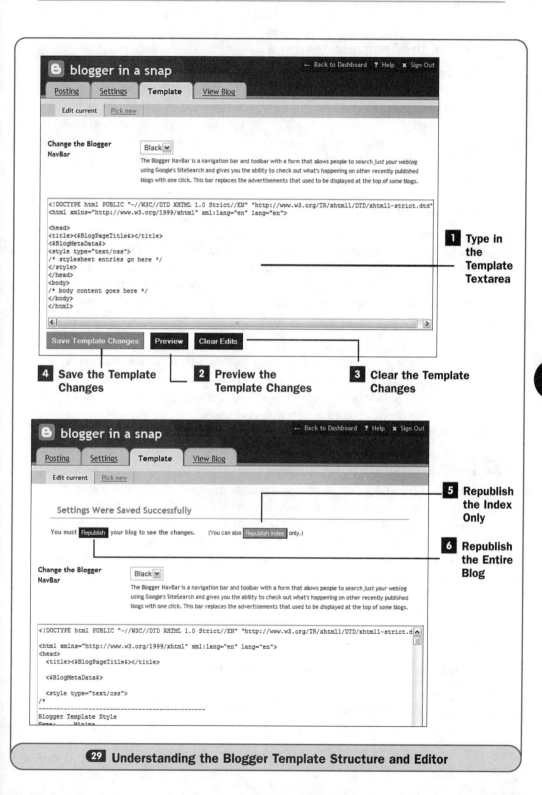

1 Type in the Template Textarea

The template textarea contains your current template. Within this template are HTML tags, style sheet entries, and Blogger template code. As you can see in this example, the structure of a Blogger template is no different from a standard HTML document: It begins with a document type declaration and opening <html> tag, followed by a <head></head> area including style sheet entries, includes a <body></body> area in which the actual blog content resides, and finishes with the closing </html> tag.

2 Preview the Template Changes

At any point in the template editing process, you can click the **Preview** button to launch a new browser window and display a representation of your blog main page with the new template applied. If you modify style sheet entries applicable to posts, previewing your template will show these new styles in action. Similarly, any modifications you make to your sidebar will also be shown in their proposed new state.

If you click through to a permalink or archive page from this preview version of your template, be aware that you will be viewing the current live version of your template, so your changes will not be reflected. Although you should preview changes to your template before republishing your blog, you have to rely on faith with regard to previewing changes applicable to archive or post pages.

3 Clear the Template Changes

Click the **Clear Edits** button to revert your template to its previous saved state. For instance, if you make several text and style sheet modifications but have not saved them, clicking the **Clear Edits** button will remove these changes. The only instance in which the **Clear Edits** functionality does not work as you might expect is when you go through the **Pick New** process and replace your existing Blogger template with a new Blogger template. In that case, the **Clear Edits** button does not revert your new template back to the former template.

▶ TIP

It is a good idea to keep a backup file of your current template at all times. Simply highlight and copy the contents of your template textarea, and paste them into a text file that is saved on your hard drive. If something goes wrong during the editing process of your template, you always have a clean backup version ready to paste in the textarea.

4 Save the Template Changes

Click the **Save Template Changes** button to save the changes you have just made to your template. After you click the **Save Template Changes** button, the **Clear Edits** button becomes moot because there will be no pending changes in the queue and nothing can be undone.

5 Republish the Index Only

If you make only cosmetic changes to items that appear on the main page of your blog, you can publish this index page simply by clicking the **Republish Index** button. Republishing only the index avoids having to republish your entire blog—which might take a few minutes if your blog is large—but be sure that the changes you make are applicable only to main page items.

6 Republish the Entire Blog

If you make style sheet modifications, which tend to be applicable to all pages within your blog, or if you make other structural modifications to the content area or your sidebar, click the **Republish Entire Blog** button. All the pages of your blog will be refreshed with the new template in place.

30

▶ NOTE

After republishing your index or entire blog, you might have to clear your browser cache or force-reload the pages to see your changes.

---

30 **Identifying Elements in the Blogger Template Source**

✔ BEFORE YOU BEGIN	→ SEE ALSO
29 Understanding the Blogger Template Structure and Editor	**31** Defining and Implementing Custom Styles
	32 Understanding the Blogger Template Language

```
1:    <!DOCTYPE html PUBLIC "-//W3C//DTD XHTML 1.0 Strict//EN"
2:    "http://www.w3.org/TR/xhtml1/DTD/xhtml1-strict.dtd">
3:    <html xmlns="http://www.w3.org/1999/xhtml" xml:lang="en"
      ➥ lang="en">
4:    <head>
5:    <title><$BlogPageTitle$></title>
6:    <$BlogMetaData$>
7:    <style type="text/css">
8:    /* stylesheet entries go here */
```

```
 9:  </style>
10:  </head>
11:  <body>
12:  <!-- To aid with the Blogger NavBar -->
13:  <div id="wrap4">
14:  <!-- Header -->
15:  <h1><$BlogTitle$></h1>
16:  <$BlogDescription$>
17:  <!-- Blog Posts -->
18:  <Blogger>
19:  <BlogDateHeader><h3><$BlogDateHeaderDate$></h3></BlogDateHeader>
20:  <a name="<$BlogItemNumber$>"> </a>
21:  <BlogItemTitle><h2><BlogItemURL><a href="<$BlogItemURL$>">
     ➥</BlogItemURL>
22:  <$BlogItemTitle$><BlogItemURL></a></BlogItemURL></h2>
     ➥</BlogItemTitle>
23:  <div class="blogPost">
24:  <$BlogItemBody$><br />
25:  <div class="byline">posted by <a href="<$BlogItemPermalinkURL$>"
26:   title="permanent link"><$BlogItemAuthorNickname$>  #
27:  <$BlogItemDateTime$></a>
28:  <MainOrArchivePage><BlogItemCommentsEnabled> 
29:  <a href="<$BlogItemCommentCreate$>"
     ➥<$BlogItemCommentFormOnclick$>>
30:  <$BlogItemCommentCount$> comments</a>
     ➥</BlogItemCommentsEnabled>
31:  </MainOrArchivePage> <$BlogItemControl$></div>
32:  </div>
33:  <ItemPage>
34:  <div class="blogComments">
35:      <BlogItemCommentsEnabled><a name="comments"></a>
36:      Comments:
37:      <BlogItemComments>
38:      <div class="blogComment">
39:      <a name="<$BlogCommentNumber$>"></a><$BlogCommentBody$><br />
40:      <div class="byline"><a href="<$BlogCommentPermalinkURL$>"
              ➥title="permanent link">#</a>
41:      posted by <$BlogCommentAuthor$> : <$BlogCommentDateTime$></div>
42:      <$BlogCommentDeleteIcon$>
43:      </div>
44:      </BlogItemComments>
45:      <$BlogItemCreate$>
46:      </BlogItemCommentsEnabled>
47:      <br /><br />
48:      <a href="<$BlogURL$>">&lt;&lt; Home</a>
```

```
49: </div>
50: </ItemPage>
51: </Blogger>
52: <!-- Archive Links -->
53: <h2 id="archives">Archives</h2>
53: <BloggerArchives>
54: <a href="<$BlogArchiveURL$>"><$BlogArchiveName$></a>
55: </BloggerArchives>
56: <script type="text/javascript" language="Javascript">
57: if (location.href.indexOf("archive")!=-1)
58:     document.write("<strong><a href=\"<$BlogURL$>\">Current Posts
                     ➥</a></strong>");
59: </script>
60: <p id="bloggerBug"><a href="http://www.blogger.com">
60: <img width="88" height="31"
61: src="http://buttons.blogger.com/bloggerbutton1.gif"
61: border="0" alt="Powered by Blogger./></a></p>
62: </div>
63: </body>
64: </html>
```

When editing your Blogger template to add links to third-party items, you might be given particular instructions to add a bit of code to the heading area of your template, or the style sheet, or within particular Blogger template tags. This topic looks at a minimal Blogger template and helps you to identify various elements.

1 Finding the Document Type Declaration

The first line or two of your template, before the opening <html> tag, typically contain a document type declaration. You can learn more about document type declarations in Appendix A, "HTML Fundamentals." Do not remove these lines; they assist in the rendering and validation of the pages that make up your blog. Lines 1 and 2 show the document type declaration within this template.

2 Identifying HEAD Elements

There are usually four sets of items within the HEAD element of a template, which is surrounded by the opening <head> tag (line 4) and the closing </head> tag (line 10). The title, surrounded by the <title></title> tag pair, is one of these elements, and can be found in this instance on line 5. Next comes the metadata for your blog. Line 6 shows the use of a Blogger template tag for metadata; you can learn more about this tag in **32 Understanding the Blogger Template Language.** One of the most important elements of metadata that is dynamically displayed in this area is a link to your site feed. Following the metadata tags are the lines containing your template's style sheet.

For the sake of brevity, the style sheet entries have been removed from this example. However, style sheets are surrounded by `<style></style>` tags, as shown on lines 7 and 9, respectively; the individual style definitions fall between these tags. Before the closing `</head>` tag, you might also find JavaScript elements that are used to control various display or functional aspects of your blog. This particular template does not show any JavaScript in the HEAD area, but if it did the code would be delineated by the `<script></script>` tag pair.

3 Locating the BODY Element

All the magic happens within the BODY element; the opening `<body>` tag can be seen on line 11, and the closing `</body>` tag does not appear until line 62 (immediately before the ending `</html>` tag). Within the BODY element are all the various Blogger template tags and `<div>` elements that control the display of your blog main page, archive page, and post pages.

4 Identifying HTML Comments

HTML comments begin with `<!--` and end with `-->`, and within these symbols contain text that is never to be rendered by the browser. Line 17 shows a good use of a comment: It indicates that the source code following this comment will be used to generate the blog posts. HTML comments are often used to provide a visual indicator of the purpose of the code that follows it, and can be very helpful when quickly scanning through source code to find a particular area.

5 Locating Blogger Content Placeholder Tags

When you see a tag that begins with `<$` and ends with `$>`, you have found a Blogger content placeholder tag. These single tags in your template represent values stored in the Blogger database that is then displayed when your template is published. For instance, line 15 shows the placement of the `<$BlogTitle$>` Blogger tag between the standard HTML `<title></title>` tag pair. When published, the actual title tag seen in the source will be `<title>Your Title Here</title>`.

6 Locating Blogger Content Container Tags

Blogger content container tags are different in appearance and usage than the Blogger content placement tags just described. These tags do not have the dollar-sign indicator (as in `<$BlogItemBody$>`) and instead look just like

HTML tag pairs (`<Blogger></Blogger>`, `<ArchivePage></ArchivePage>`, and so forth). These tag pairs are used to set apart elements of the template that will be populated with content when published. When the publishing process occurs, these tags tell the underlying Blogger application to kick into gear and do something specific based on the type of tag it encounters.

For instance, line 34 shows the `<BlogItemCommentsEnabled>` opening tag. This tag tells the Blogger application to start the process of retrieving the stored comments for this particular blog, and to continue doing so until it comes across the closing `</BlogItemCommentsEnabled>` tag in line 45.

If you have any aspirations of working with your Blogger template, it is important to be able to discern between the various elements of HTML, style sheets, and Blogger template tags found in the template. Although you have the ability to add, modify, and delete elements from your template, doing so haphazardly will have repercussions. For instance, if you remove the `<Blogger>` opening tag from your template and republish your blog, you'll find no blog content is displayed. Always be cautious when modifying your template, and always keep a backup handy.

31

31 | Defining and Implementing Custom Styles

✔ **BEFORE YOU BEGIN**

29 Understanding the Blogger Template Structure and Editor

The style sheets used in the standard Blogger templates range from simple to complex; the example shown here is one of the simplest style sheets of them all, but it does reflect the three different types of elements you will encounter: styles for tags, styles for IDs, and styles for classes. Because it's your template, after all, you can modify existing styles or add your own styles for use within your template. Style sheet entries are nothing more than sets of rules that govern the display of your content. You can learn more about the specific language of style sheets—CSS—in Appendix B, "CSS Fundamentals."

1 Locate the Style Sheet Start Tag

All style sheet entries can be found between the `<style></style>` tag pair. Some style sheets will include links to external URLs; in those instances, you will not be able to edit the styles defined in the file sitting on someone else's server. However, you can still add individual entries through the Blogger template editor and then modify your template to use your new styles.

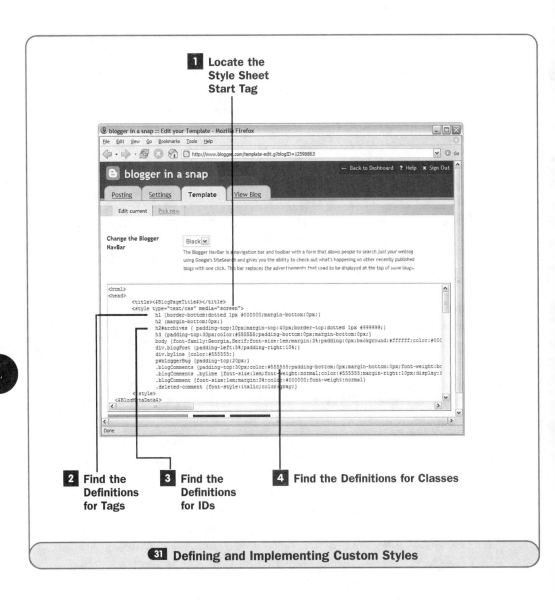

1 Locate the Style Sheet Start Tag

2 Find the Definitions for Tags

3 Find the Definitions for IDs

4 Find the Definitions for Classes

31 Defining and Implementing Custom Styles

For instance, suppose that you are using a template that includes an external link to a style sheet, and in that style sheet is a class called .headerText, which is defined as 36-point Wingdings or some such font. Because you can't modify the definition of the .headerText class in the external style sheet, simply define a new class, such as .myHeaderText, in the style sheet area of your template and replace all instances of .headerText with .myHeaderText wherever it appears in the body of the template itself.

2 Find the Definitions for Tags

Your style sheet may contain definitions for entire tags, as shown here with the definition of the <h1></h1> tag pair. In the style sheet shown here, all text surrounded by <h1></h1> tags will have a 1-pixel dotted black border at the bottom of it. If a tag is not defined in your style sheet, you may add it here; any instance of that tag in use within your template will then have the style applied to it. If you want to set a default set of styles for your content, such as font-related styles including family and size, you can do so by adding a style sheet entry for the <body></body> tag pair.

3 Find the Definitions for IDs

When a hash sign (#) precedes a style entry, it indicates an ID. In this instance, the ID is attached to a specific tag, such as h2#archives or p#bloggerBug. This type of definition specifies exactly which tags can use the particular ID. In this case, the archives ID can be applied to only an <h2> tag, and the bloggerBug ID can be applied to only a <p> tag. In other words, this text would have styles applied to it:

```
<h2 id="archives">Some Header Text for Archives</h2>
<p id="bloggerBug">Text around the Powered By Blogger credit.</p>
```

This code would not become stylized because the IDs do not apply for these tags:

```
<p id="archives">Some Header Text for Archives </p>
<div id="bloggerBug">Text around the Powered By Blogger
➥ credit.</div>
```

When you want an ID to be applied to any tag, simply define it as such in the style sheet; in the example below "style definitions" would be replaced by the actual style definitions used to create the style, such as font attributes, height and width, padding and margins, and so forth:

```
#someID {style definitions}
```

In valid code, IDs can be used only once in a template. If you want to apply the same style to more than one tag or in more than one instance, use a class instead of an ID.

4 Find the Definitions for Classes

When a dot (.) precedes a style entry, it indicates a class. In this instance, four individual classes are defined for various text elements related to Blogger comments. As with IDs, classes can be applied to specific tags, like this

31

example, where `style definitions` would be replaced by the actual style definitions used to create the style, such as font attributes, height and width, padding and margins, and so forth:

```
p.someClass {style definitions}
```

Here, the `someClass` class would be valid only when used with a `<p>` tag, so this would not be properly styled:

```
<h1 class="someClass">Important Heading!</h1>
```

However, unlike IDs, classes can be used multiple times within a template.

5   Implement Custom Styles

To add an element to your style sheet, simply type its definition between the `<style></style>` tag pair. Before you begin, review the content in Appendix B to ensure that you are using the correct syntax for the element. After you have defined a tag, ID, or class, you can use it within your template and blog posts.

31

After making any style sheet modifications, be sure to republish your entire blog and not just the index. Your archive pages and post pages use the same style sheet, and for your modifications to be accessible by all pages, all pages must be republished.

---

32   **Understanding the Blogger Template Language**

✔ **BEFORE YOU BEGIN**

30 Identifying Elements in the Blogger Template Source

Your blog's main page, archive pages, and individual post pages are all controlled by one master template. For the Blogger application to produce the various and sundry pages that make up your blog, numerous placeholder and container tags are used. This topic provides a very brief overview of the types of Blogger template tags that you might encounter and that you can use to extend your blog; additional information can be found the Blogger Knowledgebase (http://help.blogger.com/bin/topic.py?topic=39). Your basic Blogger template might include only a few of the more important tags or it might include a whole rash of these tags. Although there are definitely some tags you do not want to remove, such as the `<Blogger></Blogger>` tag pair and most of the post-related tags, other tags are optional and can be added to increase functionality or removed to streamline your template.

▶ **NOTE**

All Blogger template tags are case sensitive, so pay close attention when editing your template. For instance, if you type `<blogger></blogger>` instead of `<Blogger></Blogger>`, your posts will not appear.

Common tags found in your template's HEAD area include the following:

- `<$BlogEncoding$>`. This tag produces a content-type declaration matching the language encoding of your blog.

- `<$BlogPageTitle$>`. This tag will display the title of your page, and it is found within the HTML `<title></title>` tag pair.

- `<$BlogMetaData$>`. This tag outputs meta information for your blog.

- `<BlogSiteFeed><$BlogSiteFeedUrl$></BlogSiteFeed>`. The container tag pair wrapped around the specific site feed URL ensures the proper creation of the `<meta>` tags that control your site feed.

Tags used within the BODY area, to identify either the blog or the blog author, include

- `<$BlogTitle$>`. This tag outputs the title of your blog, stored in your account settings.

- `<$BlogDescription$>`. This tag outputs the description of your blog, stored in your account settings.

- `<$BlogOwnerFirstName$>`. This tag outputs your first name, stored in your 1account settings.

- `<$BlogOwnerLastName$>`. This tag outputs your last name, stored in your account settings.

- `<$BlogOwnerEmail$>`. This tag outputs your email address, stored in your account settings.

- `<$BlogOwnerFullName$>`. This tag outputs your full name, stored in your account settings.

- `<$BlogOwnerPhotoUrl$>`. This tag outputs the URL of your personal image, stored in your account settings.

- `<$BlogOwnerNickname$>`. This tag outputs your nickname, stored in your account settings.

- `<$BlogOwnerLocation$>`. This tag outputs your city, state, and country, or whatever location you have stored in your account settings.

32

- `<$BlogOwnerAboutMe$>`. This tag outputs the About Me text, stored in your account settings.
- `<$BlogOwnerProfileURL$>`. This tag generates a link to your complete Blogger profile.

Tags used to control elements of your posts, found within the BODY area, include

- `<Blogger></Blogger>`. This set of container tags holds most other post-related tags and Blogger template functionality.
- `<BlogDateHeader></BlogDateHeader>`. This set of tags defines the area in which the date headers are output, as defined in your Formatting settings.
- `<$BlogDateHeaderDate$>`. This tag outputs the date of the post.
- `<BlogItemTitle></BlogItemTitle>`. This set of tags contains the placeholder tags that display the post title.
- `<BlogItemURL></BlogItemURL>`. This set of tags contains the placeholder tags that display the URL of the post.
- `<$BlogItemURL$>`. This tag outputs the URL of the post.
- `<$BlogItemTitle$>`. This tag outputs the title of the post.
- `<$BlogItemBody$>`. This tag outputs the full contents of a blog post.
- `<$BlogItemAuthor$>`. This tag outputs the full name of the author of a post, as stored in your account settings.
- `<$BlogItemAuthorNickname$>`. This tag outputs the display name of the author of the post, as stored in your account settings.
- `<$BlogItemAuthorEmail$>`. This tag outputs the email address of the author of the blog post, as stored in your account settings.
- `<$BlogItemAuthorURL$>`. This tag outputs the additional URL of the author of the blog post, as stored in your account settings.
- `<$BlogItemDateTime$>`. This tag outputs the date and time attached to the post; this date and time is modifiable at the time of post creation/editing, and might not reflect the actual date and time the post was published.
- `<$BlogItemNumber$>`. This tag outputs the unique ID number of the blog post, as determined through the publishing process.
- `<$BlogItemArchiveFileName$>`. This tag outputs the archive filename of this post, which may or may not be similar to the permalink URL.

32

- `<$BlogItemPermalinkURL$>`. This tag outputs the permalink URL for this blog post.

- `<$BlogItemControl$>`. This tag outputs the Quick Edit link for this post, if **Show Quick Editing on Your Blog?** is set to Yes in your Basic settings.

- `<BlogDateFooter></BlogDateFooter>`. This set of tags defines the area in which the date footers are output, as defined in your Formatting settings.

Tags used to control the comments-related area of your posts include the following:

- `<BlogItemCommentsEnabled></BlogItemCommentsEnabled>`. This tag pair surrounds all other comment-related tags, and indicates that this chunk of code should be interpreted only if you have Blogger comments enabled in your Commenting settings.

- `<$BlogItemCommentCount$>`. This tag outputs the current number of comments for the particular post.

- `<$BlogItemCommentCreate$>`. This tag outputs the URL to the page on which you can read comments and leave comments of your own.

- `<$BlogItemCommentFormOnClick$>`. If your Commenting settings warrant it, this tag outputs a link that, when clicked, opens the comments display and forms in a pop-up window rather than a new page.

- `<BlogItemComments></BlogItemComments>`. This tag pair surrounds the code that will be output for each comment associated with this post.

- `<$BlogCommentNumber$>`. This tag outputs the number of the comment.

- `<$BlogCommentBody$>`. This tag outputs the body of the comment left by a reader.

- `<$BlogCommentPermalinkURL$>`. This tag outputs a permalink URL to this particular comment.

- `<$BlogCommentAuthor$>`. This tag outputs information identifying the author of the comment.

- `<$BlogCommentDateTime$>`. This tag outputs the date and time the comment was left by the reader.

- `<$BlogCommentDeleteIcon$>`. This tag displays the deletion icon if you are the blog administrator or the person who left the comment.

- `<$BlogItemCreate$>`. This tag outputs the link leading to the form to create a new comment.

32

▶ **NOTE**

If you are not using Blogger commenting and instead are using a third-party comment-ing system such as Haloscan, you should remove the Blogger comment-related tags from your template in addition to selecting Hide in your Commenting settings.

Tags used to display elements related to blog archives include the following:

- `<BloggerArchives></BloggerArchives>`. This container tag should surround your archive-related tags (shown in the code snippet that follows this list).

- `<$BlogArchiveURL$>`. This tag outputs the URL to an archive page.

- `<$BlogArchiveName$>`. This tag outputs the name of your archive page, as determined by your **Archive Index Date Format** setting under Formatting Settings.

A typical implementation of archives will look like the following in your template:

```
<BloggerArchives>
<a href="<$BlogArchiveURL$>"><$BlogArchiveName$></a>
</BloggerArchives>
```

For each archived time period, a link containing the URL will surrounded the text version of the time period date. In other words, although this code is only three lines long, it might represent numerous archive links.

The final set of Blogger template tags are called *conditional* tags because they allow you to display elements based on certain conditions being met. The four sets of conditional tag pairs are

- `<MainPage></MainPage>`. Place this tag pair around elements you want to appear only on your blog's main page.

- `<ArchivePage></ArchivePage>`. Place this tag pair around elements you want to appear only on archive pages.

- `<ItemPage></ItemPage>`. Place this tag pair around elements you want to appear only on individual post pages.

- `<MainOrArchivePage></MainOrArchivePage>`. Place this tag pair around ele-ments you want to appear only on your blog's main page and on archive pages.

The prime example of using conditional tags is for elements in your template's sidebar. Perhaps you have a blogroll in your sidebar, but you want it to show only on the main page and not on archive pages or post pages. In that case, you would surround the code for your blogroll like this:

```
<MainPage>
[code for blogroll]
</MainPage>
```

You will often see subsets of sidebar information on archive and post pages, with more elements retained for archive pages than individual post pages, simply because archive pages are longer and users might spend just as much time browsing through your archives as they do your main page. Individual post pages are usually quick hits, with the user returning to your main page to continue reading and perusing your site.

---

33   Implementing a Third-Party Template in Blogger

→ SEE ALSO

31 Defining and Implementing Custom Styles

32 Understanding the Blogger Template Language

33

Although Blogger provides more than thirty templates for you to choose from, and you can modify these templates to your heart's delight, you might simply want to employ the services of a design professional to create a completely custom template. Before selecting a designer, you must be absolutely certain they are familiar with the Blogger template language and have experience creating templates specifically for Blogger-based blogs. There are numerous blogging platforms, and a designer with skills and a portfolio filled with templates for Moveable Type–based blogs isn't going to do you and your Blogger-based blogs any good!

A simple Google search for *Blogger template designers* will net you thousands of results, so here are two professional design studios that have produced Blogger-based templates and happy clients:

- **Moxie Design Studios**, found at http://www.moxiedesignstudios.com/

- **E.Webscapes**, found at http://www.elegantwebscapes.com/

You need not pay for professional-grade Blogger templates; some are also freely available through what is called *linkware*. You might be familiar with the term *freeware*, in which you are free to use software without paying for a license. When utilizing linkware templates, the "payment" is typically a link to the original template designer—advertising their services, if you will.

Some examples of sites containing linkware Blogger templates include

- **Blogger Templates**, found at http://blogger-templates.blogspot.com/

- **Blogstyles**, found at http://www.blogstyles.com/

Your custom template, either one created professionally for you or one that you obtain from a linkware repository, will typically include a template file and a set of images. If you are hosting your blog on the blogspot.com domain, you have to host your images elsewhere and modify your template accordingly. If you are hosting your blog in your own web space, you must upload these images to your server and also modify your template to refer to the correct image locations.

Before implementing a custom template, be sure to back up your old template and also use the preview function in the Blogger template editor before republishing your entire blog.

33

PART III

Extending Your Blog

IN THIS PART:

6

Commenting and Trackback

IN THIS CHAPTER:

One way to increase readership and build a community around your blog is to allow users to leave comments on your posts. Comments provide an outlet for users to weigh in on posts you've written, to offer alternative perspectives on situations, or to tell anecdotes that might offer guidance in some situations. If you have a very popular or controversial blog, you might attract a swarm of negative and nasty comments—hence the topics in this chapter on comment moderation.

When comments are enabled, readers are more likely to return to your blog than if you simply publish a post and appear not to welcome additional discourse. This is especially true if you play an active role in responding to comments and continuing the conversation. Comments also allow you to discover new blogs because users typically include their blog URL as part of the signature in their comment; other people reading the comments also discover these new blogs, and the community grows. In addition, trackback pings can continue a thread; when a user writes a post that references another blog entry, he can send a ping back to the original entry, indicating the thread has been continued on his own blog. Readers interested in the topic discussed on the first blog might see the trackback ping and follow it to the second blog and onward.

34

Blogger includes comments-related functionality by default, but also allows you to turn off those functions if you so desire—such as if you do not want readers to comment on your posts or if you want to implement a third-party commenting mechanism. If you enable Blogger comments, you also have the option of turning off comments on a post-by-post basis. The Blogger commenting system does not currently offer trackback functionality. If you use a third-party commenting mechanism, you will get trackback functionality as well as additional management tools, but you will not be able to disable comments on a per-post basis.

The topics in this chapter will familiarize you with how to use the Blogger commenting systems as well as a popular third-party commenting system: Haloscan. You will learn how to modify your Blogger template to display the comment-related elements, and also how to use the various management tools offered by each system, so that your blog remains a pleasant place to visit and isn't bogged down by comment spam or nasty commenting trolls.

▶ **NOTE**

All topics in this chapter assume that you are familiar with navigating around the Blogger management interface and modifying your Blogger template.

---

34 **Using Blogger's Commenting System**

→ **SEE ALSO**

9 Configuring Blogger's Comments Settings
37 Moderating Comments with Blogger

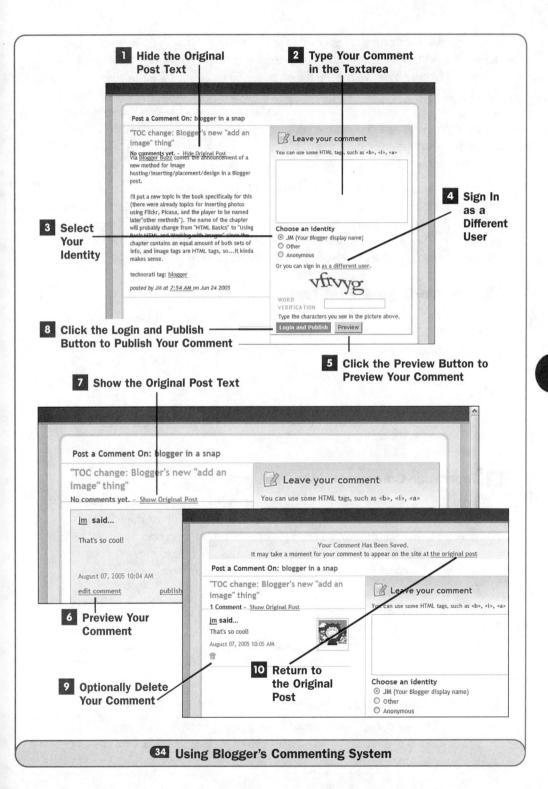

1 Hide the Original Post Text

2 Type Your Comment in the Textarea

3 Select Your Identity

4 Sign In as a Different User

8 Click the Login and Publish Button to Publish Your Comment

5 Click the Preview Button to Preview Your Comment

34

7 Show the Original Post Text

6 Preview Your Comment

9 Optionally Delete Your Comment

10 Return to the Original Post

Although **⑨ Configuring Blogger's Comments Settings** shows you how to enable the standard Blogger commenting feature within your blog, this topic shows how to use this feature to leave comments on other blogs and respond to comments on your own blog. In the following example, the comment-related settings include showing Blogger comments, allowing anyone to comment, not showing the comments in a pop-up window, and enabling profile images. If comments are shown in a pop-up window, the majority of the functionality is the same—it's just in a small pop-up window instead of a full browser window.

To leave a comment on a blog with Blogger-based comments enabled, click the **Comments** link presented for a particular post. The appearance and placement of this link can be different for every user because those options are fully modifiable through the use of Blogger template tags and style sheet entries. However, the comments link typically appears in the footer area of each post.

① Hide the Original Post Text

By default, the Blogger comments page displays the text of the original post in the left column, above any comments that have been posted. Click the **Hide Original Post** link to remove this text from view.

34

▶ **NOTE**

When comments are displayed in a pop-up window, the functionality does not include links to show or hide the original post text because the full post is in the parent browser window below the pop-up.

② Type Your Comment in the Textarea

Type the text of your comment in the textarea in the right column of the page. You can use HTML markup in your comment, such as the `<b></b>` tag pair for bold text, the `<i></i>` tag pair for italicized text, and the `<a></a>` tag pair to create hyperlinks. If you use HTML tags, be sure to preview your comment as shown in steps 5 and 6 so that you catch and correct any issues with the HTML you use.

▶ **NOTE**

When comments are displayed in a pop-up window, the textarea for leaving a comment is displayed at the bottom of the window below the comments that are already stored.

③ Select Your Identity

If your Blogger cookie is still intact from logging in to the Blogger management interface, the Blogger commenting system will preselect your display name as the identity associated with your comment. You can deselect this default action and leave a comment either anonymously or as an Other user. If you select the **Other** radio button, two additional fields will appear in the form: **Name** and **Your Web Page**.

▶ **NOTE**

When the Comments settings for a blog are configured so that only registered Blogger users or members of the blog may comment, the **Anonymous** and **Other** radio buttons will not be displayed. All users who want to leave comments will be required to log in to Blogger if they have not already.

4 Sign In as a Different User

You can sign in with a different user account than the one Blogger has currently associated with you via your login cookie. Following the link will lead you to the Blogger login form; after you've logged in, you are returned to the commenting interface with your new identity intact.

▶ **NOTE**

If the blog administrator has configured the blog to require word verification for all comments, you will see a graphical representation of a jumble of characters, followed by a text field. When you are ready to submit your comment, enter the characters you see in the graphic in the Word Verification field. Click the **Login and Publish** or the **Preview** button, as applicable. If you fail the word verification test, your comment will be saved in the textarea and you will be given another chance to pass the test, with a different image.

▶ **NOTE**

To learn how and why to enable word verification in your own blog, see **9** Configuring Blogger's Comments Settings.

5 Click the Preview Button to Preview Your Comment

After typing your comment in the textarea and using any HTML tags you choose, click the **Preview** button to display your comment as it would appear in the comment list.

6 Preview Your Comment

Your previewed comment will appear on a colored background to set it apart from the comments that are already stored for the particular post. Other than this colored background, the only difference between the previewed comment and the stored version of the comment is the appearance of two links at the bottom of the comment.

If you are pleased with the appearance of your comment, click the **Publish This Comment** link. This action publishes your comment and reloads the page. If you would like to make changes to your comment, click the **Edit Comment** link. The preview will disappear and you can edit the existing text in the textarea.

7 Show the Original Post Text

If you clicked the **Hide Original Post** link, click the **Show Original Post** link to display the text of the original post in the left column, above any comments that have been left.

8 Click the Login and Publish Button to Publish Your Comment

The act of clicking the **Login and Publish** button publishes the comment and reloads the page. Do not be confused by the *login* portion of the button: You're not actually logging in to anything—especially if you are already logged in to Blogger and are posting under your default identity.

9 Optionally Delete Your Comment

A trashcan icon will appear next to any comment you leave on any Blogger blog, as well as next to any comment left by any user on a blog you administer. Clicking this icon removes the comment from the system, which you can learn more about in **37 Moderating Comments with Blogger**.

10 Return to the Original Post

After publishing your comment, follow this link to return to the original post. If you invoked the commenting mechanism from the main page or an archive page, following this link does not return you to that page. Instead, the link returns you to the individual post page.

▶ NOTE

When comments are displayed in a pop-up window, you will see a link to close the window. By default, the link returns you to the original post below it.

---

35 Implementing Blogger's Show/Hide Comments

→ **SEE ALSO**

29 Understanding the Blogger Template Structure and Editor
30 Identifying Elements in the Blogger Template Source

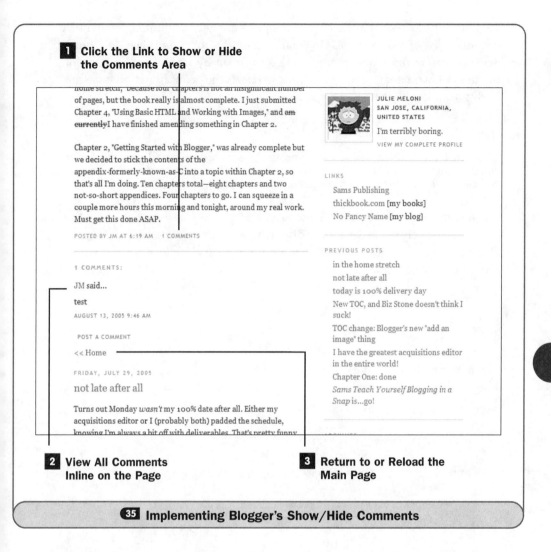

1 Click the Link to Show or Hide the Comments Area

home stretch," because four chapters is not an insignificant number of pages, but the book really is almost complete. I just submitted Chapter 4, "Using Basic HTML and Working with Images," and ~~am currently~~ I have finished amending something in Chapter 2.

Chapter 2, "Getting Started with Blogger," was already complete but we decided to stick the contents of the appendix-formerly-known-as-C into a topic within Chapter 2, so that's all I'm doing. Ten chapters total—eight chapters and two not-so-short appendices. Four chapters to go. I can squeeze in a couple more hours this morning and tonight, around my real work. Must get this done ASAP.

POSTED BY JM AT 6:19 AM   1 COMMENTS

1 COMMENTS:

JM said...

test

AUGUST 13, 2005 9:46 AM

POST A COMMENT

<< Home

FRIDAY, JULY 29, 2005

not late after all

Turns out Monday *wasn't* my 100% date after all. Either my acquisitions editor or I (probably both) padded the schedule, knowing I'm always a bit off with deliverables. That's pretty funny

JULIE MELONI
SAN JOSE, CALIFORNIA,
UNITED STATES
I'm terribly boring.
VIEW MY COMPLETE PROFILE

LINKS

Sams Publishing
thickbook.com [my books]
No Fancy Name [my blog]

PREVIOUS POSTS

in the home stretch
not late after all
today is 100% delivery day
New TOC, and Biz Stone doesn't think I suck!
TOC change: Blogger's new "add an image" thing
I have the greatest acquisitions editor in the entire world!
Chapter One: done
Sams Teach Yourself Blogging in a Snap is...go!

2 View All Comments Inline on the Page

3 Return to or Reload the Main Page

35 Implementing Blogger's Show/Hide Comments

The default method for displaying Blogger comments places the stored comments on the individual post page—even if your Comments settings are set to show comments in a pop-up window. When you click the comments link in the footer area of a post, you will either see a pop-up window containing the existing comments or you will be taken to a separate page for entering comments like the one shown in **34** **Using Blogger's Commenting System**. So, if you want to see just the comments attached to a post and not the entire commenting interface, you must click the post's permalink and view the individual post page—unless you implement a hack provided by Blogger to dynamically show or hide comments inline on the page.

Modifications to several areas of your template are necessary to implement what are called *peek-a-boo comments*. To begin, log in to Blogger and click the **Change Settings** icon in the **Blogs** section of the Blogger Dashboard. Click the **Template** tab to display navigational items; **Edit Current** is the default landing page and, in this instance, is where you should be.

▶ **TIP**

Before making modifications to your template, be sure to save a backup copy of your current template. If something goes awry while making changes to the template, you can quickly replace the messed-up version with the backup version.

The first modification sets up two additional CSS classes: `commenthidden` and `commentshown`. These classes set the display style—either `none` or `inline`—for the element containing the comment text. Within the `<style></style>` tag pair, place these two lines:

```
.commenthidden {display:none}


.commentshown {display:inline}
```

35

The next modification calls for the addition of a JavaScript function. Type the following code after the opening `<head>` tag, anywhere before the closing `</head>` tag:

```
<script type="text/javascript">

function togglecomments (postid) {

   var whichpost = document.getElementById(postid);

   if (whichpost.className=="commentshown") {
      whichpost.className="commenthidden";
   }
   else {
      whichpost.className="commentshown";
   }
}
</script>
```

This script is used to trigger the change in display for the element that holds the stored comments. When invoked, the script will change the element's display style to Inline if it is currently None, and to None if it is currently Inline. The next step in the implementation process requires some changes within the template code itself, which is found between the `<Blogger></Blogger>` tag pair.

Scroll through your template code and look for the `<BlogItemCommentsEnabled>` opening tag. It will be followed by additional comments-related template tags before the closing `</BlogItemCommentsEnabled>` tag is used. This chunk of code should be surrounded by the `<MainOrArchivePage></MainOrArchivePage>` conditional tag pair. Remove both the opening and closing `MainOrArchivePage` links around this chunk of code. Doing so ensures that the element containing the comments can be visible on all pages, not just the individual post pages.

Next, look for the `<BlogItemCommentsEnabled>` opening tag. In it you will see the HTML for a hyperlink, which is surrounded by the `<a></a>` tag pair, perhaps something like this:

```
<a href="<$BlogItemPermalinkURL$>#comments">
```

You must change the value of the `href` attribute for this link to:

```
javascript:togglecomments('c<$BlogItemNumber$>')
```

The link should end up looking something like this:

```
<a href="javascript:togglecomments('c<$BlogItemNumber$>')">
➥ <$BlogItemCommentCount$>comments</a>
```

Scroll a bit further in your template and you will see another set of `<BlogItemCommentsEnabled></BlogItemCommentsEnabled>` tags, this time surrounded by the `<ItemPage></ItemPage>` conditional tags. The final edit to your template is to replace the opening `<ItemPage>` tag with this line of code:

```
<span class="commenthidden" id="c<$BlogItemNumber$>">
```

Replace the closing `</ItemPage>` tag in this area with a closing span tag: `</span>`. Click the **Save Template Changes** button and republish your entire blog.

1 Click the Link to Show or Hide the Comments Area

From any page—the main page, an archive page, or an individual post page—clicking the **comments** link will automatically display the stored comments area for a given post. After it's displayed, click the **comments** link again to hide the stored comments from view.

2 View All Comments Inline on the Page

When visible, the comments will include author and time/date information in addition to the text of the comment. Also included at the end of the comment area is a link to post a comment. This link leads either to a pop-up window or a separate page containing the commenting interface, depending on the Comments settings for the blog.

3 Return to or Reload the Main Page

By default, the **Home** link returns you to the main page of the blog. Because this topic shows you how to dynamically display comments inline on any page of your blog, clicking this link might only reload the page and reset the comment visibility setting to None, if you are viewing the comments to a post on your main page.

---

36 Display Recent Comments Links on Your Blog

→ **SEE ALSO**

29 Understanding the Blogger Template Structure and Editor
30 Identifying Elements in the Blogger Template Source

When Blogger comments are enabled, you can display a list of the most recent comments made on your blog by pasting a bit of JavaScript code into your template. This code displays the most recent comment first in the list, and the display includes the comment author, a link to the comment, and a tooltip containing some of the comment text itself.

35

A single modification to your template is necessary to implement the "Farrago Recent Comments Hack," which was created by a Blogger user. To begin, log in to Blogger and click the **Change Settings** icon in the **Blogs** section of the Blogger Dashboard. Go to the **Comments** navigational item and modify the value of **Comments Timestamp Format** so that the mm/dd/yyyy hh:mm:ss format is selected (for example, 08/13/2005 4:28:05 PM). Click the **Save Settings** button, and then click the **Template** tab so that the Blogger template editor is visible.

▶ **TIP**

Before making modifications to your template, be sure to save a backup copy of your current template. If something goes awry while making changes to the template, you can quickly replace the messed-up version with the backup version.

The code for this particular functionality can be found at the BloggerHacks blog (http://bloggerhacks.blogspot.com/). Visit BloggerHacks and click the Farrago Recent Comments Hack link in the sidebar to obtain the code you must copy and paste into your template. Next, determine where in your template's sidebar you want the list of recent comments to appear. Wherever that placement might be, paste the code in its entirety, surrounded by <MainOrArchivePage> </MainOrArchivePage> conditional tags, like this:

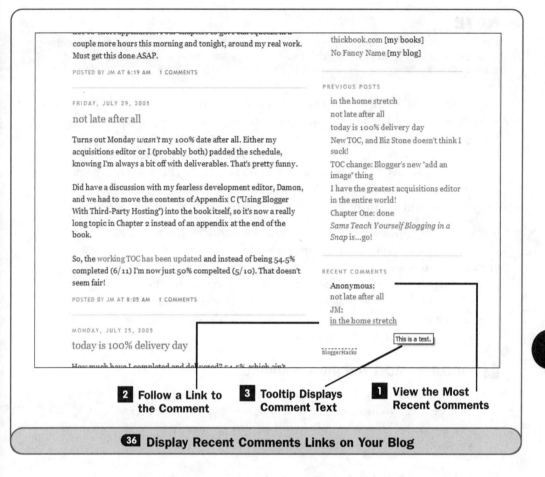

couple more hours this morning and tonight, around my real work. Must get this done ASAP.

POSTED BY JM AT 6:19 AM   1 COMMENTS

FRIDAY, JULY 29, 2005

not late after all

Turns out Monday *wasn't* my 100% date after all. Either my acquisitions editor or I (probably both) padded the schedule, knowing I'm always a bit off with deliverables. That's pretty funny.

Did have a discussion with my fearless development editor, Damon, and we had to move the contents of Appendix C ("Using Blogger With Third-Party Hosting") into the book itself, so it's now a really long topic in Chapter 2 instead of an appendix at the end of the book.

So, the working TOC has been updated and instead of being 54.5% completed (6/11) I'm now just 50% competed (5/10). That doesn't seem fair!

POSTED BY JM AT 8:05 AM   1 COMMENTS

MONDAY, JULY 25, 2005

today is 100% delivery day

thickbook.com [my books]
No Fancy Name [my blog]

PREVIOUS POSTS

in the home stretch
not late after all
today is 100% delivery day
New TOC, and Biz Stone doesn't think I suck!
TOC change: Blogger's new "add an image" thing
I have the greatest acquisitions editor in the entire world!
Chapter One: done
Sams Teach Yourself Blogging in a Snap is...go!

RECENT COMMENTS

Anonymous:
not late after all
JM:
in the home stretch

This is a test.

BloggerHacks

2 Follow a Link to the Comment

3 Tooltip Displays Comment Text

1 View the Most Recent Comments

36 Display Recent Comments Links on Your Blog

```
1:   <MainOrArchivePage>
2:   <!-- **** FARRAGO RECENT COMMENTS HACK **** -->
3:   <!-- Version 1.03 -->
4:   <!-- Copyright © 2004 Ebenezer Orthodoxy -->
5:   <!-- http://boggerhacks.blogspot.com -->
6:   <!-- ************** OPTIONS ************** -->
7:   <script type="text/javascript" language="JavaScript1.2">
8:   var titleText = "Recent Comments";
9:   var numberToShow = 5;
10:  var displayTemplate = "[name]:<br/>[title]";
11:  var nameIsLink = true;
12:  </script>
13:  <!-- ********* CODE DO NOT CHANGE ******** -->
14:  <script type="text/javascript" language="JavaScript1.2">
15:  [...]
16:  <!-- END FARRAGO RECENT COMMENTS HACK -->
17:  </MainOrArchivePage>
```

36

▶ **NOTE**

Line 15 represents the spot where a majority of the code has been snipped for presentation here, and it is code you shouldn't mess with anyway unless you are skilled in the ways of the JavaScript.

Lines 8 through 11 indicate variables that you may customize for use in your blog. By changing the value of the `titleText` variable in line 8 (for example, changing "Recent Comments" to "some other title"), you can give this area a different title. This text will be wrapped in an <h2></h2> tag pair, using the `sidebar-title` class. If you do not have a `sidebar-title` class, you can define one in your style sheet. Optionally, you can replace this value in the DO NOT CHANGE portion of the JavaScript code, being very careful when you do so.

You can change the value of the `numberToShow` variable in line 9 to any number between 1 and 10. The `displayTemplate` variable in line 10 controls the layout of the individual entries. For instance, if you want the comment author's name and title of the post to be on one line instead of two, remove the <br/> tag from the value. Line 11 controls whether the comment author's name is a link. After making your changes to your Blogger template, click the **Save Template Changes** button and republish your entire blog.

36

1 View the Most Recent Comments

Look in your sidebar for the section containing recent comments. Any comments left before the implementation of the recent comments feature will still be displayed; you don't have to wait for new comments to begin populating the Recent Comments area.

2 Follow a Link to the Comment

The links in the recent comments area are made up of the title of the blog post to which they are attached. Clicking the link takes you to the specific comment on the individual post page.

3 Tooltip Displays Comment Text

If you hover your mouse over the title link, you will notice the first 40 or so characters of the author's comment are displayed in a tooltip.

---

37 Moderating Comments with Blogger

✔ **BEFORE YOU BEGIN**

34 Using Blogger's Commenting System

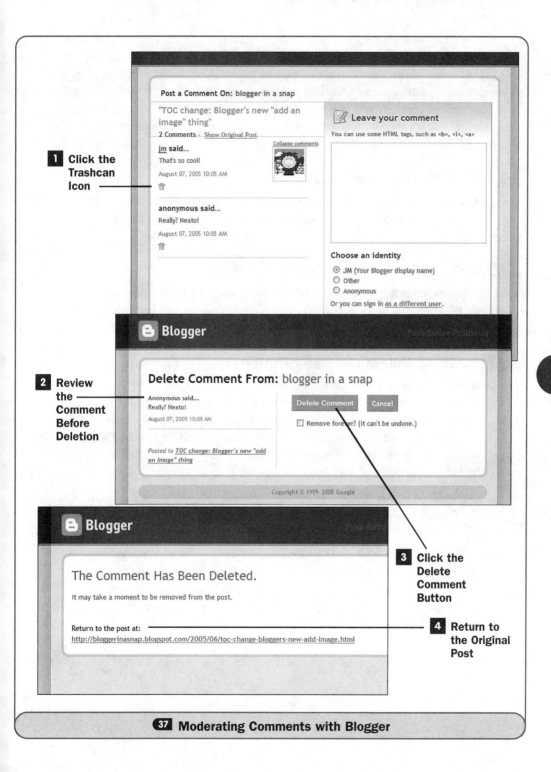

1 Click the Trashcan Icon

2 Review the Comment Before Deletion

3 Click the Delete Comment Button

4 Return to the Original Post

37

There might come a time when you want to remove a comment from your blog because it is offensive, profane, or just something you don't want to see on your blog—it's your blog, after all, and you make the rules. Unfortunately, the Blogger commenting system comes with neither a management interface for your comments nor the capability to ban specific users. Instead, when you come across a comment you want to remove from your site, you must go through a multistep process to do so.

1 Click the Trashcan Icon

Any comment left on your blog—by you or anyone else—should have a trashcan icon next to it. Clicking this icon begins the comment removal process.

2 Review the Comment Before Deletion

After you click the trashcan icon, Blogger displays the text of the comment on the deletion confirmation page. This step allows you to review the comment again before it is deleted from the system.

3 Click the Delete Comment Button

If you have decided to delete the comment, you can remove it forever by checking the **Remove Forever?** check box and clicking the **Delete Comment** button. If the **Remove Forever?** check box is not checked when you click the **Delete Comment** button, the text of the comment will be replaced with a `Comment Removed by Blog Administrator` message, but the author's name and the timestamp of the comment will remain.

If you want to exit the deletion process without removing the comment, click the **Cancel** button.

4 Return to the Original Post

After the comment has been deleted, you will see a confirmation of the action and a link to the original post. Clicking this link returns you to the original post, but you might have to force-reload the page to see that the comment has been removed.

37

38 Implementing the Haloscan Commenting and Trackback System

→ SEE ALSO

29 Understanding the Blogger Template Structure and Editor
39 Using the Haloscan Commenting System
40 Using the Haloscan Trackback System
41 Moderating Haloscan Comments and Trackback

The Haloscan commenting and trackback system is a popular alternative to the built-in Blogger commenting system. Haloscan provides a storage, display, and management method not only for comments, but also for trackbacks as well. In this topic, you'll learn how to implement the Haloscan commenting and trackback system in your blog instead of the Blogger commenting system.

But first, here is some basic information about the Haloscan service (http://www.haloscan.com/):

- **Paid versus free accounts**. There are two types of Haloscan accounts: Basic and Premium. The Basic account is free, but has some limitations. The Premium account is currently $12/year. You can begin with a Basic account and upgrade to a Premium account at any time; there will be no service interruption and you will not lose any comments or trackbacks because of the upgrade.

- **Comment lengths**. The individual comment length limit for Basic accounts is 3,000 characters per comment, whereas it's 10,000 characters per comment for Premium account holders.

- **Comment archive**. Comments older than four months are unavailable for Basic members, unless you upgrade to a Premium account and then they will be restored. Premium accountholders have access to all their comments at all times.

- **Comment link numbers on old posts**. The comment link numbers on your posts will be inaccurate *after* the 200 most recent comments for Basic members or 800 most recent comments for Premium members. The comments will still be readable to anyone who clicks the comments link; it's just that the count will be incorrect. For instance, if you visit a blog post that I wrote a year ago, the comment count will be zero. But if you click the link, you will see numerous comments in the Haloscan comment pop-up window.

38

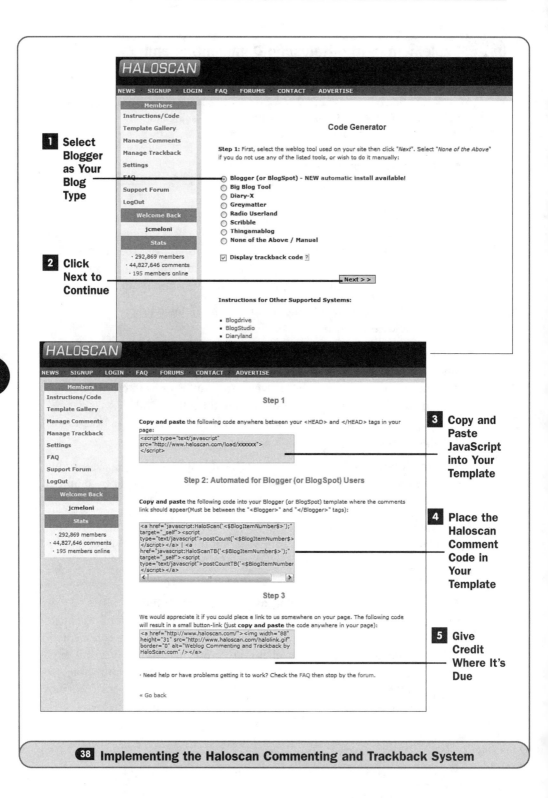

1 Select Blogger as Your Blog Type

2 Click Next to Continue

38

3 Copy and Paste JavaScript into Your Template

4 Place the Haloscan Comment Code in Your Template

5 Give Credit Where It's Due

38 Implementing the Haloscan Commenting and Trackback System

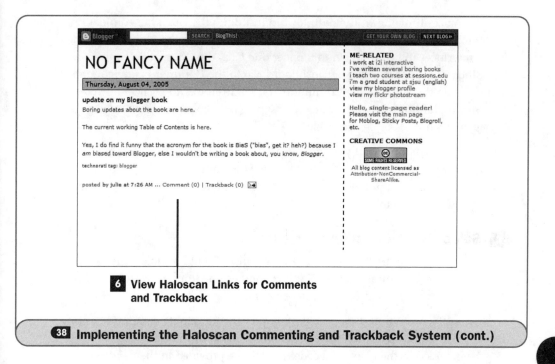

6 View Haloscan Links for Comments and Trackback

38 Implementing the Haloscan Commenting and Trackback System (cont.)

38

- **Settings.** Haloscan accountholders—both Basic and Premium—have numerous setting available in the Haloscan management interface. After logging in to Haloscan, click the **Settings** link in the left column to go to your Settings area, where you can configure all sorts of cool things such as custom text for the comments and trackback links, date formatting, time zone settings, and so forth. One very important item is the **Force Update of Comment Link** at the bottom of the **Settings** page. The Haloscan comments and trackback count will sometimes be incorrect on your blog; clicking this link forces the server to update your particular link so that after you go to your blog and refresh the page, the count is correct.

- **Comment archiving.** You can dump all your comments to a text file that you can save on your own machine. After logging in to Haloscan, click the **Manage Comments** link in the left side navigation, and then click the **Export** tab. Follow the links to dump 1,000 at a time. *Dump* does not mean *delete*; it just means *place in a text file for storage*.

- **Template gallery.** There are literally hundreds of premade Haloscan templates for the comments and trackback window if the default black-and-white template is not to your liking. After logging in to Haloscan, click the **Template Gallery** link in the left-side navigation, browse through templates until you find one that you like, and then click the **Save** link to change the template associated with your account.

Before you continue down the path toward installing the Haloscan commenting system, you must modify your Comments settings through the Blogger management interface. To begin, log in to Blogger and click the **Change Settings** icon in the **Blogs** section of the Blogger Dashboard. Go to the **Comments** navigational item and set the value of the **Comments** radio button to **Hide**. Click the **Save Settings** button to store your changes. Any previous Blogger comments you have received will no longer be accessible.

The next steps assume that you have registered with Haloscan by going to http://www.haloscan.com/ and following the **Signup** link in the top-level navigation. After registering or logging in, click the **Instructions/Code** link in the left-side navigation and follow these steps.

1 Select Blogger as Your Blog Type

Although there are links to an automatic install tool for Blogger users, please follow these manual steps so that you can become familiar with the modifications that will be made to your template.

Select the radio button next to the **Blogger (or BlogSpot)** item. Additionally, check the **Display Trackback Code** check box so that the trackback code will be included in the generated code that will be provided in the next step.

2 Click Next to Continue

After the appropriate radio button and check box have been checked, click the **Next** button to continue to the second step, which will provide code for you to paste into your Blogger template.

▶ **TIP**

Before making modifications to your template, be sure to save a backup copy of your current template. If something goes awry while making changes to the template, you can quickly replace the messed-up version with the backup version.

3 Copy and Paste JavaScript into Your Template

This first bit of JavaScript should be pasted into the HEAD element of your template. The xxxxxx in the example will be replaced by your Haloscan username during the code generation process. The placement of this code in the HEAD element of your template ensures that all commenting and trackback functionality is available throughout all pages of your blog.

4 Place the Haloscan Comment Code in Your Template

The Haloscan instructions tell you to place this code "where the comments should appear," which must be between the <Blogger></Blogger> tag pair.

38

That is a little vague because all Blogger templates are different and there is quite a bit of content between the `<Blogger></Blogger>` tag pair. Depending on your comfort level with the Blogger template language, you might decide to remove all code remotely related to Blogger comments (typically appearing between the `<BlogItemCommentsEnabled></BlogItemCommentsEnabled>` tag pair) or you might decide to have your enabled Haloscan code coexist with your disabled Blogger comments code.

You might find it easier to identify the post footer area in your Blogger template and paste the Haloscan code there, using the post footer as your point of reference rather than the vague "where the comments should appear" location. The post footer is often set apart in Blogger templates by an HTML comment such as `<!-- post footer here -->` or the use of an ID or class called `post-footer` or another similarly named item.

When you paste the Haloscan code into your template, you can click the **Preview** button and see the outcome. You can continue to modify your template and click the **Preview** button until you are satisfied that the code is in the correct place. No changes will be made to your blog until you save the template and republish your blog, so don't stress about it if you miss the mark the first time.

▶ **NOTE**

When using the Haloscan commenting system, you can choose to keep or remove any Blogger template code related to comments. If you keep the default template code as is with regard to comments, you will not see Blogger comment controls as long as the value of **Comments** is set to **Hide** in your Comments settings. If you keep the Blogger template code that refers to comments, and you do not change the **Comments** setting to **Hide**, you will have half Haloscan/half Blogger comments enabled, resulting in a big mess.

5 Give Credit Where It's Due

The final bit of code can be placed anywhere in your template; the sidebar is a good choice. This code simply places a Haloscan badge on your blog, indicating that your blog uses Haloscan comments.

When this final template modification is made, click the **Save Template Changes** button and then republish your entire blog.

6 View Haloscan Links for Comments and Trackback

Refresh your blog and then look for the links to the Haloscan comments and trackback pop-up windows in your post footer.

39 Using the Haloscan Commenting System

✔ BEFORE YOU BEGIN	→ SEE ALSO
38 Implementing the Haloscan Commenting and Trackback System	41 Moderating Haloscan Comments and Trackback

39

When the Haloscan commenting system is installed on your blog—or other blogs you read—the interface for leaving comments is much different from the default Blogger commenting system. The primary difference is that the acts of leaving a comment and reading already-saved comments occur in a single pop-up window. No matter whether you are reading a blog post on the main page, an archive page, or an individual post page, the comment link responds the same to being clicked: It launches a pop-up window.

The following steps describe the action of leaving a comment on a Haloscan-enabled blog—yours or anyone else's:

1 Click the Comment Link to Launch the Comment Window

Most users place the link to Haloscan comments in the footer area of a post. The default name of this link is **Comment (n)** where **n** is the number of comments already saved. Click this link to launch the comment window, through which you can read stored comments or leave a comment of your own.

▶ NOTE

For comment links on your own blog, you may customize the string used to make the link. Log in to Haloscan, and then click the **Settings** link in the left-side navigation. Scroll to the Comment Link Text section of the form; from there, you can change the strings used in the comment links.

2 Type Your Name

This field is optional, but if left blank it will display Anonymous when published. You can use any string—it doesn't have to be your name. You could use initials, an abbreviation, or whatever you want.

3 Enter Your Email Address

This field is optional and may be left blank. If completed, the value will be available to blog owners as part of their Haloscan comment administration area. Additionally, some Haloscan templates will display the value of this field as part of the comments, some do not, and some do so only if the person viewing them is the logged-in owner of the blog on which the comment has been left.

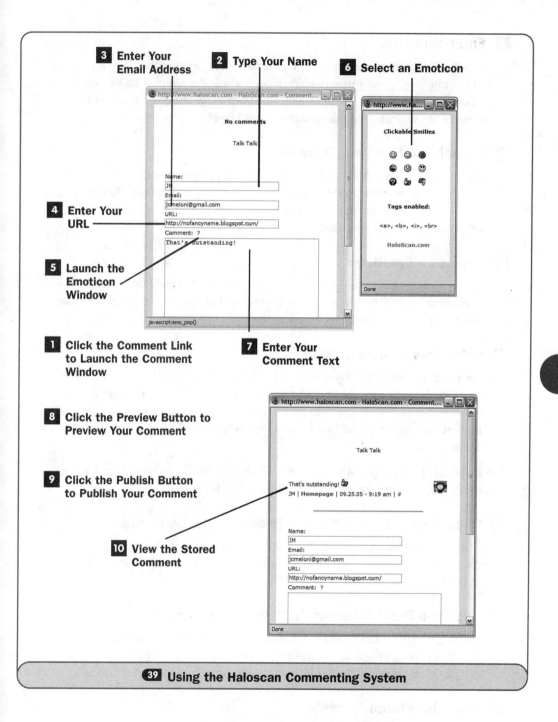

3 Enter Your Email Address

2 Type Your Name

6 Select an Emoticon

4 Enter Your URL

5 Launch the Emoticon Window

1 Click the Comment Link to Launch the Comment Window

7 Enter Your Comment Text

8 Click the Preview Button to Preview Your Comment

9 Click the Publish Button to Publish Your Comment

10 View the Stored Comment

4 Enter Your URL

This field is optional and may be left blank. But remember that leaving a URL is one way to gain new readers. Not only will the blog owner be able to follow your link and learn about you and your blog, but other comment authors or users who read the comments will be able to find you as well.

5 Launch the Emoticon Window

Haloscan converts some typed emoticons into graphical emoticons—the :) and :(emoticons are examples. Clicking the small question-mark icon launches the emoticon window in which you can view and select additional emoticons for use in your post.

6 Select an Emoticon

Click an emoticon in the emoticon window and the code will be placed in the **Comment** field of the comment window below it. Close the emoticon window when you have finished selecting emotions.

39

7 Enter Your Comment Text

Type your comment in this field. You may use HTML markup in your comment, such as the `<b></b>` tag pair for bold text, the `<i></i>` tag pair for italicized text, and the `<a></a>` tag pair to create hyperlinks. Simply click the **Return** button to produce line breaks; they will be properly converted by the system.

If you use HTML tags, be sure to preview your comment as shown in step 8 so that you catch and correct any issues with the HTML you used.

8 Click the Preview Button to Preview Your Comment

After typing your comment in the textarea and using any HTML tags you choose, click the **Preview** button to display your comment as it would appear in the Haloscan comment window.

9 Click the Publish Button to Publish Your Comment

The act of clicking the **Publish** button stores the comment in the Haloscan system and reloads the comment window. Your comment should appear in the correct chronological order, with the most recent post at the end of the list.

10 View the Stored Comment

The stored comment includes the text of the comment, the string entered in the Name fields, a premade link to the email address using the word Email as the link string (if present in the template), a premade link to the user's URL using the word Homepage as the link string, and the date and time that the comment was saved.

▶ **NOTE**

If you are a Haloscan user who is logged in to Haloscan (that is, you have a valid login cookie) when viewing your own blog, you will see additional elements in each comment entry. For instance, logged-in users with basic Haloscan accounts will see a link to edit the comment, which will take them to the Haloscan comment management form. Logged-in users with premium accounts will see the edit link as well as icons to delete one or more comments.

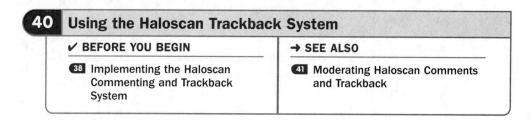

40 | **Using the Haloscan Trackback System**

✔ **BEFORE YOU BEGIN**

38 Implementing the Haloscan Commenting and Trackback System

→ **SEE ALSO**

41 Moderating Haloscan Comments and Trackback

The Haloscan commenting and trackback system fills a need unmet by the default Blogger commenting system: trackbacks. The concept of trackbacks is often confusing to new bloggers, but in fact it's a very simple process that enhances the linking mechanism between blog posts on a particular topic.

Although you'll often see (or write) blog posts that include text such as Continuing a topic found [here], where [here] is a link to someone else's blog, a trackback ping makes your post known to readers of the original post—who might not know anything about you or your blog. Readers interested in the topic discussed in the first blog post will see the trackback ping sent by you, referring to your blog post, and will perhaps follow this link to your blog where the conversation can continue and your readership will increase.

If you have a Haloscan account, you can send a trackback ping to any blog that has trackback functionality—regardless of the blogging platform or trackback type. That is, you can use Haloscan to send a trackback ping to another Haloscan-enabled blog, a Moveable Type–enabled blog, a WordPress blog, and so on. As long as a blog produces a URL that can be pinged, you can send a ping. Similarly, your Haloscan-enabled blog can accept pings from any other blogging platform. The following steps show you the process of sending and viewing trackback pings:

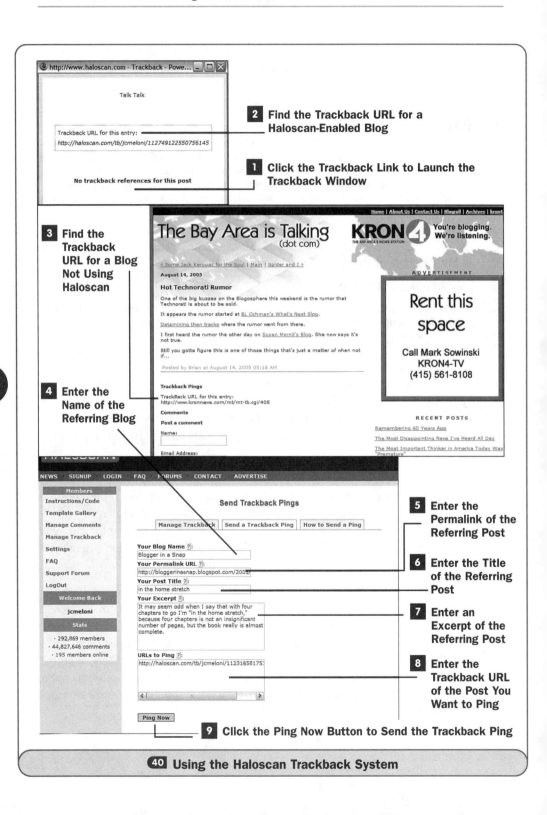

2 **Find the Trackback URL for a Haloscan-Enabled Blog**

1 **Click the Trackback Link to Launch the Trackback Window**

3 **Find the Trackback URL for a Blog Not Using Haloscan**

4 **Enter the Name of the Referring Blog**

5 **Enter the Permalink of the Referring Post**

6 **Enter the Title of the Referring Post**

7 **Enter an Excerpt of the Referring Post**

8 **Enter the Trackback URL of the Post You Want to Ping**

9 **Click the Ping Now Button to Send the Trackback Ping**

40 **Using the Haloscan Trackback System**

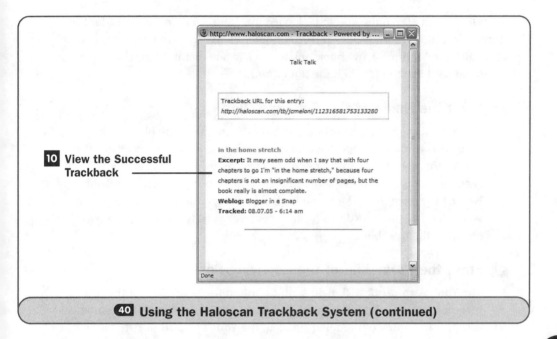

10 View the Successful Trackback

40 Using the Haloscan Trackback System (continued)

40

1 Click the Trackback Link to Launch the Trackback Window

On a Haloscan-enabled blog—your own or anyone else's—click the trackback link to launch the trackback pop-up window. In addition to listing any trackback pings that have been received for this particular post, the window also displays the trackback URL.

▶ NOTE

For trackback links on your own blog, you can customize the string used to make the link. Log in to Haloscan, and then click the **Settings** link in the left-side navigation. Scroll to the Trackback Link Text section of the form; from there, you can change the strings used in the trackback links.

2 Find the Trackback URL for a Haloscan-Enabled Blog

The trackback URL appears at the top of the trackback pop-up window. Copy and paste this URL if you want to send a trackback ping to this post.

3 Find the Trackback URL for a Blog Not Using Haloscan

Other blogging platforms publish trackback URLs, as shown in this example. The placement will differ from platform to platform and blog to blog, but the URL will be clearly marked in some way to indicate that this is the URL to use for trackback pings to this post.

Steps 4 through 10 require you to be logged into your Haloscan account for the purpose of sending a trackback ping to another blog. Log in to Haloscan, and then click the **Manage Trackback** link in the left-side menu. Next, click the **Send a Trackback Ping** tab to reach the ping form.

4 Enter the Name of the Referring Blog

The **Your Blog Name** field should contain the name of the blog sending the ping. This value will appear in the trackback ping list of the recipient blog post as the website from which the ping was received. In this example, I am sending a ping from the Blogger in a Snap blog to my personal No Fancy Name blog. Therefore, the name *Blogger in a Snap* will appear as the referrer when viewing the trackbacks for the specific post at No Fancy Name, which is receiving the trackback.

5 Enter the Permalink of the Referring Post

The **Your Permalink URL** field should contain the permalink of the specific blog post sending the ping. In this example, just as the **Your Blog Name** field contains the name of the referring blog, the **Your Permalink URL** field should contain the permalink of the specific referring post on that blog.

6 Enter the Title of the Referring Post

The **Your Post Title** field should contain the title of the specific blog post sending the ping. That is, the title of the post listed in the **Your Permalink URL** field.

7 Enter an Excerpt of the Referring Post

The **Your Excerpt** field should contain an excerpt of the referring post. No HTML tags are allowed, and you are limited to 255 characters. You can use the first 255 characters of the referring post, or you can create a new summary to use specifically for the trackback.

8 Enter the Trackback URL of the Post You Want to Ping

In the **URLs to Ping** field, enter the value copied from a Haloscan-enabled or non-Haloscan blog, as described earlier in steps 2 and 3. You can enter as many URLs to ping as you like; each URL should be on a separate line.

9 Click the Ping Now Button to Send the Trackback Ping

Click the **Ping Now** button to send the trackback ping to the URL or URLs specified in the **URLs to Ping** field. You will see a confirmation of the ping (or pings) displayed at the top of the page.

▶ **NOTE**

The Haloscan successful ping notification string appears in italicized text, not bold, or red, or something very visible. Therefore, you might miss it and think the ping as not been sent. Do not click the **Ping Now** button multiple times unless you are very sure that the ping has not been sent because you cannot manage the pings you have sent to other blogs. Only the maintainer of the recipient blog can remove duplicate trackback pings.

10 View the Successful Trackback

On a Haloscan-enabled blog, click the `trackback` link to launch the track-back window and view pings for a particular post. On non-Haloscan blogs, you will often see a `Trackbacks` or `Referring Posts` link that will take you to the same type of information that is in a Haloscan pop-up. The trackback entries typically display the title of the referring blog post, linked to the indi-vidual post page, followed by your post summary or excerpt, the name of the blog, and the timestamp of the trackback ping.

---

41 Moderating Haloscan Comments and Trackback

41

✔ **BEFORE YOU BEGIN**

38 Implementing the Haloscan Commenting and Trackback System

The Haloscan commenting and trackback system provides you with many tools for managing your comments and trackback, including the ability to edit, delete, and ban specific comments and trackback pings. In **39 Using the Haloscan Commenting System**, you saw several tools available to the blog owner when viewing a post's comments in the Haloscan pop-up window. These tools are also available to you in the Haloscan administrative interface for comments and trackbacks, which you'll see in the following steps.

Steps 1 through 4 require you to be logged in to your Haloscan account, looking at the comment management interface. Log in to Haloscan, and then click the **Manage Comments** link in the left-side menu. You will see a list of the comments left on all posts on your blog.

1 Click to Edit a Comment

Click this icon to go to a form in which you can edit all aspects of the user's comment—name, email, URL, and the comment text itself.

2 Click to Delete a Comment

Click this icon to permanently remove a comment from the system.

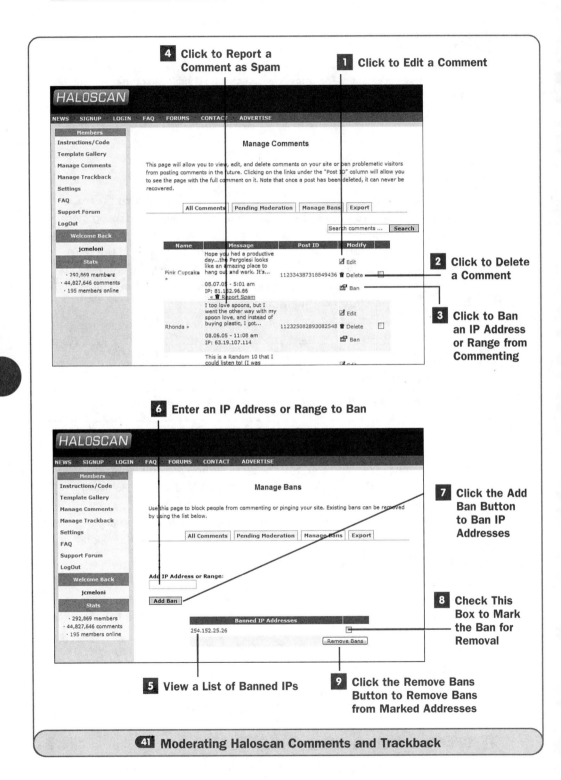

4 Click to Report a Comment as Spam

1 Click to Edit a Comment

2 Click to Delete a Comment

3 Click to Ban an IP Address or Range from Commenting

6 Enter an IP Address or Range to Ban

7 Click the Add Ban Button to Ban IP Addresses

8 Check This Box to Mark the Ban for Removal

5 View a List of Banned IPs

9 Click the Remove Bans Button to Remove Bans from Marked Addresses

41 Moderating Haloscan Comments and Trackback

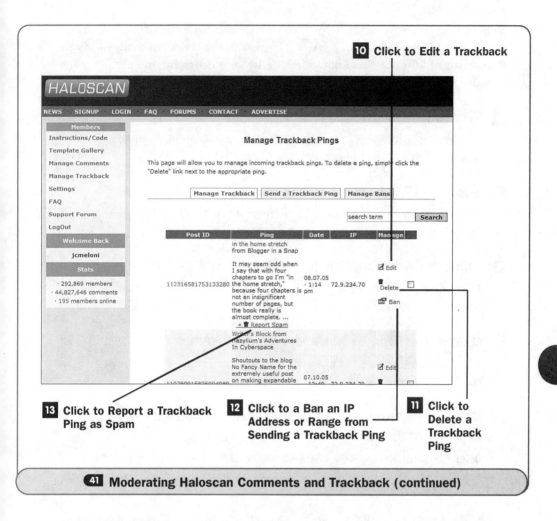

10 Click to Edit a Trackback

Manage Trackback Pings

This page will allow you to manage incoming trackback pings. To delete a ping, simply click the "Delete" link next to the appropriate ping.

13 Click to Report a Trackback Ping as Spam

12 Click to a Ban an IP Address or Range from Sending a Trackback Ping

11 Click to Delete a Trackback Ping

41 Moderating Haloscan Comments and Trackback (continued)

3 Click to Ban an IP Address or Range from Commenting

Click this icon to add the IP address of this comment author from commenting again on your site. When the icon is clicked, Haloscan asks you to confirm the ban for the single IP and offers the option to ban an extended range of IP addresses, which includes this particular IP.

4 Click to Report a Comment as Spam

If you roll over the text of the comment as well as the listing of the IP address itself, a link will appear to **Report as Spam**. This link also includes a trashcan icon because the process of reporting the comment as spam also permanently removes it from the system.

Steps 5 through 9 require you to be logged in to your Haloscan account, looking at the interface for managing bans. Log in to Haloscan, click either the **Manage Comments** or **Manage Trackbacks** link in the left-side menu, and then click the **Manage Bans** tab.

5 View a List of Banned IPs

If you have banned any IPs through the Manage Comments or Manage Trackbacks interface, the list will appear here.

6 Enter an IP Address or Range to Ban

Type the IP address or range of IP addresses in this text field to manually ban them from commenting or sending trackback pings.

7 Click the Add Ban Button to Ban IP Addresses

After entering an IP or range of IP addresses in the text field, click the **Add Ban** button to add these IPs to list of banned addresses.

8 Check This Box to Mark the Ban for Removal

Check the check box next to any IP addresses or range of IP addresses if you would like to remove them from the list of banned addresses.

9 Click the Remove Bans Button to Remove Bans from Marked Addresses

After checking one or more check boxes, click the **Remove Bans** button to remove the selected IP address or IP address ranges from the list of banned addresses.

Steps 10 through 13 require you to be logged in to your Haloscan account, looking at the trackback management interface. Log in to Haloscan, and then click the **Manage Trackbacks** link in the left-side menu. You will see a list of the trackback pings received for all posts on your blog.

10 Click to Edit a Trackback

Click this icon to go to a form in which you can edit all aspects of the user's trackback ping—blog name, permalink URL, post title, and post summary.

11 Click to Delete a Trackback Ping

Click this icon to permanently remove a trackback from the system.

12 Click to Ban an IP Address or Range from Sending a Trackback Ping

Click this icon to add the IP address of the author of this trackback ping from pinging your site again in the future. When the icon is clicked, Haloscan asks you to confirm the ban for the single IP and offers the option to ban an extended range of IP addresses, which includes this particular IP.

13 Click to Report a Trackback Ping as Spam

If you roll over the text of the trackback summary as well as the listing of the IP address itself, a link will appear to **Report Spam**. This link also includes a trashcan icon because the process of reporting the trackback ping as spam also permanently removes it from the system.

Additional Blogging Tools

7

IN THIS CHAPTER:

This chapter consists of a several topics related to extending the basic content of your blog. For instance, after creating a list of other blogs you enjoy reading, you can share these on your blog so that others can learn about them. In turn, other readers' lists of links inevitably include a link to you and the cycle of readership continues to grow. Perhaps you want to show your affiliation with a particular blogging platform, blog tool, web browser, sports team, whatever—you'll learn where to find graphics and how to place links in your sidebar to show your support. Want to provide your readers with a list of items you're currently reading or listening to? You'll learn where to find tools to manage such lists. You'll even learn how to register for and implement affiliation and advertising programs, leveraging your content to perhaps bring in a little cash. Additionally, as if the concept of blogging with the typed word weren't enough, you'll read up on how to create a moblog (photos) and an audioblog (your voice).

42

42   Using Blogrolls

✔ **BEFORE YOU BEGIN**

29 Understanding the Blogger Template Structure and Editor
32 Understanding the Blogger Template Language

A *blogroll* is nothing more than a list of blogs (or other websites) you read frequently; it is typically listed in the sidebar of your blog. By listing links to those sites, you associate yourself with the content produced by other bloggers, thereby helping your readers formulate a better picture of who you are. For instance, my personal blogroll currently lists approximately 100 blogs I read on a regular basis. These blogs run the gamut from "life blogs" to "academic" blogs to "geeky" blogs and everything in between, showing that I have a wide range of interests.

One hundred links is a lot of links to maintain statically; that is, by placing the HTML code for these links directly into my Blogger template. Because I find new blogs to add to my blogroll on an almost daily basis, that would be a lot of template editing and republishing. This is where blogroll services enter into the mix. A blogroll service provides an interface for you to store the names and URLs of blogs or other websites you read, allows you to customize the appearance of these links in some way, and also provides you with a bit of JavaScript to include in your Blogger template that will result in your blogroll being published on your blog.

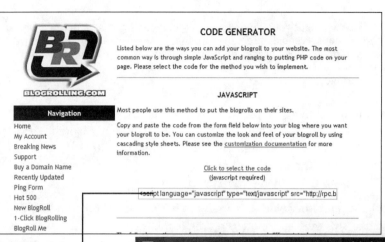

1 Obtain the JavaScript Code for Your Blogroll

2 Place the JavaScript Code in Your Blogger Template

My fingers have a mind of their own sometimes. When typing, they automatically type "g" anytime I type a word that begin "b-l-o". For instance, more than once I've typed "blog-level elements" instead of "block-level elements."

Ok, so that's not so bad. But when you're working with a database schema and you keep typing B-L-O-G instead of B-L-O-B, it gets really annoying.

[BLOB = Binary Large OBject. This is probably only funny to like one of you, if that.]

posted by julie at 10:30 AM ... Comments (4) | Trackback (0)

777 and taking a mental health moment
I'm so tired that when I saw this would be post number 777, I thought it was neat. I'm usually much harder to impress than that. Been working nonstop for awhile (by "awhile" I mean like five days of setting my alarm to get up and start working at 1 or 2am, to maximize the day). Have not sent my editor the three remaining chapters for my book, and that sucks. It's not like they're difficult to write, but real job trumps book writin' every time (and academics trump book writin' so it's a good thing my first class isn't until the 29th, by which point the book will be done done done).

BLOGROLL/LINKS
a room with a view
abdmom
academic splat!
adactio
anbruch
apostropher
apropos of something
arse poetica
asterisk
b2day
badgerbag
big brass blog
big monkey, helpy chalk
biz stone [!!]
blogger buzz
boing boing [!!]
brother kenya's paradigm [!!]
by the bayou [!!]
cheeky prof
css weblog
dan gillmor's blog
daryl sng
digital inspiration
digital web magazine
dooce
dr. laura's worst nightmare

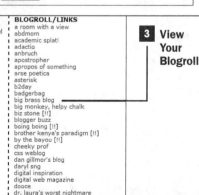

3 View Your Blogroll

▶ **NOTE**

Blogroll services typically output your blogroll in several different formats. Some of those formats require additional server-side programming that is not available to you as a Blogger user since you do not have access to the underlying server that creates the static pages making up your blog. Therefore, this topic focuses on the client-side inclusion of content in your blog.

The following example of maintaining a blogroll and implementing it on your blog uses the services of BlogRolling.com. However, there are other blogroll services that allow you to save a list of links and publish it to your site with various degrees of customization. The interfaces for these sites vary in their ease of use and the latency between the content request and display.

For example, blo.gs is another blogrolling service, backed by Yahoo! and found at http://www.blo.gs/. This free service offers a unique method for finding new blogs and adding them to your blogroll in addition to the standard client-side inclusion via JavaScript. However, the current methods of customization for blo.gs-based blogrolls are lacking for users without knowledge of XML formatting and the ability to produce their own server-side scripts.

42

▶ **TIP**

The Bloglines World Wide Web–based RSS reader, which you'll learn about in **50** **Using an RSS Aggregator**, also provides tools to export your list of feed subscriptions as a blogroll for inclusion in your Blogger template.

To get started with the BlogRolling.com service, go to http://www.blogrolling.com/ and register for a free account. After registering or logging in to the service, click the **Home** link in the navigation area. You will see your personal control panel, containing numerous items to assist you in maintaining your blogroll. Click the **Add Links** link in your control panel to begin adding links to your blogroll. You must know the title and URL of the website or blog that you want to add to your blogroll.

In addition to adding links, you can follow the **Preferences** link to customize certain aspects of your blogroll. For instance, one of my favorite aspects of the BlogRolling.com service is the ability to add an indicator next to the name of any blog that has been updated within a certain timeframe. As you can see in step 3, my personal blogroll has the [!!] characters appended to the end of the names of recently updated blogs. Other users append asterisks (*) or the word fresh!, and so on—the indicator you use is your choice, as is the "freshness" timeframe.

The next steps assume that you have registered with BlogRolling.com, added links to your blogroll, and are ready to include these links on your blog. Log in to BlogRolling.com if you are not already, click the **Home** link, and click the **Get Code** link in your control panel.

1 Obtain the JavaScript Code for Your Blogroll

The BlogRolling.com code generator provides you with several types of code snippets for obtaining your blogroll links. Blogger users should stick with the client-side method of inclusion, which is to use the JavaScript code. The additional methods for using your blogroll data require the ability to parse formats on the server side, which is not something Blogger users have access to. No fear, however: The JavaScript inclusion works wonderfully.

2 Place the JavaScript Code in Your Blogger Template

▶ **TIP**

Before making modifications to your template, be sure to save a backup copy of your current template. If something goes awry while making changes to the template, you can quickly replace the messed-up version with the backup version.

After obtaining your BlogRolling.com JavaScript code, log in to Blogger and click the **Change Settings** icon in the **Blogs** section of the Blogger Dashboard. Click the **Template** tab to access the Blogger template editor.

Determine where in your sidebar you would like your blogroll to appear, scroll through your template until you find a space for that placement, and paste the JavaScript code there. This placement should not be in the HEAD portion of your template; rather, it should be somewhere within the BODY element. In this example, I placed my blogroll after several other sections of links, including links to my Blogger archives. If you look at the top of the template editor textarea, you will see this code is within a `<MainPage>` `</MainPage>` conditional tag, meaning that my blogroll is displayed on only the main page of my blog. Using Blogger's conditional template tags, you can choose to display your blogroll on your main page, archive page, individual post pages, or some combination thereof. After making changes to your template, click the **Save Template Changes** button and republish your entire blog.

3 View Your Blogroll

After republishing your blog, view your blog to ensure that the blogroll is in its proper place. You might have to force-reload the page to obtain an uncached page before you can see the blogroll. Any blog updated within the timeframe specified in your BlogRolling.com preferences should have your chosen indicator appended to its name.

42

43   Implementing Affiliation Links, Personal Lists, or Ads

✔ BEFORE YOU BEGIN	→ SEE ALSO
29 Understanding the Blogger Template Structure and Editor	**28** Other Methods for Inserting Images into Posts

The technical requirements of implementing ads, affiliations, and other lists of favorite things are negligible compared to the processes necessary to get the code in the first place! Anyone with a website can submit an application to host ads, but you must wait for the approval process to be complete and then must customize the appearance of your ads before you even get to the point of including them in your template. Affiliation links are simpler to obtain, but in some instances you must track down graphics, or make your own, and host the images with a third-party service. Personal lists of books you're reading, movies you've watched, music you're listening to—these are, again, things that are simple to include in your template, but it takes time to compile and store the lists.

Each of the items discussed in the following topic eventually requires modifications to your Blogger template. When that time comes, log in to Blogger and click the **Change Settings** icon in the **Blogs** section of the Blogger Dashboard. Click the **Template** tab to access the Blogger template editor. Be sure to save a backup copy of your current template so that you can quickly revert to that version if something goes awry.

1   Implement Ads on Your Blog

If you look for *web advertising* in your favorite search engine or look through the directory listings at Yahoo! or Google, you'll find numerous listings for providers of click-through advertising. When thinking about placing advertisements on your site, remember you rarely have tight control over the actual content that is served; you typically can filter out advertisements from specific URLs if you know them in advance, but it might take some time and energy before you have configured your advertising settings to your liking.

The following are a few of the numerous providers of click-through advertisement placement on websites (which includes blogs). The example shown in the figure includes a Google AdSense implementation.

- **Google AdSense**, found at http://www.google.com/adsense/

- **Kanoodle**, found at http://www.kanoodle.com/

- **Pheedo**, found at http://www.pheedo.com/

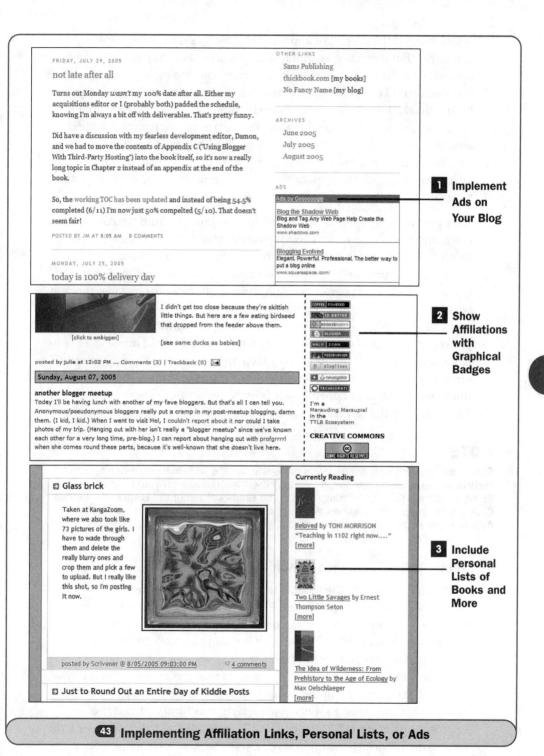

FRIDAY, JULY 29, 2005

not late after all

Turns out Monday *wasn't* my 100% date after all. Either my acquisitions editor or I (probably both) padded the schedule, knowing I'm always a bit off with deliverables. That's pretty funny.

Did have a discussion with my fearless development editor, Damon, and we had to move the contents of Appendix C ("Using Blogger With Third-Party Hosting") into the book itself, so it's now a really long topic in Chapter 2 instead of an appendix at the end of the book.

So, the working TOC has been updated and instead of being 54.5% completed (6/11) I'm now just 50% compelted (5/10). That doesn't seem fair!

POSTED BY JM AT 8:05 AM   0 COMMENTS

MONDAY, JULY 25, 2005

today is 100% delivery day

I didn't get too close because they're skittish little things. But here are a few eating birdseed that dropped from the feeder above them.

[click to embiggen]   [see same ducks as babies]

posted by julie at 12:02 PM ... Comments (3) | Trackback (0)

Sunday, August 07, 2005

another blogger meetup

Today I'll be having lunch with another of my fave bloggers. But that's all I can tell you. Anonymous/pseudonymous bloggers really put a cramp in *my* post-meetup blogging, damn them. (I kid, I kid.) When I went to visit Mel, I couldn't report about it nor could I take photos of my trip. (Hanging out with her isn't really a "blogger meetup" since we've known each other for a very long time, pre-blog.) I can report about hanging out with profgrrrl when she comes round these parts, because it's well-known that she doesn't live here.

Glass brick

Taken at KangaZoom, where we also took like 73 pictures of the girls. I have to wade through them and delete the really blurry ones and crop them and pick a few to upload. But I really like this shot, so I'm posting it now.

posted by Scrivener @ 8/05/2005 09:03:00 PM   4 comments

Just to Round Out an Entire Day of Kiddie Posts

OTHER LINKS

Sams Publishing
thickbook.com [my books]
No Fancy Name [my blog]

ARCHIVES

June 2005
July 2005
August 2005

ADS

Ads by Goooooogle

Blog the Shadow Web
Blog and Tag Any Web Page Help Create the Shadow Web
www.shadows.com

Blogging Evolved
Elegant. Powerful. Professional. The better way to put a blog online
www.squarespace.com/

COFFEE POWERED
IS BETTER
BROWSEHAPPY
BLOGGER
HALO SCAN
FEEDBURNER
bloglines
newsgator
TECHNORATI

I'm a Marauding Marsupial in the TTLB Ecosystem

CREATIVE COMMONS
SOME RIGHTS RESERVED

Currently Reading

Beloved by TONI MORRISON
"Teaching in 1102 right now...."
[more]

Two Little Savages by Ernest Thompson Seton
[more]

The Idea of Wilderness: From Prehistory to the Age of Ecology by Max Oelschlaeger
[more]

1 Implement Ads on Your Blog

2 Show Affiliations with Graphical Badges

43

3 Include Personal Lists of Books and More

Before starting the process of applying with various advertising services, remember that revenue generation is hard work: Click-through advertising depends on your blog readers to do the actual clicking-through, which means you had better keep your readers happy through a constant stream of publishing timely, informative, and otherwise thought-provoking posts that attract large audiences. Additionally, advertisements are typically context-sensitive; that is, the advertisements served tend to have something to do with the content you have written. If you write about blogging, you'll see advertisements about blog tools; if you write about religion, you'll see advertisements with religious themes, and so on.

After you are accepted into an advertising program, you are typically given a username and a password to access your ad provider's management system. Using such a management system, you should be able to customize the type of advertisement as well as the various colors and styles used in elements of the ad itself. Your ad provider's management interface also provides the snippet of JavaScript code that should be placed in your Blogger template wherever you want your ad to appear. In the example shown in the figure, I placed my snippet of Google AdSense code in the sidebar of my Blogger template after the code that displays my blog archives. You can place your ads anywhere you like, so play around with the placement until you find something that is visible but doesn't significantly detract from your content. Remember, it's the content that should drive the ads!

43

▶ NOTE

Google has made it easy for Bloggers to register for the AdSense program by placing a registration form within the Blogger management interface. After you're logged in to Blogger, click the **Change Settings** icon in the **Blogs** section of the Blogger Dashboard. Click the **Template** tab to access the Blogger template section, and then click the **AdSense** link in the subnavigation area.

2 Show Affiliations with Graphical Badges

A standard element in the Blogger template is the appearance of a Blogger graphic, indicating you indeed use Blogger to power your site. This is an example of *linkware*, in which you are taking advantage of a service in exchange for displaying an image that announces your affiliation with the service, and it costs you nothing more (that is, you are not paying cash for it). In the case of Blogger, you do not need to host this image—you are given the HTML code containing the image link to graphic on Blogger's servers. Such is often the case for service providers such as Blogger, the Halsocan commenting and trackback system, the Technorati blog indexing service, the FeedBurner RSS feed generation service, and the Amazon.com affiliation program—these companies provide you with snippets of HTML code that you just need to drop into your template, and they do the work of serving up the images.

But what if you want to announce your affiliation with services but you don't like the default graphic they provide? Or what if you want to publicize your love for coffee, tea, or the color green, using your own custom image? You can do so by creating and uploading images to any of the image hosting providers listed in **28** **Other Methods for Inserting Images into Posts**. Although you will place the links to your affiliation badges in your Blogger template rather than individual posts, the process is still the same—you need a place to store the images.

The images shown in the figure are some of my own affiliation badges, in *chiclet* format. Some are hosted on my own server whereas others, such as the FeedBurner, Bloglines, and NewsGator images, are served by the affiliated companies. A good resource for creating your own chiclets is Kalsey's Button Maker, found at http://www.kalsey.com/tools/buttonmaker/. You can define numerous elements of color as well as the text and other graphical images.

▶ KEY TERM

Chiclet—A small, rectangular graphic, typically 80 pixels wide by 15 pixels high, named for the Chiclet chewing gum.

43

After you have stored your images on an image-hosting server or have gathered the HTML code from companies serving images for you, place links to these items in your template, save it, and republish your entire blog.

3 Include Personal Lists of Books and More

Because you have complete control over any static text used in your Blogger template, you can simply type your own list of books you're reading, movies you've seen, music you're listening to, and so on. But wouldn't it be easier to have someone else maintain that list for you and, through the power of JavaScript, simply include the data? A site called All Consuming, located at http://43.allconsuming.net/, will do just that.

When you register (for free) with All Consuming, you can begin to create a list of things (books, movies, music, tasks) you want to consume or have consumed. In this case, *consume* can mean *read* or *watch* or *listen to* or *complete*. The All Consuming service provides you with a snippet of JavaScript that you can customize and include on your site. In the example shown, this blogger shares the books he is currently reading, along with an image of the book cover, a link to more information, and any personal notes he enters regarding the book.

44   Creating a Moblog

Moblog is an abbreviation of the phrase *mobile blogging* and represents a type of blogging that you can do with your cellular phone—provided you have the kind of cellular phone and service that can send an *MMS (multimedia messaging system)* message or email to the go@blogger.com email address. Think about it: How many times have you seen something in the wild, thought "I should blog this," and then realized all you have is your cellular phone and no other Internet access for the foreseeable future? No worries—enter the world of Blogger Mobile!

To get started with Blogger Mobile, you need not do anything with your current Blogger settings. The first few steps in the Blogger Mobile process create a new blog for you, which you can then merge with an existing blog or keep separate, whichever you prefer. To get started, send a blank MMS message or email to go@blogger.com from the mobile device that you plan to use for mobile blogging. Shortly thereafter you will receive a message from Blogger Mobile, containing a token you must use to register with the service. After you receive your claim token, go to http://go.blogger.com/ to continue the registration process.

44

1 Enter Your Claim Token

Enter the claim token you received from go@blogger.com in the **Claim Token** field.

2 Type the Captcha Seen Here

To verify you are a living, breathing human being and not an automated blog-creating bot, enter the value of the captcha in the **Verify Your Registration** field. The captcha you see will be different than the one shown here. Click the **Continue** button to go to the next page of the process, which requires you to identify yourself if your Blogger login cookie is not currently valid. After you identify yourself, either by logging in or clicking a link to confirm your identify, you will be presented with a list of blogs associated with your login.

3 Publish to a Separate Blog for Your Mobile Activity

When you send the initial message to go@blogger.com, a new blog is created just for you. You have the option of continuing to use this blog for all your mobile activity. If you want to do so, select the radio button next to the statement No Thanks, Keep Sending Them to [*new URL*] and click the **Continue** button. You will see a confirmation screen; click the **Finish** button to return to your Blogger dashboard.

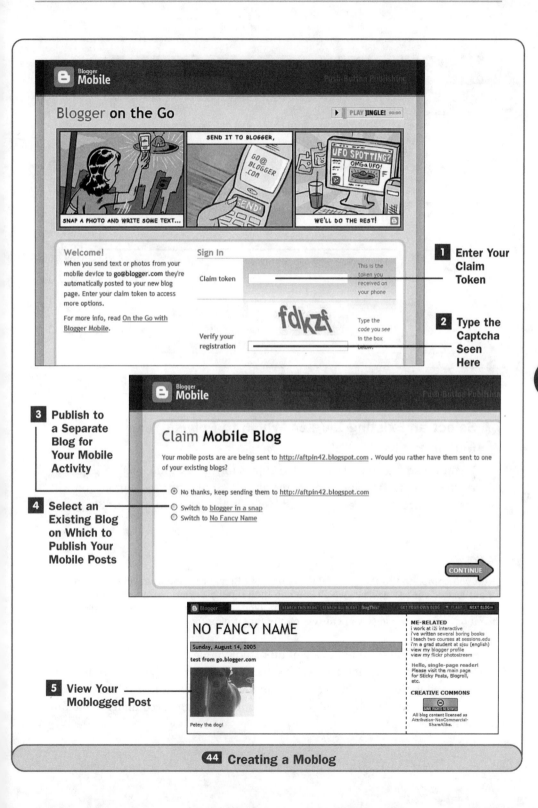

1 Enter Your Claim Token

2 Type the Captcha Seen Here

3 Publish to a Separate Blog for Your Mobile Activity

4 Select an Existing Blog on Which to Publish Your Mobile Posts

5 View Your Moblogged Post

44

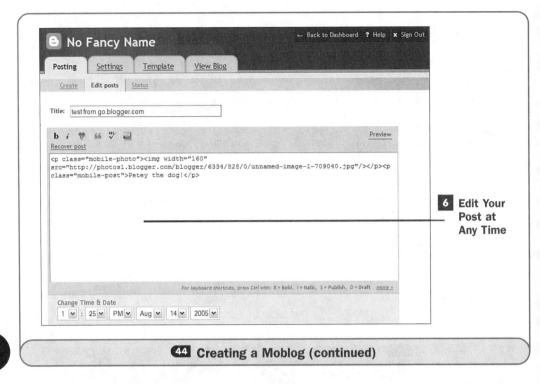

44   **44** Creating a Moblog (continued)

4 Select an Existing Blog on Which to Publish Your Mobile Posts

If you would like to post all moblog entries to your existing blog, select the radio button next to your blog name and click the **Continue** button. You will see a confirmation screen; click the **Finish** button to return to your Blogger dashboard.

▶ **NOTE**

After you complete the Blogger Mobile setup, your Blogger Dashboard will contain a list of associated mobile devices, which you can then modify or remove, if necessary. One modification available to you is to change the blog to which mobile posts are published; if you have multiple blogs, you can switch the target blog for mobile posts at any time.

Steps 5 and 6 require you to have sent an actual image and post from your mobile device. Send an email to go@blogger.com with an image attached to it for posting to your blog. The subject of your email becomes your post title and any text sent in the body of the email becomes your post text, placed under the image that you send.

5 View Your Moblogged Post

The HTML used to create a post from your email message is minimal and will not likely cause formatting issues with your blog. However, be sure to review your moblogged post after publishing it from your mobile device; you might decide to add additional text or other elements to it via the Blogger post editor.

6 Edit Your Post at Any Time

A moblogged post, after it's received by Blogger, becomes a post like any other. This means that you can edit it through the Blogger post editor and republish your post after making any changes. In the example shown here, you can see the use of two CSS styles: `mobile-image` and `mobile-post`. You can add your own style definitions to your style sheet, which would then be applied to all moblogged posts.

▶ NOTE

Mail-to-Blogger is another type of mobile blogging offered by Blogger, and should be used specifically for text-only posts. The Mail-to-Blogger functionality does not require additional registration for Blogger services; all you need to do is note the address stored in the Email settings for your blog. Any emails sent to that address, either from your mobile device or your actual email client, become posts.

---

45 Creating an Audioblog

✔ **BEFORE YOU BEGIN**

1 Creating Your Blogger Account
2 Naming Your Blog

Using the services of Audioblogger, you can post audio clips of your voice to your blog simply by placing a phone call. If you don't have access to a computer with Internet access or a cellular phone with text message capabilities, you can still blog by voice. Picture yourself traveling through the countryside, musing about the beautiful surroundings, perhaps thinking, "I should really blog this." With audioblogging, you can just pick up the phone and tell the world what you see. But before you begin to audioblog, you must register with the service. To do so, go to http://www.audioblogger.com/ and click the **Start Audioblogging Now** button.

▶ TIP

Check out Biz Stone's article "On The Road with Audioblogger" at http://help.blogger.com/bin/answer.py?answer=1050 for a great example of the usefulness of audioblogging.

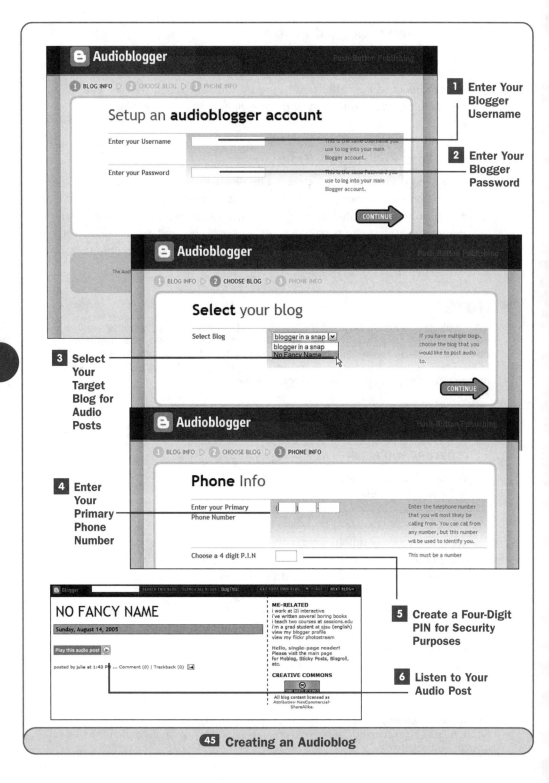

1 Enter Your Blogger Username

2 Enter Your Blogger Password

3 Select Your Target Blog for Audio Posts

4 Enter Your Primary Phone Number

5 Create a Four-Digit PIN for Security Purposes

6 Listen to Your Audio Post

45 Creating an Audioblog

1 Enter Your Blogger Username

Registering with Audioblogger requires you to have a Blogger account already created. Type your Blogger username in the **Enter Your Username** field.

2 Enter Your Blogger Password

Type your Blogger password in the **Enter Your Password** field. Click the **Continue** button to go to the next step in the process.

3 Select Your Target Blog for Audio Posts

All Blogger blogs associated with your username will be displayed in a drop-down menu. Select the blog to which you want to publish your audio posts from the **Select Blog** drop-down list and then click the **Continue** button to go to the next step in the process.

4 Enter Your Primary Phone Number

In the **Enter Your Primary Phone Number** field, enter the area code, prefix, and remaining four digits of the primary phone number that you will use to send your audio posts.

45

5 Create a Four-Digit PIN for Security Purposes

Create a four-digit personal identification number, enter it in the **Choose a 4-Digit P.I.N.** field, and click the **Finish Setup** button. You are now ready to begin audioblogging!

The final step in the audioblogging process is to actually record and publish an audio post. The call-in number is 415-856-0205, and this number is also displayed prominently on the Audioblogger home page at http://www.audioblogger.com/. Call that number from the phone you entered as the primary phone number, and follow the prompts to send the post. You will need your four-digit PIN to complete the process.

6 Listen to Your Audio Post

After you record and publish your audio post through the Audioblogger telephone interface, it is made available on your blog and looks like the figure shown here. By default, audio posts do not have titles, so you might want to edit your post to give it an actual title, as well as add any text below the graphical link to your audio file.

46 **Using the Blogger NavBar**

→ **SEE ALSO**

47 Using BlogThis! Add-Ons

The Blogger NavBar is a standard part of all Blogger templates. It contains quick links to the Blogger main page, a search form for the specific blog you're viewing as well as all blogs indexed by Google, the ability to flag content as objectionable, and a link to the Next Blog feature, which takes you to a randomly selected blog that might not be new to you. All blog readers can take advantage of the search and navigational links in the Blogger NavBar, not only those who have blogs, because the Blogger NavBar sits at the top of your blog waiting for someone to use it.

▶ **NOTE**

As the owner of a blog, you can change the color of your Blogger NavBar by logging in to Blogger, clicking the **Change Settings** icon in the **Blogs** section of the Blogger Dashboard, clicking the **Template** tab, and selecting a different color from the **Change the Blogger NavBar** drop-down list. After you make the change, click the **Save Template Changes** button and republish your blog.

46

1 Quick Link to the Blogger Dashboard

The Blogger NavBar contains two links to the Blogger home page. The Blogger logo on the left side of the NavBar takes you to the Blogger home page, as does the **Get Your Own Blog** link on the right side of the NavBar. If you click either of these links while logged in to your Blogger account, you will see your Blogger Dashboard. Otherwise, the default Blogger home page is displayed.

2 Search Within This Blog

Type a keyword or phrase into the text field and click the **Search this Blog** button. This action performs a Google search—limited to the index of the pages of the blog you are visiting—for the term you specified.

3 Search Within All Blogs

Type a keyword or phrase into the text field and click the **Search All Blogs** button. This action performs a search on all blogs indexed by Google for the term you specified.

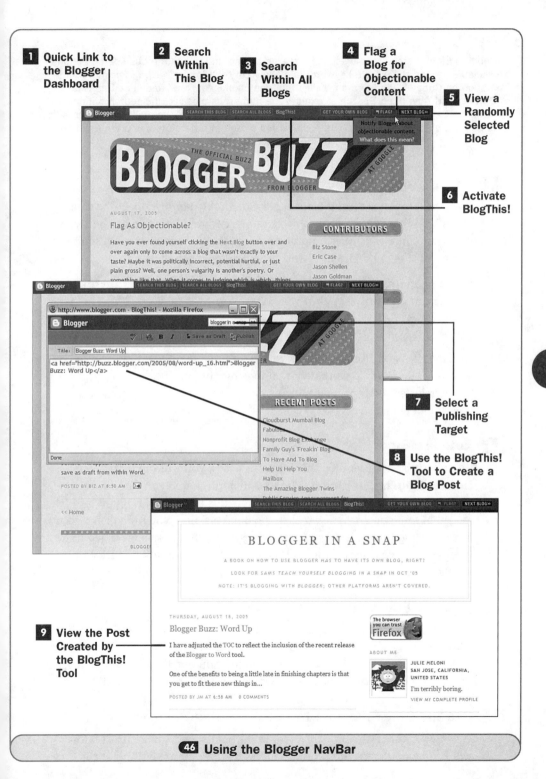

1 Quick Link to the Blogger Dashboard

2 Search Within This Blog

3 Search Within All Blogs

4 Flag a Blog for Objectionable Content

5 View a Randomly Selected Blog

6 Activate BlogThis!

7 Select a Publishing Target

8 Use the BlogThis! Tool to Create a Blog Post

9 View the Post Created by the BlogThis! Tool

46

▶ **NOTE**

Google's Blog Search is a blog-specific search engine and has numerous search options available beyond the simple keyword field shown in the Blogger NavBar. For more information on Google's Blog Search, visit http://search.blogger.com/ and click **Use Search Options** and **Advanced Search** to explore the numerous blog-specific search options available to you. These include, but certainly are not limited to, the ability to search a list of blogs, the ability to search blog posts within a certain time period, and the ability to search blog posts written in one or more selected languages.

4 Flag a Blog for Objectionable Content

If you visit a blog with the Blogger NavBar enabled and you feel the content of the blog is questionable or objectionable, click the **Flag?** link to notify Blogger. Examples of questionable or objectionable content include spam blogs and sites engaging in or encouraging illegal activities.

For more information on this tool, visit the Blogger Help page: http://help.blogger.com/bin/answer.py?answer=1200.

5 View a Randomly Selected Blog

46

Clicking the **Next Blog** link takes you to a randomly selected blog hosted by Blogger. Steps 3 and 4 work very well together; as you click through randomly selected blogs, you can flag as questionable any spam blogs or other objectionable blogs you see.

6 Activate BlogThis!

When visiting another blog that contains a post you want to blog about, click the **BlogThis!** link in the Blogger NavBar to launch an interface to the Blogger post editor. Steps 6 and 7 show how this editor works. If you are logged in to Blogger when you click the BlogThis! link, you are taken directly to the posting interface. If you are not logged in, the first step is to log in to Blogger using your username and password. This action takes place within the BlogThis! interface, so there's no need to navigate to a new page.

7 Select a Publishing Target

After you're logged into Blogger, you can select from a list of blogs associated with your Blogger account. If you have only one blog, it appears as the only item in the drop-down list. If you have more than one blog, they are all listed in the drop-down; select the blog to which this post should be published.

8 Use the BlogThis! Tool to Create a Blog Post

When you launch the BlogThis! tool from the Blogger NavBar, the textarea will be prepopulated with a link to the web page you are visiting at the time.

If you selected any text on that page before you launched the BlogThis! tool, that text will appear in the textarea as well.

You can use plain text or HTML markup in your post. Additionally, basic Blogger post editor tools such as the spellchecker, Hyperlink Wizard, and minimal post formatting buttons are present. You can choose to save your post as a draft or publish it directly to your blog.

9 View the Post Created by the BlogThis! Tool

After publishing your post with the BlogThis! tool, visit your blog to review your work. You will notice the post looks like any other blog post created through the Blogger post editor.

47 Using BlogThis! Add-Ons

BlogThis! is an interface to the Blogger post editor. Developers have tapped into the power of this small bit of software, providing methods for accessing it through web browser add-ons. For instance, the BlogThis! extension for Firefox creates a context menu option that can be selected when you are viewing a web page about which you want to write a blog post. The Google Toolbar, which is available for both Firefox and Microsoft Internet Explorer, includes a BlogThis! button as part of its standard set of user tools.

47

▶ NOTE

To download the BlogThis! Firefox extension, visit https://addons.mozilla.org/extensions/ moreinfo.php?id=261. To obtain the Google Toolbar for either Firefox or Microsoft Internet Explorer, visit http://toolbar.google.com/.

Steps 1 and 2 assume that you have installed the BlogThis! extension for Firefox or the Google Toolbar.

1 Right-Click and Select BlogThis! from the Context Menu

After the BlogThis! extension for Firebox has been installed and your browser restarted, you can right-click and select BlogThis! from the context menu. If you are logged in to Blogger when you click the BlogThis! link, you are taken directly to the posting interface. If you are not logged in the first step is to log in to Blogger using your username and password. This action will take place within the BlogThis! interface, no need to navigate to a new page.

1 **Right-Click and Select BlogThis! from the Context Menu**

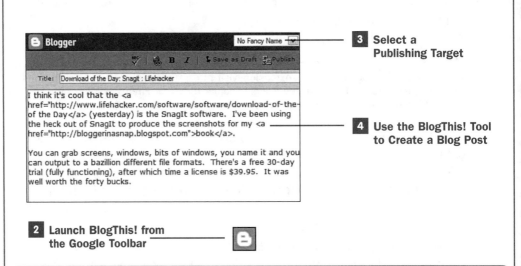

3 **Select a Publishing Target**

4 **Use the BlogThis! Tool to Create a Blog Post**

2 **Launch BlogThis! from the Google Toolbar**

47 **Using BlogThis! Add-Ons**

47

2 Launch BlogThis! from the Google Toolbar

After installing the Google Toolbar, the Blogger icon will be visible in the tool-bar directly beneath the location bar. Click the Blogger icon to launch the BlogThis! interface. If you are logged into Blogger at the time you click the BlogThis! link, you will be taken directly to the posting interface. If you are not logged in at the time, the first step is to log in to Blogger using your user-name and password. This action takes place within the BlogThis! interface, so there's no need to navigate to a new page.

Steps 3 and 4 refer to the use of the BlogThis! interface, and are valid regardless of the method used to access the tool.

3 Select a Publishing Target

After you're logged in to Blogger, you can select from a list of blogs associated with your Blogger account. If you have only one blog, it appears as the only item in the drop-down list. If you have more than one blog, they are all listed in the drop-down; select the blog to which this post should be published.

4 Use the BlogThis! Tool to Create a Blog Post

When you launch the BlogThis! tool from the context menu or the Google Toolbar, the textarea will be prepopulated with a link to the web page you are visiting at the time. If you selected any text on that page before you launched the BlogThis! tool, that text will appear in the textarea as well.

You can use plain text or HTML markup in your post. Additionally, basic Blogger post editor tools such as the spellchecker, Hyperlink Wizard, and min-imal post formatting buttons are present. You can also choose to save your post as a draft or publish it directly to your blog.

48

48 Using Blogger for Word

Blogger for Word is an add-in for Microsoft Word that allows you to compose, edit, save as a draft, and publish blog posts within Microsoft Word. If you use the Microsoft Windows XP or Windows 2000 operating system and Microsoft Word 2000 or higher, this tool is for you.

▶ **NOTE**

For more information about Blogger for Word, including FAQs and known issues, visit http://help.blogger.com/bin/answer.py?answer=1180.

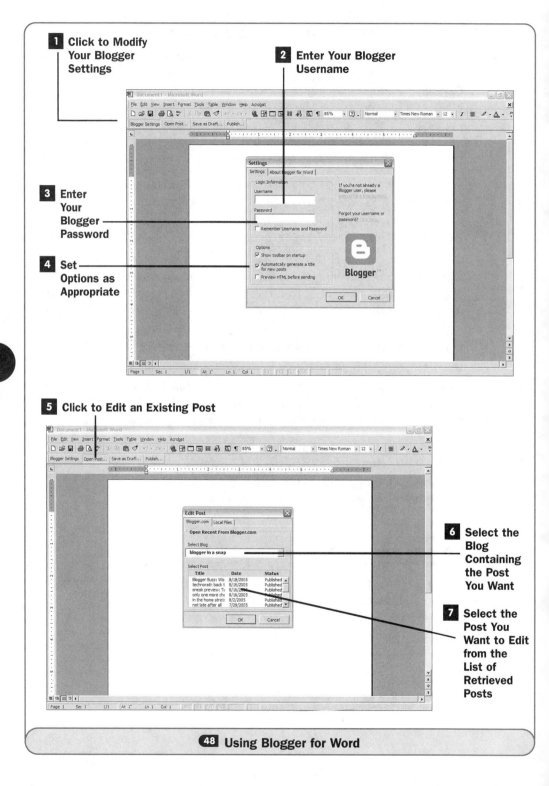

1 Click to Modify Your Blogger Settings

2 Enter Your Blogger Username

3 Enter Your Blogger Password

4 Set Options as Appropriate

5 Click to Edit an Existing Post

6 Select the Blog Containing the Post You Want

7 Select the Post You Want to Edit from the List of Retrieved Posts

 48

48 Using Blogger for Word

9 Click the Save as Draft Button to Save Your Post Without Publishing

10 Click the Publish Button to Publish Your Post

8 Type Your Post

11 Give Your Post a Title

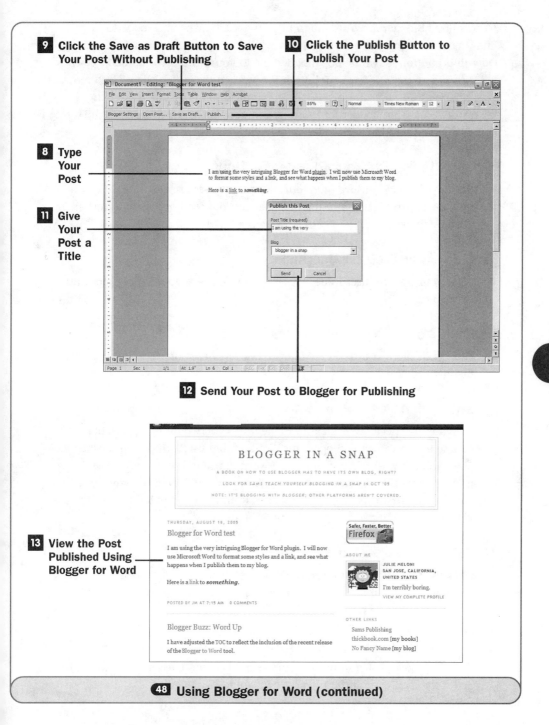

12 Send Your Post to Blogger for Publishing

13 View the Post Published Using Blogger for Word

To download Blogger for Word, go to http://buzz.blogger.com/bloggerforword. html, read the Terms of Service and Privacy Policy, and click the **Agree and Download** button. Save the downloaded file to your hard drive and double-click the filename to install. The installation process is a three-step wizard and requires little intervention on your part. When the application is installed, launch Microsoft Word. The Blogger for Word add-in appears as a toolbar near the top of your Document window.

1 Click to Modify Your Blogger Settings

Before you begin, ensure that your Blogger settings are accurate. Click the **Blogger Settings** button in the Blogger for Word toolbar, which launches the window shown here.

2 Enter Your Blogger Username

Enter your Blogger username. This is used to retrieve your list of blogs and blog posts.

3 Enter Your Blogger Password

Enter your Blogger password. Your password is necessary to validate your Blogger account.

48

4 Set Options as Appropriate

Activate the check boxes next to the features you would like to enable. If you choose not to show the Blogger for Word toolbar on startup, you must manually enable it within Word when you want to use it. If you enable the option to generate a title for your new posts, your posts are given a default title equal to the first twenty or so characters from the body of your post. When you complete your settings, click the **OK** button.

5 Click to Edit an Existing Post

Click the **Open Post** button in the Blogger for Word toolbar, which launches the window shown here. This window provides tools for retrieving existing posts for further editing.

6 Select the Blog Containing the Post You Want to Edit

This drop-down list contains the names of blogs attached to your account. Select the blog containing the post you would like to edit.

7 **Select the Post You Want to Edit from the List of Retrieved Posts**

After a blog is selected, a list of recent posts is displayed. Highlight a post to select it, and click the **OK** button to retrieve the post and edit its contents in Microsoft Word.

8 **Type Your Post**

You can begin typing at any time. Use the basic formatting elements in Microsoft Word, such as bold, italics, underline, and hyperlinks, as part of your post text. You can also type raw HTML code in your document.

9 **Click the Save as Draft Button to Save Your Post Without Publishing**

If you want to save your work but not publish it, click the **Save as Draft** button. After your work is saved, you can retrieve it via the **Open Post** tool or through the Blogger post editor.

10 **Click the Publish Button to Publish Your Post**

If you are ready to publish your post to your blog, click the **Publish** button to launch the window shown here.

48

11 **Give Your Post a Title**

If you enabled the automatic generation of post titles option, you can leave the generated title or edit it. If you did not activate the option, enter a title in this text field. Titles are required for all posts.

12 **Send Your Post to Blogger for Publishing**

Select the publishing target for this post. If you have more than one blog, all your blogs appear in this drop-down list.

13 **View the Post Published Using Blogger for Word**

After publishing your post using Blogger for Word, visit your blog to review your work. You will notice the post looks like any other blog post created through the Blogger post editor.

8

RSS, Indices, and Folksonomies

IN THIS CHAPTER:

So, you had something to say and you said it—a brilliant post sits at the top of your blog, just waiting for readers. But waiting is such a passive game, and there are ways you can be proactive in sharing your blog entries with the world. In this chapter, you will learn how to ensure that your post makes it out into the Blogosphere at large, through the use of an *RSS* feed, blog indexing, and embracing the concept of folksonomy.

There's also the tricky matter of how to keep up with the Blogosphere—all the millions of bloggers writing millions of posts each day. I personally guarantee that after a few weeks of blogging and reading blogs, you'll come to the conclusion that there is just too much interesting stuff out there and you'll never be able to keep up. You'll start to wonder just how people can read hundreds of blogs each day and still have time for their pesky jobs. One topic in this chapter introduces you to the wonderful world of RSS aggregators, the sole purpose of which is to enable you to quickly read blog postings without having to navigate to multiple websites, reload pages, search for new topics, and so on.

49 Providing an External RSS Feed

→ SEE ALSO

⑪ Enabling and Publishing Site Feeds
㉚ Identifying Elements in the Blogger Template Source

All Blogger users have the option to publish a site feed, as shown in ⑪ **Enabling and Publishing Site Feeds.** Although the feed published by Blogger is perfectly sufficient for feedreaders, providing an external feed from a company such as FeedBurner allows you to track circulation and usage, increase awareness of your blog content, and utilize additional tools for commerce-related activities.

The following steps outline the process of publishing an external site feed through the FeedBurner service. Before you begin, log in to Blogger and click the **Change Settings** icon in the **Blogs** section of the Blogger Dashboard. Click the **Settings** tab, and then click **Site Feed** in the subnavigational elements. Verify that **Publish Site Feed** is set to Yes, and then copy the value of the **Site Feed URL**. This URL is typically in the format http://*yourblog*.blogspot.com/atom.xml, such as http://bloggerinasnap.blogspot.com/atom.xml.

❶ Start the FeedBurner Process by Entering Your Blog URL

Armed with your blog's site feed URL, go to the main FeedBurner page at http://www.feedburner.com/ and enter your blog's site feed URL in the **Your Blog or Feed Address** field, as shown in the figure. Click the **Next** button to continue the registration process.

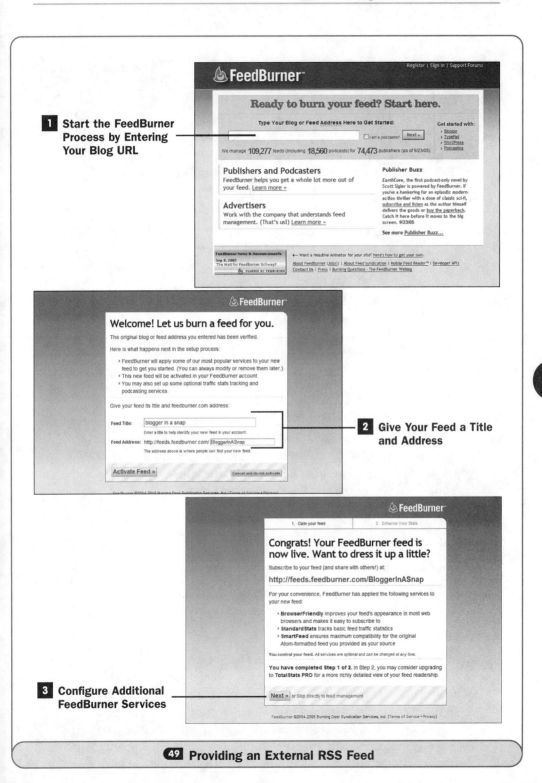

1 Start the FeedBurner Process by Entering Your Blog URL

2 Give Your Feed a Title and Address

3 Configure Additional FeedBurner Services

49 Providing an External RSS Feed

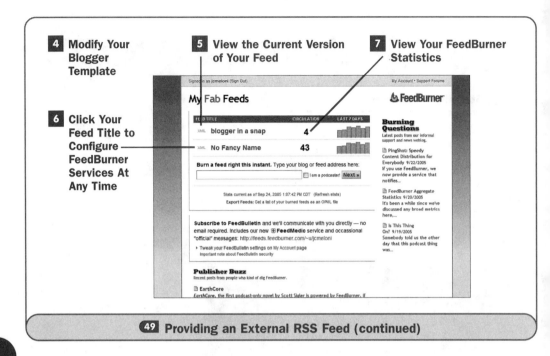

49 Providing an External RSS Feed (continued)

49

2 Give Your Feed a Title and Address

FeedBurner will retrieve your site feed from the URL provided in the previous step. FeedBurner will suggest a Feed Title and Feed Address based on this retrieved feed and place the suggested text in the appropriate text fields. If you would like to change either field, simply delete the prepopulated text and type your own text in the text fields. When you have completed these actions, click the **Activate Feed** button.

▶ NOTE

If FeedBurner encounters multiple feeds when attempting to retrieve a feed from the URL you provided in step 1, you will be asked to confirm which feed you would like to burn before moving on to the next step, shown here.

3 Configure Additional FeedBurner Services

After you click the **Activate** button at the end of step 2, you will be prompted to continue configuring FeedBurner services. FeedBurner provides a plethora of options to its users, beginning with two levels of statistics packages. If you are a statistics junkie or you are using your blog for business purposes, consider spending a few dollars each month for the Total Stats PRO package. Even though a basic FeedBurner account includes a statistics package that reports your daily feed circulation numbers, complete with a breakdown of the feed readers used, the Total Stats PRO package includes detailed item popularity and statistics related to feed resyndication. To configure an additional statistics package, click the **Next** button.

If you do not want to configure an additional statistics package, follow the **Skip Directly to Feed Management** link to view and configure even more features of your FeedBurner feed. These features are broken into several categories: Analyze, Publicize, Optimize, Monetize, and Troubleshootize. You can modify your configuration settings at this point in the process or at any time hereafter.

▶ **NOTE**

At this point you will be asked to create an account with a username and password, or to log in with existing account credentials. When you have done so, click the **Next** button to continue the registration process.

4 **Modify Your Blogger Template**

After your FeedBurner feed has been activated, you must modify your Blogger template to include a link to your new feed. First open a new browser window and visit your blog main page. Using the View Source feature of your web browser of choice, view the source code for your blog's index page. Look at the top of your blog source code, and you should see several `<meta>` and `<link>` tags, something like the ones here:

```
<meta http-equiv="Content-Type" content="text/html;
      ➥ charset=UTF-8" />
<meta name="MSSmartTagsPreventParsing" content="true" />
<meta name="generator" content="Blogger" />
<link rel="alternate" type="application/atom+xml" title="your title"
href="http://yourblogurl/atom.xml" />
<link rel="service.post" type="application/atom+xml"
      ➥ title="your blog title"
href="https://www.blogger.com/atom/yourblogID" />
<link rel="EditURI" type="application/rsd+xml" title="RSD"
href="http://www.blogger.com/rsd.g?blogID=yourblogID" />
```

Copy this entire snippet from your source code. Then access the Blogger template editor by logging in to Blogger, clicking on the **Change Settings** icon in the **Blogs** section of the Blogger Dashboard, and then clicking on the **Template** tab. Find a Blogger template tag that looks like this:

```
<$BlogMetaData$>
```

49

Remove that line, and replace it with the source code you copied. Then add the following additional code:

```
<link rel="alternate" type="application/rss+xml" title="RSS"
href="http://feeds.feedburner.com/YourFeedName" />
```

Save your template and republish your entire blog, and your new external FeedBurner feed will be available for auto-discovery.

5 View the Current Version of Your Feed

After completing the registration process, and anytime you log in to FeedBurner thereafter, you will be redirected to your personal FeedBurner home page. Follow the **XML** link to take a look at the current version of your FeedBurner feed, which can alert you to any inconsistencies or errors in its display.

6 Click Your Feed Title to Configure FeedBurner Services At Any Time

Click the linked version of your feed title to view all the various services and options available to you. Give some a try; most are available to free accountholders. If you do not like a service, you can always deselect it.

If you select no other FeedBurner options, go to the Publicize options and click the **Chicklet Chooser** link. Use this option to generate HTML code to publicize your FeedBurner feed, which you can then place in your Blogger template.

7 View Your FeedBurner Statistics

Click the number in the **Circulation** column to view the circulation statistics for your FeedBurner feed. These statistics show you the number of individuals reading your feed, the hits from your feed, and the feedreaders used to access your feed. Users who have the Total Stats PRO package will have additional circulation information available to them in this area.

50 | Using an RSS Aggregator

11 **Enabling and Publishing Site Feeds** and **49** **Providing an External RSS Feed** discuss enabling a site feed for your blog to make it easy for users to read your entries through a feedreader—also called a *feed aggregator*. If you want to keep up with reading more than a few blogs on any given day, you should employ the services of a feed aggregator.

1 Activate the Sage Extension and Show a List of Subscribed Feeds

2 Click to Highlight the Feed You Want to Read

3 View the List of Available Posts

4 Click a Post Title to Load the Original Post Page

5 Click the Auto-Discover Tool to Find Feeds on a Page

6 Select the Feed to Which You Want to Subscribe

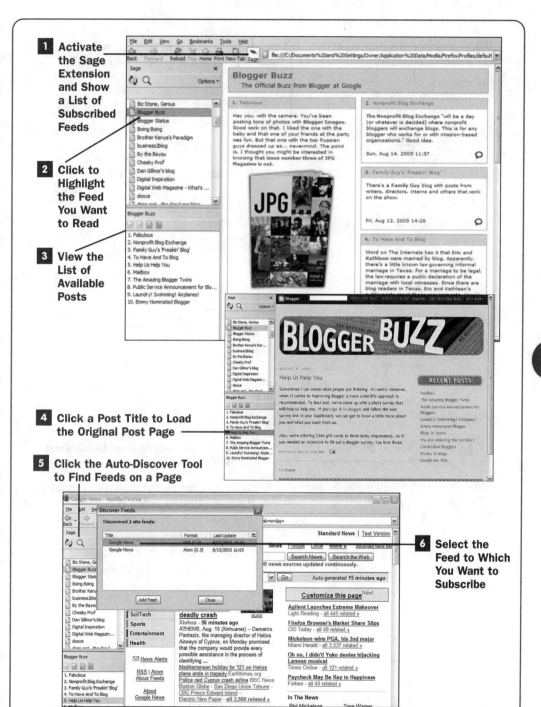

50

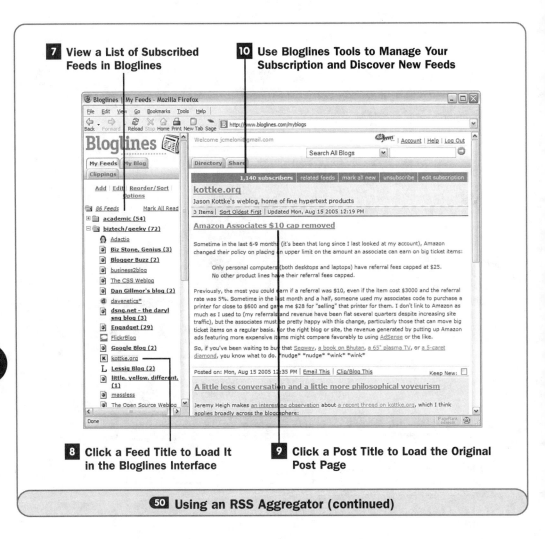

7 View a List of Subscribed Feeds in Bloglines

10 Use Bloglines Tools to Manage Your Subscription and Discover New Feeds

8 Click a Feed Title to Load It in the Bloglines Interface

9 Click a Post Title to Load the Original Post Page

50 Using an RSS Aggregator (continued)

There are three main types of aggregators: standalone software, software integrated with your web browser or email client, and World Wide Web–based applications. The process of using all three types of aggregators is conceptually similar:

1. Subscribe to a feed or automatically discover it while viewing a page.

2. Refresh your aggregator to see updated posts.

3. Click a post title to view the content or visit the original page; the post is now marked as read.

4. Continue reading new posts until you have exhausted the list.

Because the concepts are similar, the figures that follow do not cover the process in each of the various types of aggregators. Steps 1–6 show these concepts using the Sage extension for the Firefox web browser, whereas steps 7–10 look at similar tasks performed using the World Wide Web–based Bloglines service.

▶ **NOTE**

For a comprehensive list of RSS aggregators available in each of the three categories listed earlier, visit the Wikipedia page at http://en.wikipedia.org/wiki/List_of_news_ aggregators.

To install the Sage extension for the Firefox web browser, go to http://sage.mozdev.org/install/ and follow the **Click Here to Install** link. After the extension has been installed, restart Firefox. When Firefox has been restarted after a successful installation, you can access Sage via

- Menu selection: Select Tools, Sage

- Menu selection: Select View, Sidebar, Sage

- Keyboard shortcut: Press Alt+s

- Toolbar button: Select View, Toolbars, Customize, and drag the Sage icon to the desired spot

50

The following steps assume that you have installed the Sage extension in Firefox:

1 Activate the Sage Extension and Show a List of Subscribed Feeds

This example shows the Sage icon placed in the navigation toolbar. If your placement is similar, click the Sage icon to open the Sage RSS reader in your sidebar. Alternately, use the Alt+s keyboard shortcut or either of the menu selections described earlier. When Sage is opened, a list of your subscribed feeds is shown in the top pane.

2 Click to Highlight the Feed You Want to Read

If a feed contains new posts, it will appear in bold in the top pane. You can click any feed name—bold or not—to load the feed in your browser window. In this example, the feed for the Blogger Buzz blog (http://buzz.blogspot.com/) is selected.

3 View the List of Available Posts

When you click the name of a feed in the top pane, the contents of the feed will be loaded in the browser window and the individual posts will be listed in the bottom pane. Unread posts will be listed in bold text, whereas posts you have already read will be listed in plain text.

4 Click a Post Title to Load the Original Post Page

To visit the original post page for an entry, click the post title in the bottom pane of the Sage reader. You can also click the linked post title when the feed is loaded in the browser window as in step 2. You do not have to click through to the original post page unless the feed provides only a snippet of the actual text, if you want to see the formatted version of the post, or if you want to leave a comment or view trackbacks on the post.

5 Click the Auto-Discover Tool to Find Feeds on a Page

When visiting a website or blog that you enjoy, click the **Auto-Discover** icon to see whether Sage can find a feed for the site. In this example, the Sage Auto-Discover tool has found two types of feeds for the Google News page.

6 Select the Feed to Which You Want to Subscribe

From the list of available feeds, select the one to which you want to subscribe and then click the **Add Feed** button. The feed will be saved in your Sage bookmarks and its name will appear in the top pane of the Sage reader.

50

Sage includes numerous settings you can employ to make your user experience even better. For instance, click the **Reload** icon next to the **Auto-Discover** icon whenever you want to refresh your list of feeds and search for new posts. Click **Options** to produce a drop-down list of settings, preferences, and feed management tools. Visit the Sage home page at http://sage.mozdev.org/ for more information.

The next few steps show you how to use a World Wide Web–based RSS aggregator, using the very popular Bloglines tool as an example. The advantage of a World Wide Web–based RSS aggregator over a standalone application and a web browser software extension is that you can access your feeds from any computer—you needn't be on your personal machine to access your subscriptions.

The following example assumes that you have visited Bloglines at http://www.bloglines.com/ and created an account. After you have created an account, you can subscribe to RSS feeds from the websites you enjoy. For more information about Bloglines and the process of subscribing to feeds, visit the Bloglines FAQ at http://www.bloglines.com/help/faq.

7 View a List of Subscribed Feeds in Bloglines

The Bloglines interface is split into two frames: the left side pane and the body content area. The pane on the left side of your web browser contains your list of subscribed feeds, showing any folders that you have created to maintain some order inside. The body content area refreshes with content based on what you click in the left side pane.

In the left side pane, a feed containing unread posts will appear in bold with the number of unread posts in parentheses after its name. A feed that does not contain unread posts will simply display in plain text.

8 Click a Feed Title to Load It in the Bloglines Interface

When you click the name of a feed in the left side pane, the contents of the feed will load in the body content area. In addition to the name of the feed and posts contained within, the body content area will also display links to additional Bloglines tools and other information about the feed itself.

9 Click a Post Title to Load the Original Post Page

To visit the original post page for an entry, click the linked post title in the body content area. You do not have to click through to the original post page unless the feed provides only a snippet of the actual text, if you want to see the formatted version of the post, or if you want to leave a comment or view trackbacks on the post.

51

10 Use Bloglines Tools to Manage Your Subscription and Discover New Feeds

Within the body content area you can find additional tools to assist you in the management of your subscribed feeds, such as one-click deletion of a subscription and the ability to mark all feeds as read or as new. Additionally, when viewing a feed you enjoy, you can click the **Related Feeds** link and potentially discover a plethora of new and exciting feeds that match your interests.

---

51 **Using Indexing Mechanisms to Your Advantage**

✔ **BEFORE YOU BEGIN**

11 Enabling and Publishing Site Feeds
49 Providing an External RSS Feed

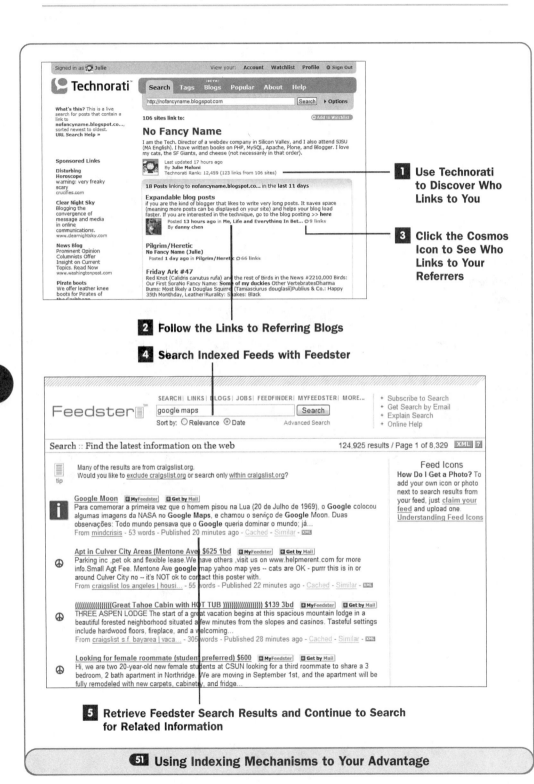

1 Use Technorati to Discover Who Links to You

3 Click the Cosmos Icon to See Who Links to Your Referrers

2 Follow the Links to Referring Blogs

4 Search Indexed Feeds with Feedster

5 Retrieve Feedster Search Results and Continue to Search for Related Information

51 Using Indexing Mechanisms to Your Advantage

Publishing an RSS feed makes it simple for readers to keep up with your posts, but there is also the added advantage of its inclusion in indexing mechanisms such as Technorati and Feedster. Both Technorati (http://www.technorati.com/) and Feedster (http://www.feedster.com/) are real-time search engines that index the constant stream of blog posts. Having a new blog created every second, and almost a million new blog posts hitting the Web every day, proves a very constant stream indeed. With your RSS feed in hand, all you need to do to ensure that your posts are indexed in these search engines is make sure that your blog is registered with the services, and ping them when you have updated your blog.

▶ **NOTE**

For information about registering your blog with Technorati, visit http://www.technorati. com/signup/ and follow the instructions.

For information about registering your blog with Feedster, visit http://feedster.com/help/ and follow the instructions.

Although Technorati and Feedster offer some of the same services, the various interfaces for searching their indexed data are quite different. The examples in steps 1–3 use Technorati to see how tools are used to discover who links to your blog, but Feedster offers some of the same services. Similarly, steps 4 and 5 use examples of a Feedster search to show how results can be displayed and used for further research; Technorati offers this feature as well. You are encouraged to register your blog with both indexing services, and utilize the toolsets available from both companies to determine which service best meets your needs.

1 **Use Technorati to Discover Who Links to You**

After registering your blog with Technorati, you can get a real-time look at the number of other blogs linking to yours. Links are typically displayed with the newest links at the top of the list rather than in alphabetical order, making it much easier to find new links.

2 **Follow the Links to Referring Blogs**

With each entry on your referring links page, you get the title of the post or blog that links to your blog, a snippet of the text surrounding the link to your blog, and a few other links to the referring blog and that blog's cosmos of links. It's a veritable bonanza of links, all of which you can follow and see how your blog is linked to—it could be in a blogroll or it could be in a blog post referring to something you've written.

51

3 Click the Cosmos Icon to See Who Links to Your Referrers

Each referral to your blog has its own cosmos of links. Just as your blog cosmos contains all the blogs that link to yours, the cosmos of a referring blog contains all the blogs that link to that blog. If you follow these links and find new blogs to read and link to, you will inevitably increase your own cosmos. The number of links and the quality of the links that link to you work together to increase your personal blog ranking.

▶ **NOTE**

Indexes of reciprocal links are not unique to Technorati; Feedster also performs such searches.

4 Search Indexed Feeds with Feedster

Enter a term or series of terms in the Feedster search field and then click the **Search** button to retrieve results of your search against Feedster's index of feeds. You can retrieve search results by relevance, which would display results more typically found in a traditional search engine, or you can retrieve search results by date, which would more accurately reflect the trend or buzz around particular topics in the Blogosphere.

5 Retrieve Feedster Search Results and Continue to Search for Related Information

Feedster search results contain the linked title of the post containing your keywords, a snippet of the text found in the post, and a few other items of use: the blog name and link, the number of words in the post, how long ago the post was published, and links to similar posts. Additionally, and depending on the search results, Feedster offers the capability to filter out repetitive results, which can help you find the information you are looking for much more quickly.

▶ **NOTE**

Technorati, like Feedster, allows similar types of keyword searches on its index of "the world live web."

---

52 Creating and Sharing Your Bookmarks	
✔ **BEFORE YOU BEGIN**	→ **SEE ALSO**
29 Understanding the Blogger Template Structure and Editor	**53** Embracing Folksonomy

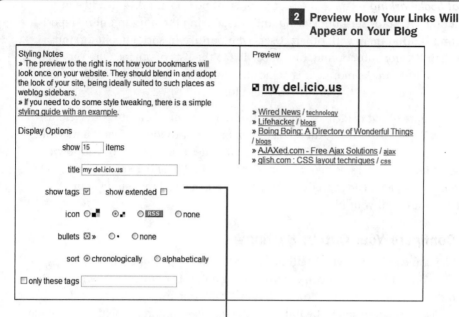

2 Preview How Your Links Will Appear on Your Blog

Styling Notes
» The preview to the right is not how your bookmarks will look once on your website. They should blend in and adopt the look of your site, being ideally suited to such places as weblog sidebars.
» If you need to do some style tweaking, there is a simple styling guide with an example.

Display Options

show [15] items

title [my del.icio.us]

show tags ☑   show extended ☐

icon ○ ■   ⊙ ■   ○ RSS   ○ none

bullets ☑ »   ○ •   ○ none

sort ⊙ chronologically   ○ alphabetically

☐ only these tags [   ]

Preview

■ **my del.icio.us**

» Wired News / technology
» Lifehacker / blogs
» Boing Boing: A Directory of Wonderful Things / blogs
» AJAXed.com - Free Ajax Solutions / ajax
» glish.com : CSS layout techniques / css

1 Configure Your Output Settings

3 View Your del.icio.us Links on Your Blog

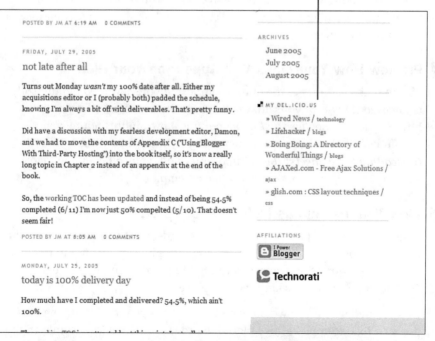

POSTED BY JM AT 6:19 AM   0 COMMENTS

FRIDAY, JULY 29, 2005

not late after all

Turns out Monday *wasn't* my 100% date after all. Either my acquisitions editor or I (probably both) padded the schedule, knowing I'm always a bit off with deliverables. That's pretty funny.

Did have a discussion with my fearless development editor, Damon, and we had to move the contents of Appendix C ("Using Blogger With Third-Party Hosting") into the book itself, so it's now a really long topic in Chapter 2 instead of an appendix at the end of the book.

So, the working TOC has been updated and instead of being 54.5% completed (6/11) I'm now just 50% compelted (5/10). That doesn't seem fair!

POSTED BY JM AT 8:05 AM   0 COMMENTS

MONDAY, JULY 25, 2005

today is 100% delivery day

How much have I completed and delivered? 54.5%, which ain't 100%.

ARCHIVES

June 2005
July 2005
August 2005

■ MY DEL.ICIO.US

» Wired News / technology
» Lifehacker / blogs
» Boing Boing: A Directory of Wonderful Things / blogs
» AJAXed.com - Free Ajax Solutions / ajax
» glish.com : CSS layout techniques / css

AFFILIATIONS

Ⓑ I Power Blogger

Technorati

52

Social bookmarking refers to the process of creating bookmarks—just like in a traditional web browser—but storing and categorizing them in an online repository and sharing them with others. Users who partake in social bookmarking offer their lists for subscription, and subscribe to the lists of others. One very popular social bookmarks manager is del.icio.us, and this topic shows you how to output your del.icio.us bookmarks to your blog.

To learn more about del.icio.us and create a free account, visit http://del.icio.us/ and click the **Register** link. After registering, browse through the bookmarks and categories of other users and find some new websites to visit or store your own pre-existing bookmarks. When you have compiled a list of bookmarks to share, go to http://del.icio.us/doc/feeds/js/ to get the code needed to include your del.icio.us links on your blog.

1 Configure Your Output Settings

You can configure several settings to control the appearance of del.icio.us links on your blog. You can control both the number of items shown and the order in which they are shown: alphabetically or chronologically by date added. You can display the link title, the link description, or neither (in which case just the URL will be shown). You can select an icon to call attention your links section, and you can choose an arrow or a bullet to precede your links. Finally, you can filter your links and show only links that have been tagged with a certain keyword.

2 Preview How Your Links Will Appear on Your Blog

As you make changes to the output settings, the preview area dynamically changes to show how your links will appear on your blog. Also on the http://del.icio.us/doc/feeds/js/ page, but not shown in this figure, you can find additional information regarding styling your output with *CSS (Cascading Style Sheets)*. Most important of all, you can copy the JavaScript snippet you have to place in your Blogger template.

3 View Your del.icio.us Links on Your Blog

Paste the snippet of JavaScript obtained from del.icio.us somewhere in your Blogger template. Access the Blogger template editor by logging in to Blogger, clicking the **Change Settings** icon in the **Blogs** section of the Blogger Dashboard, and then clicking the **Template** tab.

Find an area where you would like the links to appear and paste the code there. In this example, I have placed the code for my del.icio.us links in the area underneath my blog archives, in the sidebar of the blog template. When you have placed your code snippet in your template, click the **Save Template Changes** button and republish your blog. As you add bookmarks through the del.icio.us interface, this JavaScript snippet will display them; there is no need to modify your template every time you update your del.icio.us links.

▶ **NOTE**

del.icio.us is not the only social bookmarks management system out there. Check out the Wikipedia entry for social bookmarking at http://en.wikipedia.org/wiki/Social_ bookmarking to find a long list of services.

53 | Embracing Folksonomy

Folksonomy refers to the collection and categorization of items by the people doing the collecting and categorization. In other words, it's the "folks"—average people like you and me—who determine their own classifications and not some hifalutin' Master Classifier of All Things. Instead of writing a blog post about web design standards and looking in some reference guide how to best classify the information I just wrote, I can categorize it as I see fit—I can tag the entry with *CSS*, *web design*, *W3C standards*, *XHTML*, and so on.

Users apply categorizations through the use of tags. In some blog publishing tools, users can specifically categorize their posts, which are then interpreted as tags by blog-specific search engines, such as Technorati (http://www.technorati. com/), that rely heavily on tags to organize content. Blogger users must manually add tags to their posts, as you'll see in step 7 later in this section. In the mean-time, take a look at steps 1–6 to get a better understanding of the concept of folksonomy in action.

▶ **NOTE**

Although I consider Technorati the leader in the indexing and implementation of folksonomy-based content searching, other search engines such as IceRocket (http://www.icerocket.com/) also employ some manner of tag-based searching. del.icio.us, the social bookmarks management service, also relies on tagging to organize user content, as do image management services such as Flickr (http://www.flickr.com/) and Buzznet (http://www.buzznet.com/). Tagging is popping up everywhere!

1 | Search Tagged Content

In this example of the Technorati search interface, one of the methods of searching is by tag name. Searching by tag name is different from searching by keyword because keywords are simply words that appear in the indexed content, whereas tags are elements that have been specifically applied to the post by the author. Think of a search for tagged items as way of filtering your search to produce more precise search results.

53

1 Search Tagged Content

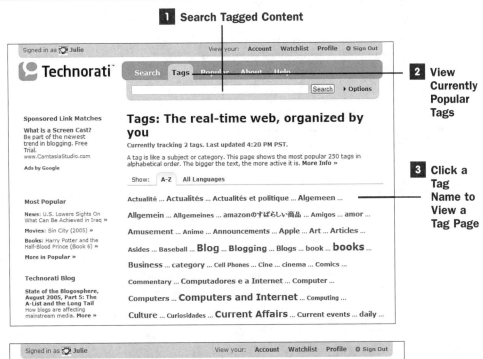

2 View Currently Popular Tags

3 Click a Tag Name to View a Tag Page

53

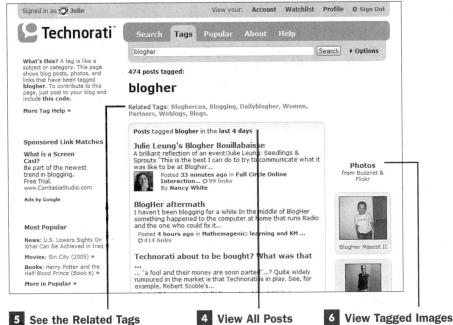

5 See the Related Tags for Your Search Term

4 View All Posts Tagged with Your Search Term

6 View Tagged Images from Other Tag-Enabled Services

53 Embracing Folksonomy

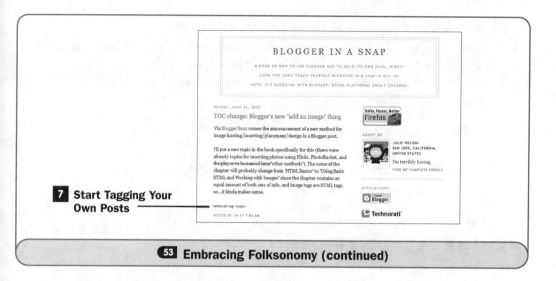

7 Start Tagging Your Own Posts

53 Embracing Folksonomy (continued)

2 View Currently Popular Tags

Technorati keeps a real-time list of the most popular tags as indexed by its service. Click the **Tags** link on the Technorati home page to access the list. A large font indicates a more popular tag. In this example, the tags *Blog* and *books* are more popular than the tags for *cinema* and *Computing*.

3 Click a Tag Name to View a Tag Page

If you click a tag name in this interface, you will be taken to a page containing the most recent posts tagged with that keyword.

4 View All Posts Tagged with Your Search Term

In this example of a tag result page, I searched for the tag *blogher*. Technorati retrieved a list of 474 posts tagged with this word, and presented the list with the most recent posts first.

▶ NOTE

In the summer of 2005, the first annual BlogHer Conference brought together hundreds of women interested in the use of blogs and social software. Attendees wrote blog posts about their experiences, continued discussions started in the official conference seminars, and took photos at the event—all these posts and photos were tagged with the term *blogher* or some related keyword. For more information about the BlogHer Conference, visit http://www.blogher.org/.

5 See the Related Tags for Your Search Term

A results page for a tag search will also present you with a list of related tags, if appropriate. For instance, the Technorati search engine determined that posts tagged with *blogher* were related to posts tagged with *bloghercon*, *blogging*, *dailyblogher*, *women*, *partners*, *weblogs*, and *blogs* because either the posts were explicitly tagged with these additional keywords or they were in some way related through linking mechanisms.

6 View Tagged Images from Other Tag-Enabled Services

When applicable, Technorati's tag results page will list images from the Flickr and Buzznet photo management sites that also include this same tag.

7 Start Tagging Your Own Posts

This example shows one of my posts tagged with the term *blogger*. Personally, I have a convention for my tagged posts, which is to explicitly state *technorati tag* followed by the tag name. That tag name is also a link to the specific Technorati tag page. You do not need to follow this convention when tagging your posts. Following the Tip, you will see examples of code to use to tag your posts.

53

▶ TIP

If you plan to use tags and want to ensure that your posts are indexed in Technorati, be sure to register with Technorati and claim your blog. Go to http://www.technorati.com/signup/ to start this process, if you haven't already.

A tag is nothing more than an <a></a> link with an additional attribute in the mix. For example:

```
<a href="http://some.link.to/some_page" rel="tag">tagname_goes_
        ➥here</a>
```

Here is a more specific example:

```
<a href="http://www.blogger.com/" rel="tag">blogger</a>
```

After adding a tag to your post, such as the one just shown, ping Technorati at http://www.technorati.com/ping/ so that it knows to add your recently published blog to its indexing queue.

In the preceding example, you'll notice I linked to http://www.blogger.com/ instead of the Technorati tag page for *blogger*. You can link to any page you want in the href attribute of the <a></a> tag. The indexing mechanism looks for the rel="tag" attribute, and then looks for the term between the <a></a> tags.

On my own blog, I use the method of linking to the Technorati tag page within my tagged elements, simply because it provides me with an easy way to jump to a category cosmos in which I am interested. For instance, when tagging a post with the blogger tag, I would use the following link:

```
<a href="http://www.technorati.com/tag/blogger"
➥ rel="tag">blogger</a>
```

A tag-indexing mechanism such as Technorati doesn't care what you put within the href attribute of your link. All it looks for is the rel="tag" attribute and the text between the <a></a> tags.

Everyone is different, so link to whatever you like, and tag your posts where appropriate to help build self-filtered search results.

53

PART IV

Appendixes

IN THIS PART:

A

HTML Fundamentals

IN THIS APPENDIX

- Plain Text Documents and HTML Tags
- Understanding the Overall HTML Document Structure
- HTML Structural Elements Within the BODY Element
- Basic Physical Markup
- Hyperlinks
- Creating Tables with HTML
- Using HTML Entities
- Putting It Together

Maintaining a blog does not required much knowledge of HTML, but a little knowledge goes a long way. With this knowledge, you can break free of the limitations placed on you when using a WYSIWYG post editor, and truly customize your blog posts. Speaking of customization, you can also use new-found HTML skills to modify your overall Blogger template so that it is more to your liking—although a totally new customization requires a combination of HTML knowledge and an understanding of CSS, which you might find in Appendix B, "CSS Fundamentals."

Plain Text Documents and HTML Tags

Although your Blogger posts are typed via the post editor, or sent via email using the Mail-to-Post feature, these are considered to be plain text HTML documents, just as if you were maintaining a website and producing single HTML documents for all the pages in your site. So, when it comes to discussing the structure of an HTML document and how to type HTML, there's little difference between how web developers and bloggers use this code.

HTML tags are the words you see in angle brackets, such as <html> and </html>. In fact, that was an example of an HTML tag pair. Tags are either paired or *self-contained*, meaning there is no ending tag. The image tag is an example of this: <img> does not have a matching </img> end tag. Instead, the <img> tag itself is closed by the forward slash at the end of the single tag: <img/>. You'll learn more about specific tags in a moment. For now, just understand that tags are usually in pairs, sometimes not, and are just words surrounded by angle brackets.

Understanding the Overall HTML Document Structure

Although your Blogger blog has an overall template into which your posts are dynamically generated, at its core is a structured HTML document. For instance, your Blogger template has the same opening and closing <html> tags and the same BODY and HEAD sections as an HTML document you'd find on a static website. In the case of your blog, you can find the core structural elements in your template, whereas your posts contain secondary structural elements as well as basic logical or physical markup.

You should understand the overall structure of an HTML document, including the elements outlined in the following sections. Because you have access to the underlying HTML document structure through your ability to edit your Blogger template, you don't want to screw up the document by deleting something that looks extraneous when it's really not!

Document Type Declarations

Your Blogger template might or might not include a document type declaration. If it does, it will be the first line of your template and will look something like this:

```
<!DOCTYPE HTML PUBLIC "-//W3C//DTD HTML 4.01//EN"
        "http://www.w3.org/TR/html4/strict.dtd">
```

or

```
<!DOCTYPE html PUBLIC "-//W3C//DTD XHTML 1.0 Strict//EN"
        "http://www.w3.org/TR/xhtml1/DTD/xhtml1-strict.dtd">
```

As its name suggests, this tag declares the version of HTML used throughout the document. The first document type shown earlier says that the document should validate against the rules of HTML 4.01 (strict), whereas the second begins a document that should validate against the rules of the XHTML 1.0 (strict).

Your Blogger template will utilize an XHTML document type declaration, which is essentially HTML 4 but with more stringent rules. XHTML-formatted documents are backward compatible with web browsers and other user agents that can render documents in HTML 4, but they also position your content so that it can be rendered in XML-compliant user agents as well.

What does this mean to you, the average Blogger user? It means very little, actually, because the Blogger application handles the vast majority of document creation chores. However, if you plan to extend your template using CSS and customize your posts using a lot of HTML, you should write your code in a manner that conforms to the document type declaration in use.

▶ **NOTE**

All markup used throughout this book is compliant with an XHTML 1.0 (strict) document type definition.

The HTML Element

After the document type declaration, your template should include the opening <html> tag. The very last line of your template should be the closing </html> tag. When your blog is published and viewed via a web browser, everything between these two tags is considered part of the HTML element and will be assumed to be valid HTML (or XHTML) markup.

The HEAD Element

After the opening `<html>` tag comes the opening `<head>` tag. Within the HEAD element come the TITLE element—surrounded by the `<title></title>` tag pair—as well as any `<meta>` and `<link>` tags you want to use, stylesheet entries, and script elements such as JavaScript functions.

When extending your blog with third-party links and applications, you will often be instructed to place specific scripts in your template. For instance, if you use the Haloscan commenting and trackback system, you will be given a snippet of code to place in your template, something like this:

```
<script type="text/javascript"
➥ src="http://www.haloscan.com/load.php?user=yourUserName"></script>
```

This code snippet will go within the HEAD element of your template. After including additional items within the HEAD element, close it using the `</head>` tag.

The TITLE Element

The title of your document is placed inside the HEAD element, contained within opening and closing `<title>` tags. For example: `<title>My Blog Title</title>`. No other information goes within the `<title></title>` tag pair. For the sake of maintaining a well-organized template, place the `<title></title>` tag pair directly after the opening `<head>` tag, before other elements within the HEAD area.

The `<meta>` and `<link>` Tags

Both `<meta>` and `<link>` tags contain various information about the document—not actual document content, just information about it. For example, a common `<meta>` tag uses the `"keywords"` value for the `name` attribute to provide keywords applicable for the document:

```
<meta name="keywords" content="open source, mozilla, firefox, blogger,
➥ flickr"/>
```

`<link>` tags work similarly, except the additional information provided is gathered from a link rather than the `content` attribute of the tag. For instance, the following `<link>` tag provides information regarding an RSS feed for my blog:

```
<link rel="alternate" type="application/rss+xml" title="RSS"
➥ href="http://feeds.feedburner.com/NoFancyName"/>
```

Your Blogger template will contain several `<meta>` and `<link>` tags related to the Blogger application and the publishing process. Do not to remove any `<meta>` or `<head>` tags unless you completely understand their purpose and, more importantly, understand what will happen to your blog if you remove these items.

Stylesheet Entries

A standard Blogger template contains stylesheet information directly in the template, located between opening and closing <style> tags, within the HEAD element. Additional stylesheet information can be imported from external URLs, such as the following code used to import the Blogger navigational bar that can be found at the top of most blogs:

```
@import url(http://www.blogger.com/css/navbar/main.css);
@import url(http://www.blogger.com/css/navbar/3.css);
```

Even if your stylesheet information is pulled in from external URLs, these lines of code will be wrapped with <style> and </style> tags and will be present in the HEAD element within your template.

The BODY Element

After the closing </head> tag comes the opening <body> tag. All document content should be placed within the BODY element, which is closed using the </body> tag. The </body> tag should be the next-to-last tag in your template, followed only by the closing </html> tag.

HTML Structural Elements Within the BODY Element

This section contains the structural elements which you could use as you create your posts via the Blogger post editor. Sometimes called *block* or *container elements*—you can think of them as the building blocks of your content, or elements which contain content—these bits of HTML markup can be found only within the BODY element of an HTML document.

Each of your blog posts is dynamically generated into a specific place in your Blogger template, already within the BODY element. However, there are also areas of your template that are within the BODY element but are not blog posts—your sidebar is a primary example. In these areas, as well as your blog posts, you can use the following container elements to hold specific page content.

Six Levels of Headings

HTML contains six levels of heading-related tag pairs: <h1></h1> through <h6></h6>. The <h1> heading is the largest, and the <h6> heading is the smallest. By default, your web browser will interpret these levels of tags using a generic style—large, bold fonts for the largest headers, smaller and nonbold fonts for the smallest headers. However, the styles for heading tags typically are outlined specifically in your stylesheet, if for no other reason than to ensure that the font family, style, and other text attributes match the overall look and feel of your template.

Headings should not be used simply to change the font size of specific blocks of text. Instead, they are meant to outline a hierarchy of content—the overall title might be a level 1 heading, a subsequent heading would be a level 2, and yet another subsection of content would be a level 3 before another level 2 heading would be used, and so on. If you are using heading tags to outline the content of a post in this manner, do not skip a level; level 2 should follow level 1, level 3 should follow level 2, and so forth.

The only content that should go between the opening and closing heading tag pair is the actual heading. For instance:

```
<h1>This is a Level 1 Heading</h1>
```

If any other content appears between the tag pair, it will all be treated as a level 1 heading. For instance:

```
<h1>This is a Level 1 Heading<br/>
Here is some content</h1>
```

Although it looks as if the user has typed some title text plus a line break plus another line of text, this entire text block would appear as a single level 1 heading.

Paragraphs

It should come as no surprise to you that paragraphs of content are often surrounded by the <p></p> paragraph tag pair. Unlike the heading tags seen earlier, paragraphs can contain other container tags such as those described later in this appendix. However, you might find that nested container elements cause more problems than they're worth—a dropped or out-of-order closing tag can wreak havoc with your content display. So, if you want to display a paragraph of content followed by a list of items, followed by another paragraph of content, be sure to close the first paragraph tag, start and finish the list, and then start and finish another entire paragraph.

One important item to remember when typing content wrapped in paragraph container tags is that indentations and line breaks in the text that you type are not displayed as such when your content is viewed in a web browser. Line breaks are handled via the <br/> tag. Indentations can be hard-coded using a number of nonbreaking space entities ( ). Better yet, in Appendix B, you'll learn to modify the style of the <p> tag so that it indents the first line by a specific number of pixels. Appendix B also contains information on numerous other paragraph attributes, including text justification and line height, just to name a few.

Blocks of Quotations

If you've ever written a paper in school, you know that if you quote a significant amount of text you should set this text apart from the surrounding text. The HTML <blockquote></blockquote> tag pair is used specifically for this purpose. By default, your web browser will display content within the <blockquote></blockquote> using a generic font and by indenting the content a standard number of pixels. However, as you will learn in Appendix B, you may style the <blockquote> tag any way you choose—you might want to indent the content by a particular number of pixels, or perhaps you want all the content to be italicized or on a differently colored background than the content which surrounds it. These attributes (and more) are all customizable.

▶ **NOTE**

Content within the <blockquote></blockquote> tag pair can contain other block-level elements, including paragraphs and lists.

Ordered and Unordered Lists

HTML includes two types of lists: ordered and unordered. Unordered lists are often referred to as bulleted lists because the default indicator before the list item is typically the bullet character. Ordered lists typically have a numbered item indicator, one that increments as a list item is added to the mix. Both ordered and unordered lists are typically indented, but that indentation—both the mere presence of it as well as the actual display—is customizable using stylesheet entries.

The structure of a list begins with the opening tag, either <ul> or <ol> depending on whether you want an unordered or ordered list. Following the opening tag are the list items, which are surrounded by the <li></li> tag pair. After the final list item, either the </ul> or </ol> closing tag is used, depending on the type of list.

This code produces a three-item unordered list, with each list item preceded by a bullet:

```
<ul>
<li>list item #1</li>
<li>list item #2</li>
<li>list item #3</li>
</ul>
```

This code produces a three-item ordered list, with the first item numbered 1, the second item numbered 2, and the third item numbered 3:

```
<ol>
<li>list item #1</li>
<li>list item #2</li>
```

```
<li>list item #3</li>
</ol>
```

▶ **NOTE**

You can use line break tags (`<br/>`) or paragraph container tags (`<p></p>`) within list items. As long as the list item has not been closed, all its content will be indented.

To create nested lists, simply start and finish another full list before closing the outer list tag. For instance, the following code produces a bulleted item followed by three numbered items underneath it:

```
<ul>
<li>list item</li>
<ol>
<li>sub item #1</li>
<li>sub item #2</li>
<li>sub item #3</li>
</ol>
</ul>
```

Your nested tables can be of the same list type, or as you see here, you can mix and match your lists. The most important aspect of lists, and especially nested lists, is that all the tags are opened and closed in the proper order.

▶ **NOTE**

Some of the styles you can use to customize your unnumbered or numbered lists include the bullet style, the indentation distance, the line height, and the starting number for numbered lists.

Line Breaks and Horizontal Rules

Two very handy bits of HTML code are the line break and horizontal rule tags. The line break tag (`<br/>`) is used to force a line break between two lines. No additional whitespace is added; it simply forces the text to stop and then continue on the next line. The use of a line break is easily seen when typing postal addresses, when the address is within a set of paragraph tags:

```
<p>Jane Doe<br/>
1234 Main Street<br/>
Sometown, SomeState 99991</p>
```

Without line breaks after the first and second lines, the output would appear as follows in your web browser:

```
Jane Doe1234 Main StreetSometown, SomeState 99991
```

However, with the line breaks the output looks like this:

```
Jane Doe
1234 Main Street
Sometown, SomeState 99991
```

I'm sure you'll agree that the second example looks much more like a postal address than the first example! For additional space between lines, you may use two `<br/>` tags in succession or you can style your `<br/>` tag so that the line height is greater than the default used.

Like the line break, you can use the horizontal rule to insert a break in your content, but in this case the break comes with a visible line. The width, color, and style of this line can be customized via your stylesheet; you will learn options for doing so in Appendix B. In the meantime, just know that the horizontal rule tag (`<hr/>`) will produce a visible line with a forced line break above and below it.

Basic Physical Markup

When working within blog templates and individual posts (as well as both the Blogger and Haloscan commenting systems, among others), you will likely use a lot of physical markup in your HTML. You might not know it's called *physical markup*, but whenever you surround text with a tag pair intended to alter the appearance of content rather than the meaning of the content, you're using a physical style.

For instance, think about the tag pair for bolded text: `<b>` and `</b>`. You use this bit of physical markup specifically because you want that text to be bold, not because you want it to represent a specific level within the overall content hierarchy. Other elements of physical markup include the `<i></i>` tag pair for italicized text, `<tt></tt>` for typewriter text, `<u></u>` for underlined text, and `<s></s>` for strikethrough text. You can define the standard physical markup tags any way you'd like, via your stylesheet. Suppose that you want all text surrounded by the `<b></b>` tag pair to have a `font-weight` attribute of `bold` but also to appear colored red, regardless of the other text colors used in your document. You can style the bold tag to always be red, just as you can style the typewriter text tag to always appear in the Courier New font, and so on. You will learn numerous options for styling items in Appendix B.

Hyperlinks

Internet content without hyperlinks would be very boring indeed, especially when it's blog content. A large part of blogging involves the hyperlinking of content to and from other content available in the Blogosphere. Hyperlinks are created using the `<a></a>` tag pair, using the `href` attribute to provide the actual target to which you want to link. The text between the opening and closing tag becomes the clickable text of the tag. For instance, I would use the following to create a link that would take you to the blog for this book using the text `visit my blog!` as the clickable link:

```
<a href="http://bloggerinasnap.blogspot.com">visit my blog!</a>
```

Unless you are linking to a file on the same server as your blog, you must use the full protocol and domain name in the link—for example, `http://` and `bloggerinasnap.blogspot.com`. If you publish your blog on your own server, you need only specify the directory and page or image name as part of your link, such as

```
<a href="/directory/page.html">sample link</a>
```

▶ **TIP**

The `<a></a>` tag pair has four different states, all of which can be specifically styled through the stylesheet. You can define a specific appearance for links that are normally displayed on the page, links that have been visited, links as they are being hovered over by the user's mouse, and links as they are being clicked. You will learn more about link styles in Appendix B.

In addition to linking to specific pages, you might want to provide a hyperlink to an email address. The act of clicking a hyperlinked email address typically launches the default email application for the end-user. The format of this type of link is

```
<a href="mailto:someaddress@domain.com">e-mail me</a>
```

Clicking the words `e-mail me` will launch the user's default email application, creating a blank email with the `To:` field prepopulated with the value in the `href` attribute of the `<a>` tag.

Image Tags

In Chapter 4, "Using Basic HTML and Working with Images," you learned several methods for inserting inline images into your blog posts. The image tag (`<img>`) has several attributes, but the only required attribute is src or source. The image source attribute contains the URL at which the image can be found. The URL can be to an external server, such as

```
<img src="http://photos2.flickr.com/3623668_0743b16eda_m.jpg"/>
```

or it could be to an image on your own server:

```
<img src="/images/petey.jpg"/>
```

Other attributes that you should use, but are not required, include height, width, and alt text attributes. For instance, the following defines an image that is 180 pixels wide, 240 pixels high, with alternative text of petey:

```
<img src="http://photos2.flickr.com/3623668_0743b16eda_m.jpg"
➥ width="180" height="240" alt="petey"/>
```

Specifying the height and width of the image allows the browser to render the page while leaving the correct space for the photo that might or might not be ready to load at the time the browser encounters the <img> tag.

▶ **NOTE**

When images are used as hyperlinks (that is, they are surrounded by the <a></a> tag pair), use the border attribute in the <img> tag. If the attribute value is set to 0, no border will appear. A border value of 1 will display a 1-pixel border, a border value of 2 will display a 2-pixel border, and so forth.

In Appendix B, you'll learn how to set additional properties for <img> tag attributes.

Creating Tables with HTML

Creating tables with HTML requires the use of three main table-related tag pairs:

- <table></table> surrounds all the table-related code and defines it as part of a table; within this tag pair are table rows and table data cells.

- <tr></tr> defines a table row and contains table data cells.

- <td></td> defines a table data cell. Cell content resides between the opening and closing table data tags, which are ultimately contained within a table row.

For instance, you would use the following code to create a basic table with three rows containing three columns each:

```
<table border="1">
<tr>
        <td>row 1, cell 1</td>
        <td>row 1, cell 2</td>
        <td>row 1, cell 3</td>
</tr>
```

```
<tr>
        <td>row 2, cell 1</td>
        <td>row 2, cell 2</td>
        <td>row 2, cell 3</td>
</tr>
<tr>
        <td>row 3, cell 1</td>
        <td>row 3, cell 2</td>
        <td>row 3, cell 3</td>
</tr>
</table>
```

The table, table row, and table data tags each have numerous attributes which can be controlled via a stylesheet, including alignment, border size and colors, cell background colors and font attributes, and much more—you'll learn about these in Appendix B. However, two attributes that are typically part of the HTML code are the colspan and rowspan attributes because these attributes are table-specific in that their usage depends on the content you are presenting.

The colspan attribute defines the number of columns spanned by a cell, whereas the rowspan attribute defines the number of rows spanned by a cell. You can see an example of each of these items in action in the listing at the end of this appendix.

Using HTML Entities

You can use HTML entities in place of special characters that will not display properly when typed natively in HTML. The primary examples of these characters are the less-than (<) and greater-than (>) signs, also known as the left and right angle brackets that make up HTML tags.

For these tags to be displayed, you must type the entity names for them: < and > respectively. So, if you want the following text to be displayed on your blog (literally):

```
<a href="http://www.somedomain.com">Link here!</a>
```

you would have to type the following the in the post editor:

```
&lt;a href="http://www.somedomain.com"&gt;Link here!&lt;/a&gt;
```

Special characters are not the only instances in which HTML entities are used. Accented characters from languages other than English often provide instances in which HTML entities are necessary. Suppose that you're creating a blog post containing a recipe and one of the steps in the recipe is to sauté something. Sauté contains an accented character: é. The corresponding HTML entity for this character is é and therefore the word would be typed as follows in the post editor:

sauté

▶ WEB RESOURCE
http://www.bbsinc.com/iso8859.html
Here you can find links to numerous resources regarding HTML entities.

Putting It Together

The following code listing uses most of the basic HTML tags described in this appendix. You can match some of the items to the visual display in the figure following the listing.

```
 1:  <!DOCTYPE html PUBLIC "-//W3C//DTD XHTML 1.0 Strict//EN"
 2:          "http://www.w3.org/TR/xhtml1/DTD/xhtml1-strict.dtd">
 3:  <html>
 4:  <head>
 5:  <title>HTML Markup Example</title>
 6:  </head>
 7:  <body>
 8:
 9:  <h1>This is a Level 1 Heading</h1>
10:
11: <p>Here is a paragraph of content, followed by a line break. <br/>
12: Accumsan at qui augue quis dolore diam, wisi nulla molestie tation
13: iusto, in nostrud, tation. Facilisis consequat ut delenit feugait
14: ullamcorper eu tincidunt eros.</p>
15:
16: <blockquote>More content, blockquoted. Feugiat feugait vel,
    ➥ laoreet lobortis
17: feugait commodo adipiscing dignissim aliquam in aliquip iriure at
    ➥ ullamcorper.
18: </blockquote>
19:
20: <p>An unordered list:</p>
21: <ul>
22: <li>list item #1</li>
23: <li>list item #2</li>
24: <li>list item #3</li>
25: </ul>
26:
27: <p>An ordered list:</p>
28: <ol>
```

```
29: <li>list item #1</li>
30: <li>list item #2</li>
31: <li>list item #3</li>
32: </ol>
33:
34: <p>An example of nested lists:</p>
35: <ul>
36: <li>list item</li>
37: <ol>
38: <li>sub item #1</li>
39: <li>sub item #2</li>
40: <li>sub item #3</li>
41: </ol>
42: </ul>
43:
44: <b>bolded text</b><br/>
45: <i>italicized text</i><br/>
46: <u>underlined text</u><br/>
47: <s>strikethrough</s> text<br/>
48: <tt>typewriter text</tt><br/>
49:
50: <p>Here's a hyperlink:<br/>
51: <a href="http://bloggerinasnap.blogspot.com">visit my
    ➥ blog!</a></p>
52:
53: <p>Here's an image:<br/>
54: <img src="http://photos2.flickr.com/3623668_0743b16eda_m.jpg"
55: width="180" height="240" alt="petey"/></p>
56:
57: <p>A basic table:</p>
58: <table border="1">
59: <tr>
60:         <td>row 1, cell 1</td>
61:         <td>row 1, cell 2</td>
62:         <td>row 1, cell 3</td>
63: </tr>
64: <tr>
65:         <td>row 2, cell 1</td>
66:         <td>row 2, cell 2</td>
67:         <td>row 2, cell 3</td>
68: </tr>
69: <tr>
70:         <td>row 3, cell 1</td>
71:         <td>row 3, cell 2</td>
72:         <td>row 3, cell 3</td>
```

```
 73: </tr>
 74: </table>
 75:
 76: <p>A table using rowspan:</p>
 77: <table border="1">
 78: <tr>
 79:        <td rowspan="3">row 1, cell 1</td>
 80:        <td>row 1, cell 2</td>
 81:        <td>row 1, cell 3</td>
 82: </tr>
 83: <tr>
 84:        <td>row 2, cell 2</td>
 85:        <td>row 2, cell 3</td>
 86: </tr>
 87: <tr>
 88:        <td>row 3, cell 2</td>
 89:        <td>row 3, cell 3</td>
 90: </tr>
 91: </table>
 92:
 93: <p>A table using colspan:</p>
 94: <table border="1">
 95: <tr>
 96:        <td>row 1, cell 1</td>
 97:        <td colspan="2">row 1, cell 2</td>
 98: </tr>
 99: <tr>
100:      <td>row 2, cell 1</td>
101:      <td>row 2, cell 2</td>
102:      <td>row 2, cell 3</td>
103: </tr>
104: <tr>
105:      <td>row 3, cell 1</td>
106:      <td>row 3, cell 2</td>
107:      <td>row 3, cell 3</td>
108: </tr>
109: </table>
110:
111: <p>Display HTML entities:<br/>
112: &lt;a href="http://www.somedomain.com"&gt;Link here!&lt;/a&gt;</p>
113:
114: </body>
115: </html>
```

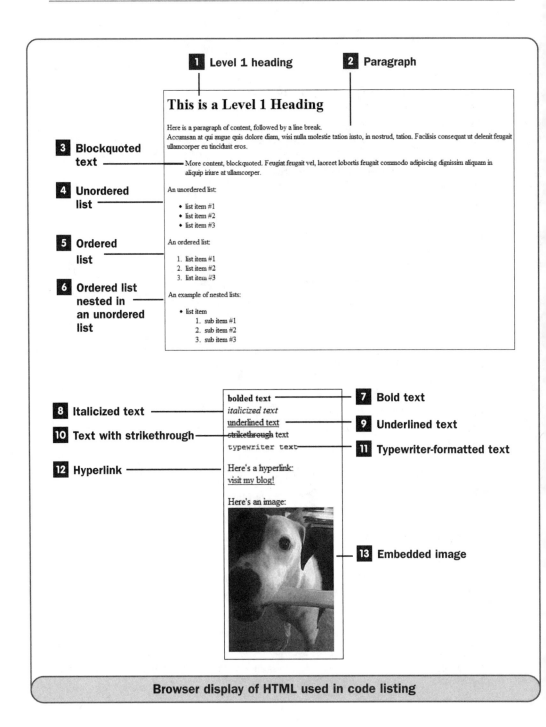

1 Level 1 heading   **2** Paragraph

3 Blockquoted text

4 Unordered list

5 Ordered list

6 Ordered list nested in an unordered list

7 Bold text

8 Italicized text

9 Underlined text

10 Text with strikethrough

11 Typewriter-formatted text

12 Hyperlink

13 Embedded image

Browser display of HTML used in code listing

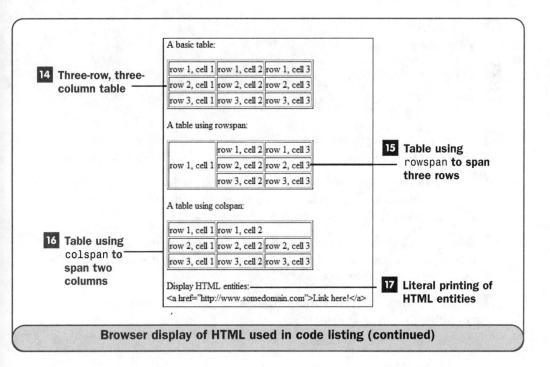

14 Three-row, three-column table

15 Table using rowspan **to span three rows**

16 Table using colspan **to span two columns**

17 Literal printing of HTML entities

Browser display of HTML used in code listing (continued)

1 **Level 1 heading**. The code in line 9 of the listing produces a level 1 heading.

2 **Paragraph**. The code beginning in line 11 of the listing produces the first line of the paragraph. A line break separates the text in lines 12–14 of the listing from the opening line of the paragraph.

3 **Blockquoted text**. The code in lines 16–18 is used to create an indented chunk of text called a *blockquote*.

4 **Unordered list**. The code in lines 21–25 is used to create an unordered list with the default bullet indicator before line items.

5 **Ordered list**. The code in lines 28–32 is used to create an ordered list using standard numbering before line items.

6 **Ordered list nested in an unordered list**. The code in lines 35–42 displays an ordered list inside an unordered list.

7 **Bold text**. The code in line 44 displays as bold.

8 **Italicized text**. The code in line 45 displays as italicized.

9 **Underlined text**. The code in line 46 displays as underlined.

10 **Text with strikethrough**. The code in line 47 displays one portion of the phrase with strikethrough text, one portion with plain text.

11 **Typewriter-formatted text**. The code in line 48 displays as if it were typed on a typewriter.

12 **Hyperlink**. The code in line 51 is used to create a hyperlink.

13 **Embedded image**. The code in lines 54–55 embeds an image with a specific height and width.

14 **Three-row, three-column table**. The code in lines 58–93 displays a table with three columns and three rows, with text in each of the individual cells.

15 **Table using** rowspan **to span three rows**. The code in lines 77–91 displays a table; the first column spans all three rows, whereas the second and third columns have cells in each of the three rows.

16 **Table using** colspan **to span two columns**. The code in lines 92–108 displays a table; the second and third cells in the first row appear merged, through the use of the colspan attribute.

17 **Literal printing of HTML entities**. The code in line 112 displays HTML entities rather than rendering them.

B

CSS Fundamentals

Blogging applications such as Blogger depend heavily on the underlying templates that control the overall look and feel of the final, published product. By separating the content from the presentation, even bloggers without HTML and CSS skills can produce aesthetically pleasing websites; those with a modicum of HTML and CSS knowledge can extend their sites and customize the appearance of their blog, even further.

In short, style sheets enable you to create your own set of presentation rules for HTML tags, classes, and other elements. By creating a thorough style sheet, you can rest assured that the content you surround with specific tag pairs will always look the same. If you want to create your own custom classes for existing HTML tags, you can do that as well. In this appendix you'll learn the basics of creating a style sheet, including the various attributes available for tags, classes, and other elements.

▶ **NOTE**

CSS stands for *Cascading Style Sheets*. The idea is that you might import styles from several different style sheets into your master template, and these internal styles or imported styles will then cascade seamlessly into one master style sheet.

This appendix is by no means a complete reference to all things CSS. Instead, it outlines most of the elements you will encounter when working with style sheet-based Blogger templates, thereby enabling you to perform numerous customizations for your blog.

Basic Format of Style Sheet Entries

Various methods for importing or placing style sheet entries in the HEAD element of an HTML document were discussed in Appendix A, "HTML Fundamentals." Now let's move on to the nitty-gritty of the style sheet rules themselves. Style sheet rules consist of two parts. The first part is the selector, which can be a tag name, an *identifier* name, or a *class* name. The second part is the declaration, which describes exactly how the selector should appear.

▶ **KEY TERMS**

Create an *identifier* for use with a single container element, such as a paragraph you want to identify as p1 or a <div> you want to identify as object1. Identifiers can be used only once per document, so there can only be one <p id="p1"></p> container, for example.

A *class* can be used numerous times in a single document and can be attached to any bit of structural or physical markup unless otherwise indicated.

Take, for instance, the standard <b></b> tag pair. If you wanted to ensure that all text within this tag pair was always displayed in a red, bold, Verdana font, you would use the following rule:

```
b {
        color: #FF0000;
        font-weight: bold;
        font-family: Verdana;
}
```

You could also write the rule on one line:

```
b {color: #FF0000; font-weight: bold; font-family: Verdana;}
```

Rules written on multiple lines and in an indented style are much easier to read, but if you prefer your rules all on one line, there's no detrimental effect (except perhaps to your eyes when you're straining to track down a rule).

The three items within the rule—color, font-weight, and font-family—are called *properties*, whereas #FF0000, bold, and Verdana are the values of the properties. Notice that the rule for the <b></b> tag pair does not have any information related to font size. In this instance, the font size will be inherited from within whatever element the content is contained. For instance, if font size information is indicated at the paragraph level (for example, in the declaration for the <p></p> tag pair) and bolded text appears within a paragraph, the bolded text will also be the same font size as all the rest of the content in the paragraph.

You can see that it would be advantageous to declare as many constant variables at the highest level possible. For instance, if you know the base font family, font weight, font color, and font size for all the content in your document, define these items as part of the rule for the <body></body> tag pair:

```
body {
        font-family: Verdana, Arial, Helvetica, sans-serif;
        font-weight: normal;
        font-size: 12px;
        color: #000000;
        background-color: #FFFFFF;
}
```

You've seen several examples of properties and values, but before listing all of them, you should understand the proper notations for different types of values.

Value Syntax

The values of style sheet properties can be

- **Strings**, such as `"Verdana"` as a font family

- **Color notation**, such as `#FF0000` or `rgb(255,0,0)`

- **Lengths**, such as `450px` (pixels)

- **Percentages**, such as `80%`

- **URLs**, with or without protocol and domain name

String Values

String values are seen mostly in lists of font families, such as

```
body {
        font-family: "Times New Roman";
}
```

or

```
body {
        font-family: Verdana, Arial, Helvetica, sans-serif;
}
```

or

```
body {
        font-family: "Times New Roman", Times, serif;
}
```

In the first instance, you see a string containing multiple words with whitespace between them. This type of string must be surrounded by quotation marks. In the second instance, several strings are used as values but none is of the multiple-word variety, so no quotation marks are needed around any of the words. In the third instance, one value requires quotation marks and the others do not. All are valid representations of values.

Color Notation

Color is expressed in hexadecimal notation for *RGB* (*red, green, blue*) values. RGB values range from 0 to 255. After conversion to hexadecimal, the two-character value of each color is used to create the hexadecimal color code. For instance, pure red has a value of 255 red, 0 green, and 0 blue. Its hexadecimal notation becomes FF for red, 00 for green, and 00 for blue, or FF0000.

▶ **WEB RESOURCE**
http://webmonkey.wired.com/webmonkey/reference/color_codes/
This web resource provides a chart of 216 standard colors, but you can convert any color you choose to hexadecimal values using a scientific calculator, your image editing program, or any of numerous RGB-to-hex calculators available online.

There are three common methods for representing color values in style sheets. In the following examples, pure blue is represented three different ways:

```
body {
        background-color: #0000FF;
}
```

and

```
body {
        background-color: #00F;
}
```

and

```
body {
        background-color: rgb(0,0,255);
}
```

In the first example, all six hexadecimal entries are used to represent the three colors: 00, 00, and FF. In the second example, only three characters are used because the hexadecimal notation includes values that are the same; if the hexadecimal notation for the color were ADC0DA, you could not use the three-character notation. Similarly, if the hexadecimal notation were AD00DA, you could not use the three-character notation because only one of the three colors (G or green) has a hex value with two identical characters.

Finally, the third example uses the RGB values themselves. In a value such as rgb(0,0,255), the first slot (0) represents zero red values, the second slot zero green values, and the third slot 255 blue values, which amounts to pure blue. Something like rgb(200,200,200) would produce a light gray, whereas something like rgb(170,170,255) would produce a pleasant periwinkle color.

▶ **NOTE**
There are sixteen colors that may be referred to by name: aqua, black, blue, fuchsia, gray, green, lime, maroon, navy, olive, purple, red, silver, teal, white, and yellow.

No rule exists that says you must use the same notation throughout your style sheet, but try to do so for the sake of consistency within your work.

Lengths

The syntax for displaying length includes the number and the unit of measurement, with no whitespace between the two. For instance, 14px is a value length but 1.5 em is not. After you have committed that rule to memory, you're ready to tackle the numerous types of relative and absolute lengths you can use. Following are common lengths you will encounter:

- **em** is a relative length; its length is equal to the font height in use. For instance, if the font height is 10px, 1em is equal to 10px.

- **px** is a relative length, where 1px equals one pixel.

- **in** is an absolute length measured in inches.

- **cm** is an absolute length measured in centimeters.

- **mm** is an absolute length measured in millimeters.

- **pt** is an absolute length where 1pt equals 1/72 of an inch.

Working with absolute values can get pretty tricky because you control neither the size of the visible area of a user's web browser nor the resolution under which the display is made. Therefore, sticking to relative values offers greater flexibility for both you as the designer as well as your readers.

Percentages

Like length values, the syntax for displaying a percentage value includes the number and the percentage sign with no whitespace between the two. For instance, 75% is a value length but 35 % is not. All percentage values are relative. For instance, the following defines a level 1 heading as 200% of the base font size in use:

```
h1 {
        font-height: 200%;
}
```

Another common instance for the use of percentages is in the use of classes or IDs for <div> tags when you want to define the width of the block element as a certain percentage of the element in which it is contained (the body, another <div>, and so on):

```
#halfDiv {
        width: 50%;
}
```

URLs

The URL value is not used nearly as often as other types of values, but when used, it requires a specific syntax. Namely, the URL appears within a url() structure and must be quoted. For instance:

```
body {
        background: url("images/someimage.gif");
}
```

In this example, the background of the body of the page will include a graphic found in the images directory, in a location relative to the style sheet source. With no leading forward slash or indicator to go up one directory level ("../"), it is assumed that the images directory is a subdirectory found in the same location as the style sheet itself.

You may also use the full URL, including protocol and domain name. For instance:

```
body {
        background: url("http://www.mydomain.com/images/someimage.gif");
}
```

Of course, do not link to anything on an external web server unless you have permission to do so.

Text Properties

You've seen some text-related properties in the examples used in this appendix, but without much explanation. The following items are common properties you'll encounter as you attempt to set style sheet rules for your blog.

- font-family. This property is used to define the font in which you want your content to be displayed. Remember, the font must be something the user has on his system, otherwise there's no way for the browser to display the intended look. So, if you intended to use some expensive proprietary font that matches your corporate branding, don't! Stick to the basics, and provide alternatives by providing a list of possible matches. For example:

  ```
  font-family: Verdana, Arial, Helvetica, sans-serif;
  ```

  The browser will first try to display content in Verdana, and if that is not successful, it will use Arial. If using Arial is unsuccessful, the browser will attempt to display in Helvetica. If using Helvetica fails, the browser will use any sans-serif font family to which it has access.

- `font-style`. This property has three possible values: `normal`, `italic`, and `oblique`. You may use only one at a time, such as

  `font-style: italic;`

- `font-weight`. This property relates to the thickness of the font, and you will typically see one of two possibilities here: `normal` and `bold`. For instance:

  `font-weight: bold;`

  However, there are actually four string values for `font-weight`: `normal`, `bold`, `bolder`, and `lighter`—the "-er" values being relative to the inherited `font-weight` of the element. For the sake of browser compatibility, it's best to stick to `normal` and `bold` for this property.

- `font-size`. The `font-size` property has numerous possibilities for both absolute and relative size definitions. If using an absolute size, you can use the keywords `xx-small`, `x-small`, `small`, `medium`, `large`, `x-large`, and `xx-large`. If using a relative size, the keywords are `larger` and `smaller`. For instance:

  `font-size: medium;`

  or

  `font-size: larger;`

  Personally, I try to stick to length or percentage values for font-size, such as

  `font-size: 12px;`

  or

  `font-size: 75%;`

  My preference is only because I understand "12px" and "75% of inherited font size" more than I do "medium," which could mean anything.

- `font`. You can combine all of the `font-*` properties into one definition. The syntax is

  `font: style weight size family;`

  For instance:

  `font: normal bold 12px Verdana, Arial, Helvetica, sans-serif;`

If you intend to use the font property, pay close attention to the syntax because the order does matter.

Text-related properties do not end with the font-* properties; there are several additional elements that you might find useful when working with your blog template.

- word-spacing. This property defines the spacing that will appear between words. The default value is normal and therefore you do not have to define the word-spacing style explicitly if you simply want it to be normal. However, if you want additional spacing between words, you can use something like

  ```
  word-spacing: 0.2em;
  ```

- letter-spacing. This property works like word-spacing in that it defines spacing between elements, except in this case it defines the space between letters and not between entire words. The default value is normal and therefore you do not have to define the letter-spacing style explicitly if you simply want it to be normal. However, if you want additional spacing between letters, you can use something like

  ```
  letter-spacing: 0.1em;
  ```

  You might see a letter-spacing style implemented in headers or labels.

- text-decoration. A common use of the text-decoration property is with the <a> tag, to remove the standard underline from a hyperlink:

  ```
  text-decoration: none;
  ```

  However, there are other possible values for the text-decoration property, including underline, overline, line-through, and blink. You can use this value in place of the physical HTML tag pair <s></s> to achieve a strike-through effect.

  Please don't ever use blink.

- text-transformation. This property is quite useful for headings and footer text because it forces the typed text to take on the look defined in the style as opposed to the text that is actually typed. The possible values for this property are capitalize, uppercase, lowercase, and none. Imagine that you are defining a heading or creating a class to be used in a heading, and you want all the text to be uppercased. You would define the class as such:

  ```
  .upper {text-transformation: uppercase;}
  ```

When used in your document, such as

```
<p class="upper">This is my heading</p>
```

you will see the following output:

```
THIS IS MY HEADING
```

Regardless of the case in which the text was typed, the style overrides the typed text and transforms the display into all-caps.

- `text-align`. The `text-align` property is akin to the justification settings used when creating a document in a word-processing program. The possible values for the `text-align` property are `left`, `right`, `center`, and `justify`. To ensure that all content paragraphs are justified, you might use the following in your rule for the `<p></p>` tag pair:

```
text-align: justify;
```

- `text-indent`. The `text-indent` property specifically affects only the first line of an element. If you would like the first line of your paragraphs to be indented by 10 pixels, you would place the following in your rule for the `<p></p>` tag pair:

```
text-indent: 10px;
```

- `color`. Do not confuse this property with the `background-color` property; they are quite different. The `color` property is valid only for text elements, and affects the color of the text. You can use any of the color notation methods previously described. For instance, black text could be written in any of the following ways:

```
color: #000000;
color: #000;
color: rgb(0,0,0);
```

List Properties

In Appendix A, you learned the basics of numbered and unnumbered lists. In this section, you'll learn some of the styles that can be applied to those list elements. The first item has to do with the overall display, and indeed it is called `display`.

- `display`. This property defines whether an element should be displayed inline, as a `block` element, as a list-item, or not at all. For example:

```
ul {display: block;}
li {display: list-item;}
.hidden {display: none;}
```

An element defined with an `inline` display will be placed on the same line as the preceding element, whereas an element defined with a `block` display will show up as a new chunk of content next the preceding element. The `list-item` and `none` display values are easily understood: The former places some sort of marker before the item and the latter does not display the content at all.

- `list-style-type`. When using a list-item display value, you may also use the `list-style-type` to define the marker that will be placed in front of the list item. For example, the following rule states that content surrounded by the `<li></li>` tag pair will be displayed as a list with each line preceded by a circle:

```
li {
        display: list-item;
        list-style-type: circle;
}
```

Other values for the `list-style-type` property are `disc`, `square`, `decimal`, `lower-roman`, `upper-roman`, `lower-alpha`, `upper-alpha`, and `none`.

- `list-style-image`. Suppose that you don't want your list items to have the standard disc, circle, number, or letter at the beginning of the line. No problem: The `list-style-image` property enables you to specify an image using `url()` notation. For example:

```
li {
        display: list-item;
        list-style-image: url("myArrow.gif");
}
```

- `list-style-position`. What happens when you have a lovely bulleted list but your lines are too long and the content must wrap? Does the second line begin at the start of the element, or does it indent and begin directly beneath the first line? The `list-style-position` enables you to control the placement of wrapped text in list items, using `inside` and `outside` as the available values.

```
li {
        display: list-item;
        list-style-type: square;
        list-style-position: inside;
}
```

In the preceding definition, long lines of text within the list item will wrap under the marker and will indent to the position of the line above it. If you were using the `outside` value, the line would wrap under the marker but would not be indented.

- `list-style`. Just as with all the `font-*` properties, you can combine all the `list-style-*` properties into one definition. The syntax is

```
list-style: type position image;
```

For instance:

```
list-style: outside url("myArrow.gif");
```

or

```
list-style: square inside;
```

Pseudo-Class Properties

At the beginning of this appendix you learned the difference between identifiers and classes. Pseudo-classes are like classes in that they can be used multiple times within one document, but the difference is that the names of these classes are already standardized. The main element that contains pseudo-classes is the anchor element, also known as "the tag you use to make a link" or `<a></a>`.

The anchor tag has four pseudo-classes: `link`, `visited`, `hover`, and `active`. The order in which these classes are defined is actually important, so you can remember the order using the acronym LVHA or "LoVe-HAte." The syntax for pseudo-classes is similar to other rules:

```
selector:pseudo-class {property-value;}
```

You might be wondering, "But isn't a link is a link is a link?" Links actually have four distinct states represented by the four pseudo-classes. Take a look at this example set of style sheet entries:

```
a {
        font-family: Verdana, Arial, Helvetica, sans-serif;
        font-size: 9pt;
        font-weight: normal;
}

a:link   {
        color: #3366CC;
        text-decoration: underline;
}
```

```
a:visited {
        color:#DDDDDD;
        text-decoration: none;
}

a:hover {
        color:#FF6600;
        text-decoration: underline;
}

a:active {
        color:#FF6600;
        text-decoration: none;
}
```

The first entry is for the overall appearance of the content within the <a></a> tag pair, which is to be normal weighted and in a 9pt Verdana font. The next entry is for the pseudo-class link and defines the additional styles to be applied to a link sitting on the page—in this case, the text should be a lovely blue and underlined. The third entry will be applied to any link sitting on a page that has been visited by the user at any time since her browser history has last been cleared. In this case, the visited link will be displayed as a dull gray with no underline.

The final two entries are for the hover and active pseudo-classes. Hovering occurs when the user's mouse is placed over the link; in this case, the link turns orange. The active pseudo-class is triggered when the user clicks on the link. From the time the click occurs until the mouse button is lifted up, the link will be orange but will not be underlined.

Box Properties

Block-level elements adhere to what is known as "the box model," which basically describes how each block essentially starts out as an invisible box to which visible borders and padding inside the box may be added, and margins outside the box may be implemented. As you can imagine, there are several styles you can use to control the display of your box. We'll start with borders because they're the easiest to understand.

▶ **WEB RESOURCE**
http://adactio.com/articles/display.php/CSS_based_design/8
This article manages to clearly describe the box model in only two pages!

- `border-[location]-width`. A border is made up of four locations: top, right, bottom, and left. Again, order is important and there's an acronym you can use to remember it: TRBL or "trouble"—as in "if you screw up the order of locations, your template will be in trouble." The general syntax for the `border-[location]` settings is

  `border-[location]:` *type* OR *size*

  The possible types for border width are `thin`, `medium`, and `thick`, or you can use pixel-based measurements such as 1px for a one-pixel border, 2px for a two-pixel border, and so on. To define the borders of a block element in a rather ugly way, you could use

  ```
  border-top-width: thin;
  border-right-width: medium;
  border-bottom-width: thick;
  border-left-width: 10px;
  ```

  You can also combine the width-related elements using the proper order, like so:

  ```
  border-width: thin medium thick 10px;
  ```

  I advocate the use of absolute sizes for borders, such as 1px or 2px, because doing so puts the responsibility for the design in your hands and is not left up to the whims of the web browser.

- `border-color`. You can set the color of the borders individually using the `border-color` style and the order (top, right, bottom, left) described in the preceding item. For example:

  ```
  border-color: #FFF #000 #FFF #000;
  ```

  If you specify only one color, it will be used for all four locations. If two colors are specified, the first color will be used for the top and bottom borders and the remaining color for the right and left borders. If three colors are specified, the first color will be used for the top border, the second color will be used for the right and left borders, and the third color will be used for the bottom border.

- `border-[location]` **and** `border`. As you have seen with other styles, you can combine the various elements that make up a border into a single rule— either for a location or for a border as a whole. The syntax for this rule is

  `border[-location]:` *width style color*;

For instance, if you wanted to set the top border of a block element to a 1px solid black line, you could use:

```
border-top: 1px solid #000;
```

If you wanted to set the border for an entire box to a 2px dashed blue line, you would use

```
border: 2px dashed #00F;
```

With borders out of the way, we can tackle margins and padding. For such simple styles, margins and padding cause a lot of headaches—primarily because it's difficult to imagine invisible space inside and outside a box, and secondarily because this space is sometimes rendered differently by different web browsers. Within both styles, you will again use the order of locations: top, right, bottom, left (TRBL).

- `margin-[location]` **and** `margin`. Margins can be set using relative or absolute units of measurement, from pixels (px) to percentages (%). Both are common, but other units such as ems and inches can also creep into a style sheet. Margins are definitely something you'll want to try hands-on to get a feel for how the spacing is applied. The syntax for the margin style is simply

  ```
  margin[-location]: length OR percentage;
  ```

  For instance, if you wanted to set the bottom margin of a block element to 10px you could use

  ```
  margin-bottom: 10px;
  ```

  If you wanted to set the margin for an entire block element to 5px all around, you would use

  ```
  margin: 5px;
  ```

  If you wanted to set the margin to different sizes for all four locations you would use something like

  ```
  margin: 1px 2px 3px 4px;
  ```

  As in the border example, if you specify only one size, it will be used for all four locations. If two sizes are specified, the first size will be used for the top and bottom margins and the remaining size for the right and left margins. If three sizes are specified, the first size will be used for the top margin, the second size will be used for the right and left margins, and the third size will be used for the bottom margin.

- `padding-[location]` **and** `padding`. Padding is represented exactly like margins, using relative or absolute units of measurement, from pixels (px) to percentages (%). The difference between padding and margins is where the space is located relative to the invisible box around the blog element. Padding surrounds the content within the borders, whereas margins surround the box outside the borders.

The syntax for the padding style is simply

```
padding[-location]: length OR percentage;
```

For instance, if you wanted to set the bottom padding within a block element to 10px, you could use

```
padding-bottom: 10px;
```

If you wanted to set the padding within an entire block element to 5px all around, you would use

```
padding: 5px;
```

If you wanted to set the padding to different sizes for all four locations, you would use something like

```
padding: 1px 2px 3px 4px;
```

As in the border and margin examples, if you specify only one size it will be used for all four locations. If two sizes are specified, the first size will be used for the top and bottom padding and the remaining size for the right and left padding. If three sizes are specified, the first size will be used for the top padding, the second size will be used for the right and left padding, and the third size will be used for the bottom padding.

- `width` **and** `height`. Boxes need to have dimensions, and you can specify widths and heights of your block elements using the `width` and `height` styles, respectively. Any unit of measurement can be used, but pixels and percentages are most common. For instance, the following class specifies an element that is 150 pixels wide and 50 pixels high.

```
.someBox {
        width: 150px;
        height: 50px;
}
```

Suppose that you wanted padding within elements of this class, such that 10 pixels of padding would appear on the left side and 15 pixels of padding on the right. You would add this line to the class definition:

```
padding: 0px 15px 0px 10px;
```

But you would also have to reduce the width of the class by 25 pixels because the actual display width of the element is going to be the width style plus the value of left padding (and margins) plus the value of right padding (and margins). So, if you also wanted 5 pixels of margin on either side, you would have to reduce the width even further:

```
.someBox {
        width: 120px;
        height: 50px;
        margin: 0px 5px 0px 5px;
        padding: 0px 15px 0px 10px;
}
```

The same rule applies to the `height` property; if you use top and/or bottom margins and/or padding, reduce the value of the `height` property appropriately.

Floating and Clearing

Now that you have been introduced to the box model, you can begin to understand how floating and clearing works. When block elements are adjacent, such as images within paragraphs or two `<div>` elements next to each other, the `float` and `clear` properties control the overall flow of the content on the page.

- `float`. There are three values for the `float` property: `left`, `right`, and `none`. The syntax is simply

  ```
  float: value;
  ```

  If the `float` value is `left`, the element floats to the left of the display and all subsequent elements wrap around it to the right. If the `float` value is `right`, the element floats to the right and text wraps around it to the left.

- `clear`. There are four values for the `clear` property: `none`, `left`, `right`, and `all`. The syntax is simply

  ```
  clear: value;
  ```

The `clear` style is used in conjunction with `float` styles so that the block elements are not running into each other on the page. You will often see a `<br/>` tag with the attribute `clear="all"` used to separate `<div>` elements from each other, but you can also define a value for the `clear` style in the rule for the tag, ID, or class itself.

The `<div>` and `<span>` Tags

You will undoubtedly find within your template two sets of HTML tags that you might not have seen before: the `<div></div>` and `<span></span>` tag pairs. These elements are discussed in this appendix rather than Appendix A because they're most often used in conjunction with a thoroughly style-sheeted site.

The `<div>` is a division of content, which is like a paragraph (`<p></p>`), but without the hard-coded line breaks that come along with using that tag pair. Most of the block-level elements you'll find in your Blogger template will be within the `<div></div>` tag pair, often with an ID, class, or both applied to it. For instance, the following identifies a sidebar area and applies the `"sidebar"` class to all the content contained within:

```
<div id="sideBarArea" class="sidebar">some content</div>
```

The `<span></span>` tag pair is an inline tag rather than a blog-level element. This tag pair essentially enables you to create your own physical markup tags. Because there's no standard HTML tag for "very small moss green text on a light purple background," you can create your own class:

```
.mossonpurple {
        font-size: 7pt;
        color: #669966;
        background-color: #CC99FF;
}
```

With the style defined, you can apply it to the text spanned with the appropriate tag:

```
<p>This is <span class="mossonpurple">horrible-looking</span> text!</p>
```

Putting It Together

The following code listing uses some of the CSS described in this appendix. You can match some of the items to the visual display in the figure that follows the listing.

```
 1:  <!DOCTYPE html PUBLIC "-//W3C//DTD XHTML 1.0 Strict//EN"
 2:        "http://www.w3.org/TR/xhtml1/DTD/xhtml1-strict.dtd">
 3:  <html>
 4:  <head>
 5:  <title>CSS Markup Example</title>
 6:  <style>
 7:  body {
 8:        font-family: Verdana, Arial, Helvetica, sans-serif;
 9:        font-weight: normal;
10:        font-size: 12px;
11:        color: #000000;
12:        background-color: #FFFFFF;
13:  }
14:
15:  b {
16:        color: #FF0000;
17:        font-weight: bold;
18:        font-family: Verdana;
19: }
20:
21: .crazytext {
22:        font: normal normal 22px ZapfDingbats;
23: }
24:
25: li {
26:        display: list-item;
27:        list-style-type: square;
28:        list-style-position: inside;
29:  }
30:
31: #myBox {
32:        border: 2px dashed #00F;
33:        padding: 15px;
34:        width: 150px;
35: }
36: .mossonpurple   {
37:        font-size: 7pt;
38:        color: #669966;
39:        background-color: #CC99FF;
40: }
41:
42: </style>
43: </head>
44: <body>
45:
```

```
46: <p>Text in the body has a default style.</p>
47:
48: <p><b>bolded text, with style</b></p>
49:
50: <p class="crazytext">the crazytext class in action.</p>
51:
52: <p>An unordered list with square item indicator.</p>
53: <ul>
54: <li>item #1</li>
55: <li>item #2</li>
56: <li>item #3</li>
57: </ul>
58:
59: <div id="myBox">This is a bordered box with padding.</div>
60:
61: <p><span class="mossonpurple">This is icky colored.</span></p>
62:
63: </body>
64: </html>
```

1 **Default body text style.** The <body> tag is given a style in lines 7–13, and as such this style becomes the default for any markup within the BODY element that does not have its own style definition.

2 **Specific style for bold text.** The <b> tag is styled in lines 15–19 and used in line 48. If you were viewing this screenshot in color, it would appear as bold red text.

3 **Custom style using a crazy font.** A custom class is defined in lines 21–23 and used in line 50.

4 **Custom list item indicator.** Lines 25–29 define the styles used for all list items. When used, as in lines 54–56, a square item indicator will appear before the text of each line item.

5 **Border and padding styles to create a box.** Lines 31–35 define an ID called myBox that creates the bordered and padded box shown here.

6 **Custom style using text and background colors.** A custom class is defined on lines 36–40, which produces a green text on a purple background when used as in line 61.

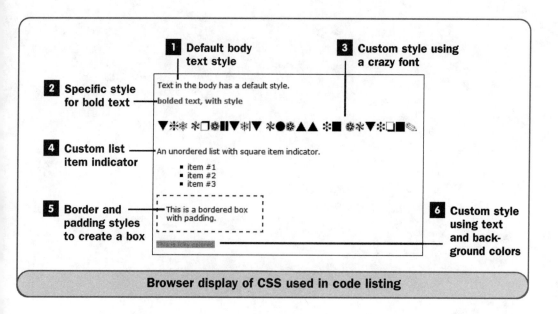

Browser display of CSS used in code listing

Index

C

RGB values (style sheets), 244

rowspan, 234

RSS feed aggregators, 208-209

RSS feeds, providing, 200-204

rules (style sheets), 242-243

string values, 244-245

text properties, 249-250

URL values, 247

values, 244

styles in Blogger templates, 129-132

S

Sage RSS aggregator, 207-208

search engines, 211

SFTP, utilizing, 24

shortcuts (Blogger editor), 74

site feeds (Blogger), publishing, 48-50

sources, citing, 10

<span>, 258

string values (style sheets), 244-245

<style>, 227

style sheets

  box-level elements

    borders, 254-255

    floating and clearing, 257-258

    margins and padding, 255-257

  classes, utilizing, 242

  color notations, 244

  <div> and <span> tags, 258

  font properties, 247-249

  format of, 242-243

  HTML tags, 227

  identifiers, 242

  lengths, 246

  list properties, 250-252

  percentages, 246

  pseudo-class properties, 252-253

  sample code, 258-260

T

tables, creating

  with HTML, 233-234

  in posts, 103-107

tags (Blogger content), identifying, 128. *See also* HTML

Technorati, 8, 211-212

templates

  Blogger template editor, 122-125

  Blogger templates

    custom styles, 129-132

    elements of, 127-129

    new templates, applying, 29-31

    post templates, creating, 41-42

    selecting, 19

    tags, 132-137

  third-party templates, 137-138

text documents (HTML), 224

text properties (style sheets)

  font-* properties, 247-249

  overview, 249-250

textarea (Blogger editor Compose mode), 65

third-party

  hosting, 19-25

  templates, 137-138

time zones, selecting, 39

timestamp formats, 39, 44